International Management and Intercultural Communication

International Management and Intercultural Communication

A Collection of Case Studies; Volume 1

Edited by

Elizabeth Christopher
Charles Sturt University, Australia

First published 2015 by
PALGRAVE MACMILLAN

Palgrave Macmillan in the UK is an imprint of Macmillan Publishers Limited,
registered in England, company number 785998, of Houndmills, Basingstoke,
Hampshire RG21 6XS.

Palgrave Macmillan in the US is a division of St Martin's Press LLC,
175 Fifth Avenue, New York, NY 10010.

Palgrave Macmillan is the global academic imprint of the above companies
and has companies and representatives throughout the world.

Palgrave® and Macmillan® are registered trademarks in the United States,
the United Kingdom, Europe and other countries.

ISBN: 978–1–137–47989–1

This book is printed on paper suitable for recycling and made from fully
managed and sustained forest sources. Logging, pulping and manufacturing
processes are expected to conform to the environmental regulations of the
country of origin.

A catalogue record for this book is available from the British Library.

A catalog record for this book is available from the Library of Congress.

This collection is dedicated to the memories of my beloved daughter, Anne Dunn, and my good friend and colleague, Larry E. Smith

Contents

List of Figures

List of Tables

Acknowledgements

Many thanks to Palgrave Macmillan's UK editorial staff, especially Liz Barlow and Kiran Bolla, and Vidhya Jayaprakash of Newgen Knowledge Works, for much help and support. Grateful thanks also to all contributors for their unfailing generosity.

Notes on Contributors

Somayeh Alizadeh is a cross-cultural consultant in the health service sector in Sydney, Australia, working with the Ethnic Community Services Department. She holds degrees in Biomedical Engineering and Information Technology Management and was a consultant in the corporate sector as an expert in turnkey design and construction of new hospital buildings, medical equipping, and the operation and management and administration of healthcare facilities. She has conducted research to identify key factors for successful telemedicine technology transfer in the Middle East. She lectures in marketing and cross-cultural management at Macquarie University, Sydney. somayeh.alizadeh@mq.edu.au

Smriti Anand is Assistant Professor of Management at the Stuart School of Business, Illinois Institute of Technology, Illinois, USA. Her research interests include leadership, diversity and non-traditional work arrangements with particular focus on multi-level and cross-cultural frameworks. Her research has been published in leading management journals, such as the *Academy of Management Journal*, the *Journal of Applied Psychology* and the *Leadership Quarterly*. Smriti won the Society for Human Resource Management (SHRM) dissertation grant award and the Society for Industrial and Organizational Psychology (SIOP) dissertation grant award in 2011. She is an SIOP scholar and has received the 2012 Emerald/EFMD Outstanding Doctoral Research Award in Human Resource Management. sanand12@stuart.iit.edu

Dharm P.S. Bhawuk is Professor of Management and Culture and Community Psychology, Shidler College of Business, University of Hawaií, Manoa, Honolulu. His research interests include indigenous psychology and management; intercultural training (also study abroad); culture theories (especially individualism and collectivism); diversity in the global workplace (also intercultural sensitivity, multiculturalism); culture and creativity, leadership, ethics and entrepreneurship. A recent publication is *Spirituality and Indian Psychology: Lessons from the Bhagavad-Gita* (2011). bhawuk@hawaii.edu

Meena Chavan is a senior lecturer in the Department of Marketing and Management at the Macquarie University, Sydney, Australia, and her teaching and research focus on international business strategy, cross-cultural management, strategic management and entrepreneurship. Her work has been published in the *Journal of Management Development, International Journal of Entrepreneurship and Innovation, Journal of Equal Opportunities* and *Journal of Industry and Higher Education* and the *Journal of Teaching in International Business*. She is an exponent of the experiential method of teaching. meena.chavan@mq.edu.au

Choon-Hwa Lim is a PhD candidate in the Department of Marketing and Management at the Macquarie University, Sydney, Australia, where she teaches cross-cultural management. She was awarded Macquarie Graduate School of Management (MGSM) Scholarship and is a member of the Australian Psychological Society. Her publications include a number of refereed journal articles. contact@peopleinvest.com.au

Elizabeth Christopher is a cross-cultural specialist in international management, communication across cultures, and online teaching and learning. She is a visiting academic with Charles Sturt University, NSW, Australia; a reviewer of academic publications and publishing proposals; a member of various editorial boards and a Chartered Fellow of the Australian Human Resource Institute (AHRI). She presents papers at international conferences and her awards include the Chartered Institute of Management (UK) Management Book of the Year Award (2013) for *International Management: Explorations across Cultures* and in 2012 she edited a collection *Communication across Cultures* for Palgrave Macmillan. echristopher051@gmail.com; www. ElizabethChristopher.net

Daniel Dauber is an assistant professor at the University of Warwick, UK. After finishing the doctoral programme at the Vienna University of Economics and Business (WU), he became a faculty member at the Centre for Applied Linguistics, University of Warwick. His doctoral thesis "Hybridization in Mergers and Acquisitions" (January 2011) was the result of investigation into the process of blending organizational cultures. Since October 2009, he has been Executive Editor of the *European Journal of Cross-Cultural Competence and Management* (EJCCM). d.dauber@warwick.ac.uk

Vincent Ferravanti is the IT Director of L-3 Communications S&DS global manufacturing company. He is an information technology (IT) executive with global experience in aligning IT departments to support company growth and reduce costs. He has held several senior leadership positions in global corporations, developing systems architectures that are both flexible and sustainable allowing companies to absorb acquisitions and support rapid growth business models. With an MBA and hands-on experience, he is "bi-lingual" in "techy" and business language, allowing him to bridge the gap between technology and business. He has published numerous articles on IT management and systems implementations. vincent@ferravinti.com

Dániel Z. Kádár is Professor of English Language and Linguistics at the University of Huddersfield, UK. He previously worked at the Research Institute for Linguistics of the Hungarian Academy of Sciences, simultaneously holding a post in Taiwan. He is the series editor of the Pragmatic Interfaces series for Equinox and holds membership on the editorial boards of various journals. Since 2005, he has received many major research grants from international funding bodies, and his research won the Hungarian Academy of Sciences Award for Young Outstanding Researchers, one of the most prestigious awards for excellence in Hungary, given to very few researchers in humanities. d.z.kadar@hud.ac.uk

Andrew Kakabadse is Professor of Governance and Leadership at Henley Business School and Emeritus Professor at Canfield University. He was a visiting professor at the Australian National University, and Hangzhou University; a visiting fellow at Babson College, Boston; Honorary Professorial Fellow at Curtin University of Technology, Perth; and the H. Smith Richardson Visiting Fellow at the Centre for Creative Leadership, North Carolina. Currently, he is a visiting professor at the University of Ulster; a visiting scholar in residence at Thunderbird, School of Global Management; and an adjunct professor at Southern Cross Business School. He is Fellow of the International Academy of Management, British Psychology Society and British Academy of Management. andrew. kakabadse@heneley.ac.uk

Nadeem Khan is a PhD student at Henley Business School, University of Reading, UK researching in the field of Strategy and Strategic Behaviour of the firm. He has professional experience in the UK and international multinational environments prior to running his own business. His research interests include corporate behaviour, strategy and leadership, policy development and governance, ethics and CSR, and sustainability. Nadeem has co-authored papers published in academic journals and book chapters. nadeem.khan@henley.ac.uk

Nada Korac-Kakabadse is Professor of Policy, Governance and Ethics at the Henley Business School, University of Reading, UK, and was previously Professor of Management and Business Research at the University of Northampton, UK. She has written many scholarly articles and book chapters and worked for international organizations and the federal government. Her consultancy clients have included Citigroup, Microsoft and the public sector UK. She is the co-editor of two journals and has won an award for the best article written by an academic in the *Public Administration Review* (PAR) in 2003. Her paper in *Journal of Managerial Psychology* (JMP) was adjudged the paper of the year in 1998. nada. kakabadse@heneley.ac.uk

Rosina Márquez-Reiter is Reader in Communication at the University of Surrey, UK, and a researcher in Linguistic Practices and Ideologies. She is a member of the University Postgraduate Academic Board, the University Student Progress and Assessment Board (Research), the AHRC Peer-Review College, the International Pragmatics Association Consultation Board, the Executive Committee of the International Association for the Study of Spanish in Society, the International Pragmatics Association and the Asociación Española de Lingüística Aplicad. She is the founding editor of *Spanish in Context*, an international peer-reviewed journal, and advisory board member of the *Journal of Politeness Research* (Mouton de Gruyter). r.marquez-reiter@surrey.ac.uk

Sara Orthaber is a member of the Faculty of Logistics at the University of Maribor, Slovenia. Her research interests are workplace studies, linguistic impoliteness, computer-mediated discourse analysis, sociolinguistics, conversation analysis, interactional linguistics and pragmatics. sara.orthaber@uni-mb.si

Catherine Pereira is Head of the Negotiation and International Trade/ International School of Economics and Management, University of La Sabana, Bogota, Colombia. She has held management positions at various private and public sector firms. Her appointments include those of Mayor in Pension and Financial Oversight; Media Prima Regime; and Economic Advisor to the Superintendent of Banks. catherine.pereira@ unisabana.edu.co

Helen Spencer-Oatey is Director of the Centre for Applied Linguistics, University of Warwick. Her main research interests are the interrelationships between language use and the management of interpersonal relations; intercultural interaction, the interface between culture, language and behaviour; and intercultural adaptation and change, including issues of identity and hybridity, culture shock, intercultural competence and development. At the University of Luton, she established the first MA in Intercultural Communication in the UK. In 2002, she started managing the major inter-governmental eChina-UK Programme on behalf of the Higher Education Funding Council for England and joined the University of Warwick in September 2007. helen.spencer-oatey@warwick.ac.uk

Lucy Taksa is Professor of Management, Head of Department, Marketing and Management, Macquarie University, Sydney. Previously, at the University of New South Wales, she was Head of School, Organization and Management, and Associate Dean (Education) in the Faculty of Commerce and Economics. She is internationally recognized for her work on gendered workplace cultures in transport and finance, migrant employees, multiculturalism, identity and diversity management. She is currently working on the Australian Research Council funded "Affinities in Multicultural Australia" project. She is on the Australian Research Council College of Experts and is an associate editor of the *European Management Review* and the *Economic and Labour Relations Review*. lucy.taksa@mq.edu.au

Jiayi Wang is Lecturer in Chinese Language, Cultural Studies and Interpreting and Translation Studies at the University of Central Lancashire, UK. Her focus is on official/business intercultural communication. Her research interests include pragmatics, intercultural interaction and the interface between intercultural communication and translation/interpreting studies. Formerly, she was an international project manager and official interpreter/translator in a Chinese government ministry, and she also worked as an interpreter/translator for a wide range of organizations such as Deutsche Bank and *Fortune* Magazine. She has published research articles on comparative law and professional translations, and previously edited a ministerial journal on international exchange. jwang11@uclan.ac.uk

Geoffrey Webb is President of Figaro Systems, Inc, the inventors of Simultext®, the electronic text delivery system for presenting simultaneous translations of opera librettos. An Australian citizen, he attended Yale University, USA, in 1985 and received a master's degree in Technical Design and Production from the Yale School of Drama in 1988. He is a graduate of the University of New South Wales School of Architecture. He served as design engineer at the Metropolitan Opera House, New York, for ten years, and as a visiting professor, he taught a graduate course in Finite Element Analysis at Yale University for three years. gjhwebb@gmail.com

Anne Marie Zwerg-Villegas was awarded a doctoral degree in International Business from Uppsala, Sweden, and a Master of International Management from Baylor University Texas. She was an economist at Virginia Tech, USA, before being appointed as Profesor-Investigador, Jefe de Àrea Negociación y Comercio Internacional, Universidad de La Sabana, Colombia. anne.zwerg@unisabana.edu.co.

About the Book

The nature of case studies

Case studies represent a form of research that is qualitative and descriptive. It examines individuals and groups by participant and direct observation and by interviews, tests and records. Thus cases are compiled from a wide range of detailed information about a particular participant or group, to provide as complete a picture of an event or situation as possible.

This kind of comprehensive understanding is achieved through "thick"[1] description. It involves in-depth examination of given situations or events, relevant circumstances, characteristics of those involved and the nature of the community in which it is located.

Thick description also involves interpreting the meaning of demographic and descriptive data such as cultural values as well as individual attitudes and motives. Its objective is to achieve a degree of external validity by which to evaluate the extent to which conclusions might be transferable to other times, settings, situations and people; and to identify patterns of cultural and social relationships and put them in context.[2]

Case studies are the preferred method of investigation when researchers have little control over relevant events, and where a holistic, real-life, contemporary view is needed to reason from specific to more general terms. To this extent, case studies are interchangeable with ethnography, field study and participant observation. All these types of qualitative research take place in natural settings such as offices, classrooms, neighbourhoods or private homes. Where case studies differ from other qualitative research is that essentially they are narratives. They describe real, complicated and contextually rich situations that usually involve dilemmas, conflicts or problems that one or more of the characters must negotiate. As an instructional strategy, these stories create links between theory and practice, between what is taught in the classroom and enacted in "real life".

The case studies in this collection have been chosen carefully for variety in subject, length and detail, to provide guidelines for further research, to illustrate lectures or to promote classroom discussions, depending on users' goals. Some are quite short, others much longer; some are real, with details of actual people and circumstances, others are simply realistic. Each is followed by a discussion that attempts to set the case into a wider theoretical framework; and all topics relate to one or more aspects of international management and intercultural communication.

Material for these case studies has been drawn from the writers' professional experiences. Each case, relatively concisely, tells an engaging story; raises a thought-provoking issue; contains elements of conflict; promotes empathy by providing plenty of information about characters, locations, context and action; but lacks an obvious or clear-cut right answer. They all encourage readers to think about the situation and take a position regarding it.

The format of the book

The book is presented in two volumes, the first consisting of case studies concerning different aspects of international management and intercultural communication in business, marketing and politics. Volume 2 deals with cases of international management in social and educational settings.

Thus, in Volume 1, Chapter 1, Dauber writes of the need for careful times to minimize culture shock resulting from a domestic acquisition. In Chapter 2, Lim *et al.* provide a study of cross-cultural communication problems in selection interviews; and the same theme is sounded in Chapter 3 by Alizadeh and Chavan in their cases of international health care.

In Chapter 4, Christopher's case concerns leadership motivation tactics when leader and follower approach a problem from very different perspectives; and Bhawuk and Anand's study in Chapter 5 also concerns motivation in cross-cultural management when there are discrepancies between corporate policies and individual interpretations. Wang and Spencer-Oatey follow in Chapter 6 with an account of challenges in building professional relations across cultures, and Márquez-Reiter *et al.* in Chapter 7 supply a case of customers' culture-based responses to corporate social media marketing. Kakabadse *et al.* (Chapter 8) provide comparative cases of official and unofficial business practices across national cultures, and Pereira and Zwerg-Villegas in Chapter 9 continue the ethical debate with their account of an expatriate's moral dilemma.

In Chapter 10, Webb writes of communication trials and tribulations of project management in an international setting.

Finally in Chapter 11 Ferravanti puts the case for games and iconography in multicultural technology training.

Volume 2 begins with Lindstrom's case of a campaign to limit tobacco consumption by members of minority cultures in mainstream USA (Chapter 1). This is followed by a study by Gillis of an anti-opium social lobby group in Singapore (Chapter 2); then, in Chapter 3 Goodenow writes of the emerging role of communications technology in rotary international. Li's case (Chapter 4) is set in an academic environment and deals with the intercultural experience of a Chinese teacher. Fujimori *et al.* present a complementary case in Chapter 5, of an international student's cross-cultural adjustment, as do Stone and Stone in Chapter 6 with their case of cultural differences in communication cues and perception of time.

In Chapter 7, Szczepek Reed offers a study of bilingual supervision meetings between a lecturer and her international students, while Pu's case in Chapter 8 is of adjustment by a western-trained Chinese teacher after she returns to her native land.

McKinney *et al.*'s Chapter 9 account is of managing the learning of new arrival children in mainstream schooling, and Leigh in Chapter 10 writes of "playing" the way to shared understanding. Finally, in Chapter 11, Harrison's case study illustrates the importance of space in communication, especially in learning environments.

All case studies conform to the same format:

- Title and name of author;
- editor's introduction;
- abstract;
- key words;
- case description;
- outcomes;
- legends;
- references;
- endnotes.

How to use case studies as teaching tools

The use of case studies depends on teaching goals and the structure of the learning environment. For example, a short case might illustrate and enrich a lecture to a large group. On the other hand, classes may be divided into small groups or pairs to discuss a relevant case – if so, more detailed and complex cases will provide opportunity for students to explore them in some depth; perhaps integrated with other instructional strategies such as role playing or debate.

The following is a set of guidelines for leading case-based discussions:

Students need plenty of time to read and think about the case before discussing it, especially if some or all of them are working in a second language. Therefore, longer cases might be set in advance as a homework exercise, perhaps accompanied by a set of questions to direct students' thinking.

1. In class, the case should be introduced briefly and students told about the approach to be taken
2. Small groups should be set up and members of all groups advised to identify the constraints on the various characters in the case, their opportunities and the quality of their decisions. In the same situation, what do the students think they might have done differently and why?
3. When time is up, lecturers might ask a representative from each group to present members' responses. Again depending on time, questions may be solicited from the listening groups, and the lecturer may probe for deeper analysis by requests to substantiate arguments.
4. At the end of such sessions, it will be the lecturer's responsibility to collate, summarize and synthesize the issues that were raised, to reinforce students' learning.

Notes

1. G. Ryle, 1949, *The concept of mind* (Hutchinson, UK).
2. Clifford Geertz, 1993, *The interpretation of cultures: selected essays* (Fontana Press).

1

Timing of Communication in Organizational Culture Change Processes: The Case of a Domestic Acquisition

Daniel Dauber

Editor's introduction

This case study meticulously charts a commercial acquisition, with the objective of demonstrating the importance of synchronizing organizational communication with organizational change, if both parties are not to suffer traumatic culture shocks. Dauber clearly illustrates the need to find common ground before implementing major decisions, in order to create synergies and harmonize operations that will ease the transition from two companies into one.

His study reveals how open communication is particularly necessary if there are major cultural differences between the relevant firms, otherwise employee commitment, motivation and efficiency will suffer. The more dissimilar the culture, the more the likelihood of misinterpretation, that is, noise.[1] Communication, therefore, is a complex process of linking up or sharing perceptions: this requires understanding, and trust promotes it. This is not to say that trust is essential. All over the world, every day, business and government transactions take place between people who wouldn't trust each other further than they could throw them.[2] Nevertheless, as Dauber demonstrates, collaboration and alliances do depend to some degree on trust developed between parties over time.

Schwartz's research[3] identified hierarchy versus egalitarianism (author-itarian leadership vs democratic decisions) as a major dimension of indi-vidual work values; and Dauber's study supports this. He found BIGFISH to own a strong and formal organizational hierarchy, whereas that of

BIZCOM was flat and friendly: and these cultural differences resulted in unnecessary conflict because they were poorly handled by senior management.

These are some of the ways in which Dauber follows and analyzes the process of the BIGFISH/BIZCOM acquisition; and he offers suggestions for organizational communication, and for the timing of such communication, that might have made for a smoother ride.

Abstract:

The presented case study sheds light on timing and communication dilemmas caused by organizational change and organizational culture differences. Since the case study is of a national acquisition, factors such as organizational culture can be analysed more systematically and reliably. It is particularly suitable for lecturers and students who wish to analyse intercultural communicative challenges that individuals and groups face in workplace contexts where organizational and sub-organizational cultures differ substantially. By drawing on 19 narrative interviews with members of the acquiring and target company, a systematic analysis of communication processes was undertaken using the configuration model of organizational culture.

Keywords: acquisition, communication, configuration model of organizational culture, cultural differences, M&A.

Introduction

Setting the scene for the case of a domestic acquisition

Mergers and acquisitions (M&As) are by far the most popular market entry strategy, and yet their success rate is considered to be stunningly low.[4] Prior research has pinpointed the relevance of proper post-M&A integration management and intercultural communication as decisive factors to determine whether expected synergies will ultimately unfold and pre-defined goals can be achieved.[5]

While several studies have focused on cross-border M&As, less is known about domestic acquisitions. Although these do not "suffer" from language barriers, they nevertheless suffer from what could be considered as the "single-layered acculturation shock" and the unexpected cultural differences between organizations experienced by people exposed to changes in an acquisition.

This case study sheds light on organizational culture differences and their interaction and goes beyond communication issues resulting from differences in languages. In particular, emphasis is put on the concept of "timing" as well as dilemmas of timing in communication and how it affects the change process and those people involved. By drawing on 19 narrative interviews with members of the acquiring and target company, evidence from a real acquisition will be used to highlight issues emerging from organizational culture differences, rather than national culture differences.

In a first step, the background of both organizations involved will be outlined and key differences that reflect their organizations' culture, including values, strategies, structures, and ways of doing business, will be explored. In a second step, the experiences in the first year after the acquisition are critically reviewed, and two common communication issues related to timing of communication will be showcased and analysed in greater detail. This chapter closes with an analysis of the situation using the configuration model of organizational culture[6] as an analytical frame of reference.

Case presentation

The acquirer: BIGFISH Global Austria

BIGFISH Global Austria is the Austrian subsidiary of an American communication technology company and counts as one of the top market players in Austria. Their success is largely based on their technology advantage that allowed them to offer their services on a reliable basis to thousands of customers. With a primary focus on business-to-customer (B2C) business, their entire philosophy and strategy are geared towards mass production and therefore a high level of standardization.

Another major reason for their success lies in the independent service delivery infrastructure that they built over the past years. While other competitors were forced to pay third companies to deliver services to their customers, BIGFISH Global Austria decided to build their own infrastructure. This required substantial investment over several years, but offered (1) independence from third-party organizations, (2) total control over distribution channels, (3) technological innovations to provide faster and better communication services and (4) lower prices for customers in the long run.

BIGFISH Global Austria's strategy allowed them to compete with the market leader at that time, and it can be considered the foundation for their continuing success.

However, more recently, BIGFISH Global Austria recognized that if they want to grow further and stay competitive, they need to expand.

While profitable, the current infrastructure and technology limited the company's reach to a certain capacity of customers. Further expansion using their traditional approach, that is, building more infrastructure themselves, would have been too costly.

Apart from that, a new, small and innovative organization, BIZCOM, shook up the market and developed a new technology that promised better quality at the same price and was not so dependent on such infra-structures. Soon BIGFISH Global Austria realized that acquiring this new technology would not only allow them to further grow their customer base, but also add business customers to their clientele, which consti-tuted the core business of BIZCOM. The idea to undergo an acquisition was born.

The target: BIZCOM

BIZCOM started as a small company, founded by two engineers who had the brilliant idea for a new communication technology that was very well received by companies, which later on became their core business. As the business grew, so did the company, and soon BIZCOM became one of the most relied-on communication solutions for organizations in Austria. Their strong business-to-business (B2B) operations shaped the organization's future path and organizational culture.

The rapid success in the B2B segment triggered the idea to expand into the B2C segment, using their much more advanced technology, compared to the competition, such as the one used by BIGFISH Global Austria. Therefore, it was less surprising to see that BIZCOM started to gain more and more ground in the B2C business and was mainly perceived as the new positive driving force in the industry, that offered new technology at a fair price. This was also reflected in their main slogan "We are the GOOD ones!," clearly separating themselves from the competition.

New employees that joined the company did so because they appreci-ated the small, family-like atmosphere allowing for maximum creative freedom and not being overburdened with administrative structures. This positive spirit certainly added to the success of the company, its quality of products and drive for innovation.

Despite this positive trend, the two owners realized that the initial vision of creating technology started to become less of a major task for them. Instead, they were confronted with an organically growing organ-ization that required pro-active management of staff and, in general, made it necessary to restructure the organization. When BIGFISH Global Austria offered to buy the company and its technology, the two owners considered this a unique opportunity to hand over a healthy business that had started to become too big for them. When the offer was made, the two owners gladly accepted.

Communicative context: organizational cultures, philosophies, structures and ways of doing business

In view of the above, it becomes apparent that the differences between both organizations are manifold. In the course of the interviews, several differences between the organizations were mentioned that seemed to have had a considerable bearing on the efficiency of communication after the acquisition. Table 1.1 highlights these differences as perceived by employees of BIGFISH Group Austria and BIZCOM.

Table 1.1   Operational differences between BIGFISH Group Austria and BIZCOM

BIGFISH Group Austria		BIZCOM	
As perceived by BIGFISH	**As perceived by BIZCOM**	**As perceived by BIGFISH**	**As perceived by BIZOM**
Strong hierarchy	Strong hierarchy	Small and responsive	Flat hierarchy
Structured approach to customer service	Slow processes	More share decision-making	Less controlled/monitored
Formal communication processes	High complexity	Flat hierarchy	Fast and responsive
Slow decision-making	Large company		Young
High complexity	International		Dynamic
	Poor customer service		Family business
	Inflexible		Small company
	Employees are specialized		Direct contact with customer
			Strong customer service
			Employees are generalists

Source: Author's own.

Two of the interviewees summarized the differences and the associated problems as follows:

P10$_{\text{BIZCOM}}$: Today you call an employee and say: "Yes, I would need this and this," and you say: "Well, I am sorry. I know how to do it, but I am not allowed to do it. You need to create an entry in the ticketing system." This will then be assigned, I don't know, maybe to the right or otherwise to the wrong person. If it [the entry in the ticketing system] will not be assigned it returns to the big collecting point and there it will be re-assigned and some day it will be done. And even though you know that it would have all been done within 20 seconds during a phone call, you are not allowed to do it.

P4$_{BIGFISH}$: These were business customers and we had private customers. Business customers are a different type of customer care. With respect to the call-center, in general, they [BIZCOM] had a different service. Because, a business customer cannot wait. If he needs something he needs it now and not the day after tomorrow, if something is not working. And, ahm, also with respect to contracts, because a private customer is bound to it for a year, at maximum. Then he can do what he wants. A business customer, this goes up to three, one, three, five year lasting annual contracts and [...] we do not have extensions of a contract for the private segment. There is no extension of a contract.

The first year of the acquisition

The following sections outline the takeover before and after the deal was signed. Apart from that, the day the acquisition was announced and the contract had been signed will be illustrated since it had a considerable impact on the entire narrative of this case. Figure 1.1 summarizes the events in chronological order, including the reported issues in terms of communication.

Pre-acquisition	Announ-cement	Post-acquisition
BIZCOM workshop	Day before Christmas	Structural change after one year
Secrecy	Negative emotions	Conflict of strategies, structures and values
Competitiors	Anxiety of losing job	Lack of identity with new company
	No change promised	Autonomy partially remained

Figure 1.1 Chronological order of events that took place in the acquisition
Source: Author.

Pre-announcement: rumours and false information

The acquisition was officially signed and announced on December 23. As usual for every acquisition, there was only a small group of people who knew about the acquisition in advance and the members were mainly responsible for the due diligence, that is, the evaluation of the target company prior to the takeover. This was true for both sides, BIGFISH Group Austria and BIZCOM. The latter involved only the two owners, and therefore none of the other employees at BIZCOM expected an acquisition. The signs of a potential takeover were not visible for a long time.

In contrast, the owners of BIZCOM even organized events to discuss their joint future as if they were about to continue as an independent company. Great plans were forged to establish themselves further in the years to come and to become more competitive, in particular compared to BIGFISH Group Austria. This workshop was entirely contradictory in its messages to the employees at BIZCOM, since it was clear at that time that the company will most likely be acquired.

A member of BIZCOM described it as follows:

P19$_{BIZCOM}$: In October the managers of BIZCOM started to present the mission, vision and where are we in two years. And we worked that well up to now. And there were workshops for that and the employees were so much motivated. And those who worked for BIZCOM made it very well, I say. The employees were so fascinated: "Yes, we are BIZCOM. We are allowed to work here. We stick together." And so on. And not even two months later we were already sold.

Given the fact that employees in BIZCOM considered themselves as a small family and many of them knew the owners personally, it was a huge shock when suddenly the acquisition was announced publicly. There were feelings of betrayal as well as a huge loss in loyalty to and trust in the two owners. The lack of prior communication also infused feelings of anxiety combined with utter irritation. The workshops two months earlier were now not perceived as an effort to shape their joint future, but as a huge lie that nobody could understand.

One of the managers of BIGFISH Group Austria, who was present on the day of the announcement at BIZCOM, remembers this moment as follows:

P15$_{BIGFISH}$: But what they [the members of BIZCOM] held against their former owners was that they [the former owners] did not inform them. Because it was a company, which within five years grew from zero to 300 people. This means, many people were in a friendly contact with the owners. It was more or less a "friends and family business." Except the call-center, which [consisted of] some agents, who came from university, but the group of engineers were all friends and acquaintances of the ex-owners. And actually they expected that their friends, with whom they went out to eat privately and at weekends, I don't know, made LAN-parties, would inform them about it and that they will cream off X Million Euro. [...] The former owners did actually say in two sentences: "So, we sold the company. These are the new owners. I may introduce [names of new owners]." And then they left without explaining people why all this happened. And this made people that angry that they were more or less taken by surprise and that the former owners left them more or less alone that they relatively quickly adjusted, I have to say.

At the other end of the deal, employees at BIGFISH Group Austria were much less surprised and there were even several rumors that signalled a takeover in a not-too-distant future. Their emotions about the acquisition itself remained fairly neutral and even positive, largely due to the fact that they were aware that they might not be affected as much as employees of the target company.

The day before Christmas = the day of the announcement of the acquisition

The managers at BIGFISH Group Austria faced a dilemma when they had to decide when they wanted to personally announce the takeover at BIZCOM. Since the acquisition took place on December 23, they only had two choices: First, they could have waited until after Christmas and New Year and then arrange a larger meeting to talk to the newly acquired members of BIGFISH Group Austria. Second, they could call in employees on December 23 and inform them on the day of signing the deal.

The managers of BIGFISH Group Austria decided to announce the acquisition as soon as possible, and therefore, they drove four hours by car to reach the BIZCOM facility to introduce themselves. The major reason for doing so was the fear that employees of BIZCOM would find out about the takeover through the news, which, according to the CEO of BIGFISH Group Austria, could have had even worse effects in the months to come:

P6$_{BIGFISH}$: Now you were able to say: "Well, we could have informed them on January 6th as well." Well, what is better about that?

Nothing. Then people read it in the newspapers and this always excites the feeling [...]: "Well, now they sell me and this I read [short pause] I get notified about that in the newspapers." This you cannot make undone. You have for this kind of communication no second chance. There is no other way.

However, BIZCOM managers who had to come in on December 23 interpreted the situation and the timing of the announcement considerably differently. For them, it was more an inconvenience having to leave their families during their holidays for a business meeting as well as the shock that overshadowed their Christmas holidays after the announcement:

P12$_{BIZCOM}$: Well, I think that such things just before Christmas, as well as lay-offs are never a good idea. [...] on the one hand it was good that we got informed, on the other hand we partly did not know how to cope with these news. [...] and the wildest fantasies [emerged] about what will happen in the future.

P14$_{BIZCOM}$: It was Christmas and then it was announced officially. So it was rather inconvenient, the whole situation. We all were shocked.

P19$_{BIZCOM}$: Exactly before Christmas, because everyone was afraid about what will happen now. Will we all lose our jobs, fear for our existence. And is this necessary now, just before Christmas? And on January 1st we have no job anymore.

In this already emotionally heavily loaded context, it turned out to be fairly difficult for BIGFISH Group Austria to communicate their message properly. Several employees of BIZCOM questioned the phrases used in their presentation of not being laid-off, although BIGFISH Group Austria emphasized that nothing would change, because they needed them and their expertise to run the business.

P1$_{BIZCOM}$: There were [...] the common phrases and clichés, which are known from this area [i.e., M&As]: "We are good, we are nice and you have the technology, which we do not have and there will change nothing and everything stays as it is. And of course the brand BIZCOM will remain and of course you continue to do what you have been doing until now, because you are so successful. Otherwise we would have not bought you. Nothing will change. But the owners need to change [...]. And everything is beautiful and so well and so great! Merry Christmas! [very sarcastically]"

Post-acquisition: separation and partial changes to BIZCOM with a time-lag

After the acquisition, BIGFISH Group Austria lived up to their promise that no major changes would be introduced to BIZCOM. This eased the emotions of BIZCOM employees slightly and since there were no changes announced within an entire year, business seemed to continue as usual.

The main reason for no fast changes to BIZCOM was due to the fact that BIGFISH Group Austria was entirely unfamiliar (1) with the technology of BIZCOM as well as (2) the new B2B customer segment. In order not to interfere with ongoing business and various projects, BIGFISH Group Austria waited an entire year before introducing first structural changes, which caused severe disruptions in BIZCOM.

As a first major step, several changes to the reporting system in BIZCOM were necessary, since BIGFISH Group Austria had to report back to their American headquarters. Apart from that, several other operational and structural changes were introduced.

Employees of BIZCOM were irritated and confused at that time. They were not able to make sense of these new structures and modes of communication that were more "hierarchical," "bureaucratic," "complex" and "unnecessary." Due to the lack of communication by managers of BIGFISH Group Austria, the newly imposed patterns of doing business and modes of operating as a company were bewildering to them and also contradictory to their philosophy and overall strategy for the B2B segment. In addition, the technical integration of BIZCOM with their new technology was also an issue when communication started to fall short.

> P16$_{BIZCOM}$: Well, it was actually, it was never really sufficiently communicated to colleagues or employees that it is a cooperation, a cooperation with equal rights. But it was rather like: "We are the big network people [...], we are the huge BIGFISH Group Austria and we tell you now how it works." [...] Because I experienced it a little bit that certain objections, doubts, help, support, [by employees of BIZCOM] now with respect to the integration of systems, were not really dealt with [...] but rather were played down and therefore this created already barriers. Because it was quite a belly-landing. The integration of systems went quite wrong. Now the members of BIZCOM or the former members of BIZCOM were even more confirmed regarding their doubts. And this created an even larger gap.

The sudden imposition of new structures that were not compatible with B2B products and the business clientele resulted in a lock-down in communication between the two companies. BIZCOM employees partly decided to hold back their knowledge, knowing that BIGFISH Group Austria would not be able to easily operate BIZCOM's business by themselves. One of the interviewees very vividly describes the subversive behaviour by BIZCOM employees as follows:

P2$_{BIGFISH}$: [...] the creditor department of BIZCOM, it is very much, there is a noticeable difference. It is still: "We are BIZCOM and belong together." They never do something as it should be, or as the regulations are. This means, if they order something like a rubber [they do it like they did before ignoring the pre-defined processes]. [...] The people of BIZCOM resist it. As it was in BIZCOM: No permission, they order what is needed, every one of them and then there are problems, because I need to call and ask every time the responsible person of the creditor department and say: "Who has ordered what?" Because with 1,300 employees, it is difficult to call everyone: "Did you order something?" [...] This is the typical BIZCOM behaviour: It will stay as it was. And partly I have the feeling they do this on purpose to make my life difficult.

Nevertheless, BIZCOM employees tried to explain why certain changes will be dysfunctional to their business, but it was felt that BIGFISH Group managers are not willing to listen. One of BIZCOM's managers reflects on one of his meetings as follows:

P1$_{BIZCOM}$: And he [an acquired employee] tried to explain with arms and legs to "ladies and gentleman" [sarcastically] that this is something different. That you need to take care of certain basic conditions and that an orchid needs to be treated differently from a rose, because otherwise it will die. The grower of roses [used as a synonym for the acquirer in the following metaphor by P1] says: "Don't tell me about flowers. I know about flowers. Flower is flower. That's that!" The grower of orchids says: "No, flower is not flower. Take care. If you do not take care about that, that and that, this thing [orchid] will die." "Bull shit. Don't tell me." [Answers the grower of roses]

[...] This integration was already in the beginning shaped by a remarkable ignorance. [...] that there exist requirements and necessities of business customers, which go beyond the performance description of sold products was not recognized. They did not care as long as cash was flowing. That one thing depends on the other was ignored [by the acquirer].

This and similar situations resulted in complete misunderstandings on both sides and also unfolded negative side-effects on both of their businesses. For example, while BIGFISH Group Austria was required to harmonize communication procedures to comply with standards set by the American headquarters, employees of BIZCOM felt that these changes imposed limitations to their operations and technology. Since BIGFISH Group Austria did not deviate from their plan to change certain structures, they were perceived as being arrogant, because of their company size and large customer base, compared to BIZCOM.

For some employees, the reasons why they worked for BIZOM, for example, creative freedom, personal and family-like operation of business, were suddenly replaced by hierarchical structures and time-consuming, slow and impersonal communication structures. As a result, some employees decided to leave the company, while others stayed, but primarily because they either were dependent on their income or feared to find no other job in the current economic situation.

BIZCOM and BIGFISH Group Austria today

Several years later, BIGFISH Group Austria still struggled with a full integration of BIZCOM, and it was decided to pursue a separation strategy. Thus, BIZCOM maintained a fairly high level of autonomy. The geographic distance between BIGFISH Group Austria and BIZCOM also contributed to this situation, since only one manager was sent to this new organizational unit to report back to BIGFISH Group Austria.

Apart from that, the composition of employees largely remained the same and only the reporting system was changed. While some employees expressed positive feelings about the new situation, the majority of them were rather negative about all those changes that were introduced and the conflicts they caused. Nevertheless, they learned to accept to work for BIGFISH Group Austria, but certainly lacked the same motivation they had when they worked for BIZCOM.

The following section will look behind the dynamics of this case study and aims to provide insights into social dilemmas as well as timing of communication in such drastic organizational change processes.

Outcomes

Organizational culture differences and timing of integration and communication as sources for conflicts

A large amount of research has highlighted the importance of efficient communication in M&As,[7] in particular when companies located in different countries are concerned. However, as this case study shows, not only national culture but also organizational culture can be found as a disruptor in acquisitions. The relevance, timing and consistency of information and communication were of particular importance in this case.

In many ways, the presented case study can be considered stereotypical for a technology-driven acquisition. A big company, BIGFISH Group Austria, aimed to grow organically by gaining access to the new business customer segment as well as an entirely new technology.

Companies who seek to acquire non-tangible assets need to pay particular attention to the "human integration" after an M&A deal. The knowledge of employees in the target company is by far the most valuable "asset" of such small and innovation-driven organizations. From a strategic perspective, BIZCOM was the ideal choice for BIGFISH Group Austria to gain a substantial competitive advantage in the Austrian market and secure a prosperous future. However, several of the expected synergies did not unfold due to issues that emerged during the attempted integration stage.

While this issue is particularly accentuated in this case study, similar approaches to acquisitions can be found with other cases. Indeed, a plethora of prior research identified that strategic fit between organizations is very important and a major source of synergies, but ultimately cultural fit between organizations might dictate whether these synergies can be realized. Therefore, it can be argued that strategic benefits are most likely a requirement for every M&A to be successful. However, cultural fit is equally, if not even more, important.[8]

Considering the outlined acquisition, two major reasons for a rather low level of success can be determined: (1) organizational culture differences and (2) timing of integration and communication.

Organizational culture differences: different values, different strategies, different operations/ways of doing business

Besides the obvious difference in company size, several other differences between BIGFISH Group Austria and BIZCOM can be identified.

All interviewees in this study reported about differences between the organizations, which were sources of or reasons for conflicts that would need to be addressed through communication between the organizations.

Some examples for these perceived differences were shown in Table 1.1 and can be analyzed more systematically using the configuration model of organizational culture[9] as an analytical frame of reference. This model allows mapping organizational dynamics related to four different domains: organizational values, strategy, structure and operations. These are connected through different modes of communication and learning processes. These domains also reflect the four major areas of differences identified in this case study.

While Figure 1.2 shows both organizations before the acquisition, Figure 1.3 demonstrates the communication issues when the structural changes were introduced. The incompatibility between BIZCOM's strategy and BIGFISH Group Austria's structures and operations is illustrated by an "X." Figure 1.3 also showcases the hybrid state of BIZCOM that required resolution to allow for a stable social system again.

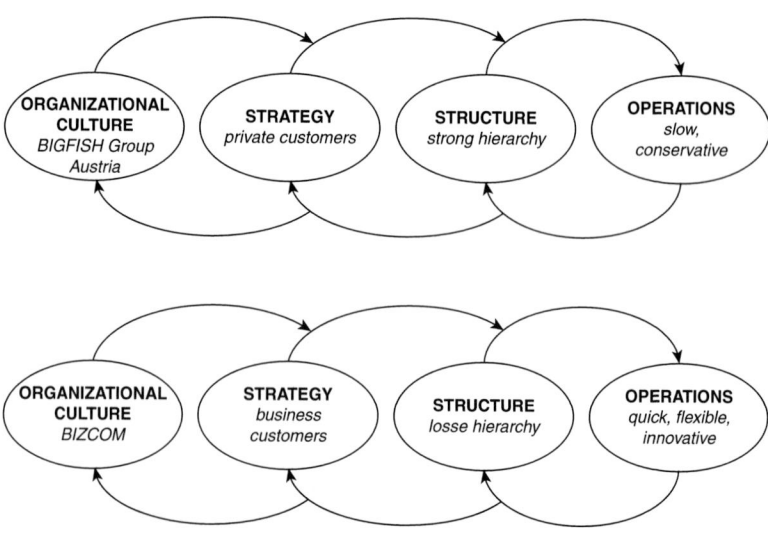

Figure 1.2   BIGFISH Group Austria and BIZCOM before the acquisition using the configuration model of organizational culture

Source: Dauber *et al.*, 2012.

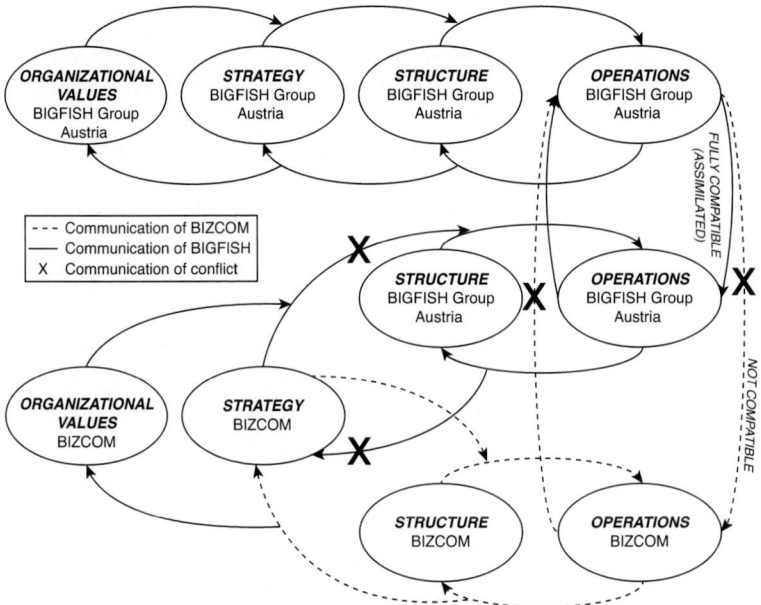

Figure 1.3   BIGFISH Group Austria and BIZCOM during the integration process using the configuration model of organizational culture

Source: Dauber *et al.*, 2012.

Operations in both organizations are deeply rooted in their organizational values and strategies that are well aligned with their respective structures. Each organization by itself was perfectly in tune and in balance before the acquisition. In particular, in BIZCOM, the identity of employees with the organization was very strong and constituted a major source for their intrinsic motivation as well as their desire to become bigger. Imposing changes to elements of an organization might turn out to be detrimental, if these changes should result in unstable states of such social systems, for example, when strategies do not fit structures anymore or vice versa.

A whole field of research exists that explores the notion of "strategy-structure-fit" and it highlights the importance of compatibility of strategies and structures to allow companies to function properly and ensure not only financial viability, but also social viability.[10]

In light of the case study, BIGFISH Group Austria found itself in a dilemma, because they needed to change the structures in BIZCOM to make them conform to their own organization and ensure it is in line with their American headquarters. On the other hand, they had to face the issue that the new structure did not fit the established operations and strategy of BIZCOM, which were geared towards a market segment that was also different to that of BIGFISH Group Austria. This explains why both organizations managed to continue to operate well prior to the introduction of larger structural changes, which took place a year after the announcement of the acquisition.

Besides the issue of structural changes, it is worth mentioning that BIGFISH Group Austria and BIZOM were not only competitors in the Austrian market, but also used different technologies and operated on different business models. In addition, the differences in philosophy, in particular regarding "Who is my customer?" and "How do I treat my customers?," were substantially different. Therefore, their understanding of how business should be done on an operational level also contributed to several misunderstandings and conflicts as outlined before.

Timing of integration and communication: the need for a synchronous approach

All these differences in values, strategies, structures and operations between these organizations, as well as the fact that they were competitors prior to the acquisition, made efficient and successful communication between employees very difficult.

The need to harmonize organizations can pose severe challenges for managers since they are required to accommodate their headquarters as well as the newly acquired organization. This dilemma can only be resolved by sharing knowledge between organizations and making employees understand why certain changes are necessary.

This will have to go beyond explaining operations, structures and strategies, but may also involve cultural training, that is, building an understanding for organizational culture differences. By only explaining how certain processes look like, employees will not be able to attach meaning to these procedures and just follow instructions. This is even more so the case if the introduced practices are contradictory to other parts of the organization, such as existing strategies, which could result in either open revolt or subversive ways of resistance to change.

Having a holistic understanding of both organizations seems crucial. The necessary learning process to achieve this has to take place on both sides, since all parties involved in an M&A need to understand their prior operations in order to allow for the emergence of maybe a third way of doing business. This is commonly considered as "integration."[11] With respect to BIGFISH Group Austria and BIZCOM, no particular integration attempts were made in the first year, thus keeping their businesses separate and only allowing for a fairly simple, loose, rather unidirectional and less integrated communication policy.

In such situations, the level of communication between companies tends to be rare and certain synergies cannot unfold, for example, structural synergies, because two autonomous structures need to be maintained and managed independently. Also, differences between organizations tend to be less of an issue, since they are not interacting or conflicting with each other if organizations are kept separately.

However, as soon as BIGFISH Group Austria aimed to more fully integrate BIZCOM, communication broke down since there was a lack of understanding for each other in all domains (i.e., values, strategy, structure and operations). It was not clear to employees of BIZCOM how the new structures and operations fit their strategy. BIGFISH Group Austria was not at all interested in changing BIZCOM's strategy, because it was successful in the past and they held no knowledge about the B2B business. However, this disconnection of structures and operations from strategies and organizational values ultimately led to communication breakdowns and even conflicts between members of both organizations.

The situation was defined by confusion on both sides: BIZCOM employees could not make sense of the change process and the purpose of it, while BIGFISH Group Austria was not able to make sense of BIZCOM's resistance to change. This dilemma resulted in negative emotions and resentments against the entire acquisition, making it even more difficult to achieve planned synergies.

In view of this, the timing of change and the timing of certain ways of communication are crucial and need to be in "sync." The call for action with respect to a more intercultural approach to communication between organizations coincides with the moment integration or assimilation of organizations sets in.

In M&As where a separation strategy is pursued, companies involved would not suffer from such communicative shortfalls, since organizations will remain largely autonomous and preserve the values, strategies, structures and operations that are aligned to each other. However, as soon as changes are made to both or at least one system, communication becomes vital to allow for sense-making.[12]

Timing of announcement of an acquisition to staff: an unresolvable dilemma

Besides the need for appropriate timing in communication when it comes to integration endeavours, it is also possible to identify another, less easily resolvable issue in communication within the M&A context: timing of announcement of an acquisition.

Admittedly, the presented case study is very special in this respect and has to be considered an extreme case. Not only was the day of the year unfortunate, but also the activities (i.e., the future strategy meeting) that were set prior to the acquisition by the former owners of BIZCOM. There was no way for BIGFISH Group Austria to monitor or control activities prior to the signing of the contract. It was clearly a management mistake to run such activities if the future of the organization was uncertain.

The reasons why the former BIZCOM owners arranged such an event remains unclear, since it was not possible to collect information from them. From the perspective of the acquirer, it certainly had two effects:

- BIZCOM employees slightly dissociated themselves from their former organization; and
- frustration and anger towards the new situation.

In particular, the latter requires attention when aiming to shift peoples' mindsets. The strategy chosen by BIGFISH Group Austria to not change the current organizational structures and aim for temporary separation was helpful in easing emotions among employees. However, the decision to postpone the structural integration had a negative impact on the changes that were introduced a year later and would have required a bi-lateral dialogue.

Considering that BIZCOM's former owners were found to be dishonest by their own employees, at the time when BIGFISH Group Austria introduced their changes, some employees felt that, yet again, a promise was not kept.

In this case study, most of the issues emerged when changes were introduced, and this once more emphasizes the need to consider the timing of communication as well as the timing of introducing changes as an essential component of acquisitions.

Concluding remarks

This case study aimed to highlight the importance of timing in communication and the necessity to synchronize communication with planned change processes. The relevance of appropriate and efficient communication has been highlighted by previous empirical studies,[13] but less is known about the timing of communication within national contexts. It would certainly be wrong to believe that determining the right timing of communication is easy or the most important element in change processes, but it surely requires attention by those responsible for change management.

Acquirers who find themselves in similar situations to that of BIGFISH Group Austria might wish to consider the timing aspect of communication and the importance of ensuring that both parties are able to find a common ground. Only through this common ground will it be possible to explore each other's organizational cultures before making final decisions on how and what to change. This way it will be possible to realize expected synergies more likely and harmonize operational processes.

Open communication is particularly necessary if organizations differ strongly with respect to all domains: organizational values, strategy, structure and operations.[14] Failing to achieve it would cause instability in the target company, not only in terms of systems and operations, but also with respect to employees' commitment, motivation and efficiency due to the inability to make sense of these changes. A successful acquisition is certainly not only determined by its financial achievements, but also by its social coherence and viability in the future.

Notes

The names of all organizations referred to in this case study are entirely fictitious and bear no relation to those of any real firms. All quotations are from anonymous commentators who cannot be identified. All tables and figures are the author's own.

1. Helen Deresky and Elizabeth Christopher, 2012, *International management; Managing cultural diversity* (Australia: Pearson), Chapter 1.
2. Ibid.
3. Shalom H. Schwartz, 1999, 1 January, "A theory of cultural values and some implications for work applied psychology," *Applied Psychology*, 48(1), 23–47.
4. J. Child, D. Faulkner and R. Pitkethly, 2001, *The management of international acquisitions* (Oxford: Oxford University Press).
5. See, for example, "Faites vos jeux," *Economist*, December 4, 1999, p. 63; M.J. Epstein, 2004, "The drivers of success in post-merger integration," *Organizational Dynamics*, 33(2), 174–189; M.E. Graebner, 2004, "Momentum and serendipity: how acquired leaders create value in the integration of technology firms," *Strategic Management Journal*, 25(8/9), 751–777. A.C. Inkpen, A.K. Sundaram and K. Rockwood, 2000, "Cross-border acquisitions of U.S. technology assets," *California Management Review*, 42(Spring), 50–70; M.H. Kavanagh and N.M. Ashkanasy, 2006, "The impact of leadership and change management strategy on organizational culture and individual acceptance of change during a merger," *British Journal of Management*, 17, 81–103; C.B. Meyer, 2008, "Value leakages in mergers and acquisitions: why they occur and how they can be addressed," *Long Range Planning*, 41, 197–224.

6. D. Dauber, G. Fink and M. Yolles, 2012, "A configuration model of organizational culture," *SAGE Open*, 2(1), 1–16. DOI: 10.1177/2158244012441482.
7. For example, Epstein, 2004; Inkpen *et al.*, 2000; Kavanagh and Ashkanasy, 2006.
8. S. Cartwright and C.L. Cooper, 1993, "The role of culture compatibility in successful organizational marriage," *Academy of Management Executive*, 7(2), 57–70; S. Chatterjee, M.H. Lubatkin, D.M. Schweiger and Y. Weber, 1992, "Cultural differences and shareholder value in related mergers: linking equity and human capital," *Strategic Management Journal*, 13(5), 319–334; D. Dauber, 2012, "Opposing positions in M&A research: culture, integration and performance," *Cross Cultural Management: An International Journal*, 19(3), 375–398; Y. Weber, 1996, "Corporate cultural fit and performance in mergers and acquisitions," *Human Relations*, 49(9), 1181–1202. Y. Weber and N. Pliskin, 1996, "The effects of information systems integration and organizational culture on a firm's effectiveness," *Information & Management*, 30, 81–90.
9. Dauber *et al.*, 2012.
10. For example, K. Andrews, 1971, *The concept of corporate strategy* (Homewood, IL: Dow Jones-Irwin); H.I. Ansoff, 1965, *Corporate strategy: an analytic approach to business policy for growth and expansion* (New York: McGraw-Hill); T.L. Amburgey and T. Dacin, 1994, "As the left foot follows the right? The dynamics of strategic and structural change," *Academy of Management Journal*, 37(6), 1427–1452; L. Donaldson, 1987, "Strategy and structural adjustment to regain fit and performance: in defense of contingency theory," *Journal of Management Studies*, 24(1), 1–24. L Donaldson, 1996, *For positive organization theory: proving the hard core* (London, England: SAGE); R.T. Hamilton and G.S. Shergill, 1992, "The relationship between strategy-structure fit and financial performance in New Zealand: evidence of generality and validity with enhanced controls," Journal of Management Studies, 29: 95–113.R.T. Hamilton and G.S. Shergill, 1993, *The logic of New Zealand business: strategy, structure, and performance* (Auckland; New Zealand: Oxford University Press); I.C. Harris and T.W. Ruefli, 2000, "The strategy/structure debate: an examination of the performance implications," *Journal of Management Studies*, 37(4), 587–604; O.E. Williamson, 1975, *Markets and Hierarchies analysis and antitrust implications: a study in the economics of internal organization* (New York: Free Press).
11. See also J.W. Berry, 1980, "Acculturation as varieties of adaptation," in A. Padilla, *Acculturation, theory, models and some new findings* (Boulder and Co; Westview Press); P.C. Haspeslagh and D.B. Jemison, 1991, "The challenge of renewal through acquisitions," *Planning Review*, 19(2), 27–32.
12. K.E. Weick, 1995, *Sensemaking in organizations* (Sage Publications: Thousand Oaks).
13. For example, S.H. Appelbaum, H. Gandell, H. Yortis, S. Proper and F. Jobin, 2000, "Anatomy of a merger: behavior of organizational factors and processes throughout the pre- during- post- stages" (part 1), *Management Decision*, 38(9), 649–662; Epstein, 2004; Kavanagh and Ashkanasy, 2006; Meyer, 2008; D.M. Schweiger and A.S. DeNisi, 1991, "Communication with employees following a merger: a longitudinal field experiment," *Academy of Management Journal*, 34(1), 110–135; T.J. Tetenbaum, 1999, "Beating the odds of merger &

acquisition failure: seven key practices that improve the chance for expected integration and synergies," *Organizational Dynamics*, 28(2), 22–35.
14. Dauber *et al.*, 2012.

References

T.L. Amburgey and T. Dacin, 1994, "As the left foot follows the right? The dynamics of strategic and structural change," *Academy of Management Journal*, 37(6), 1427–1452.

K. Andrews, 1971, *The concept of corporate strategy* (Homewood, IL: Dow Jones-Irwin).

H.I. Ansoff, 1965, *Corporate strategy: An analytic approach to business policy for growth and expansion* (New York: McGraw-Hill).

S.H. Appelbaum, H. Gandell, H. Yortis, S. Proper and F. Jobin, 2000, "Anatomy of a merger: behavior of organizational factors and processes throughout the pre-during- post- stages" (part 1), *Management Decision*, 38(9), 649–662.

J.W. Berry, 1980, "Acculturation as varieties of adaptation," in A Padilla, *Acculturation, theory, models and some new findings* (Boulder, CO: Westview Press).

S. Cartwright and C.L. Cooper, 1993, "The role of culture compatibility in successful organizational marriage," *Academy of Management Executive*, 7(2), 57–70.

S. Chatterjee, M.H. Lubatkin, D.M. Schweiger and Y. Weber, 1992, "Cultural differences and shareholder value in related mergers: linking equity and human capital," *Strategic Management Journal*, 13(5), 319–334.

J. Child, D. Faulkner and R. Pitkethly, 2001, *The management of international acquisitions* (Oxford: Oxford University Press).

D. Dauber, 2012, "Opposing positions in M&A research: culture, integration and performance," *Cross Cultural Management: An International Journal*, 19(3), 375–398.

D. Dauber, G. Fink and M. Yolles, 2012, "A configuration model of organizational culture," *SAGE Open*, 2(1), 1–16. DOI: 10.1177/2158244012441482.

H. Deresky and E. Christopher, 2012, *International management; Managing cultural diversity* (Pearson Australia), chapter 1.

L. Donaldson, 1987, "Strategy and structural adjustment to regain fit and performance: in defense of contingency theory," *Journal of Management Studies*, 24(1), 1–24.

———, 1996, *For positive organization theory: proving the hard core* (London, England: SAGE). *Economist*, 4 December 1999, "Faites vos jeux," 63.

M.J. Epstein, 2004, "The drivers of success in post-merger integration," *Organizational Dynamics*, 33(2), 174–189.

M.E. Graebner, 2004, "Momentum and serendipity: how acquired leaders create value in the integration of technology firms," *Strategic Management Journal*, 25(8/9), 751–777.

R.T. Hamilton and G.S. Shergill, 1992, "The relationship between strategy-structure fit and financial performance in New Zealand: evidence of generality and validity with enhanced controls," *Journal of Management Studies*, 29, 95–113.

———, 1993, *The logic of New Zealand business: strategy, structure, and performance* (Auckland; New Zealand: Oxford University Press).

I.C. Harris and T.W. Ruefli, 2000, "The strategy/structure debate: an examination of the performance implications," *Journal of Management Studies*, 37(4), 587–604.

P.C. Haspeslagh and D.B. Jemison, 1991, "The challenge of renewal through acquisitions," *Planning Review*, 19(2), 27–32.

A.C. Inkpen, A.K. Sundaram and K. Rockwood, 2000, "Cross-border acquisitions of U.S. technology assets," *California Management Review*, 42 (Spring), 50–70.

M.H. Kavanagh and N.M. Ashkanasy, 2006, "The impact of leadership and change management strategy on organizational culture and individual acceptance of change during a merger," *British Journal of Management*, 17, 81–103.

C.B. Meyer, 2008, "Value leakages in mergers and acquisitions: why they occur and how they can be addressed," *Long Range Planning*, 41, 197–224.

S.H. Schwartz, 1 January 1999, "A theory of cultural values and some implications for work applied psychology," *Applied Psychology*, 48(1), 23–47.

D.M. Schweiger and A.S. DeNisi, 1991, "Communication with employees following a merger: a longitudinal field experiment," *Academy of Management Journal*, 34(1), 110–135.

T.J. Tetenbaum, 1999, "Beating the odds of merger & acquisition failure: seven key practices that improve the chance for expected integration and synergies," *Organizational Dynamics*, 28(2), 22–35.

Y. Weber, 1996, "Corporate cultural fit and performance in mergers and acquisitions," *Human Relations*, 49(9), 1181–1202.

Y. Weber and N. Pliskin, 1996, "The effects of information systems integration and organizational culture on a firm's effectiveness," *Information & Management*, 30, 81–90.

K.E. Weick, 1995, *Sensemaking in organizations* (Sage Publications: Thousand Oaks).

O.E. Williamson, 1975, *Markets and hierarchies analysis and antitrust implications: a study in the economics of internal organization* (New York: Free Press).

2
Intercultural Communication in Selection Interviews

Choon-Hwa Lim, Meena Chavan and Lucy Taksa

Editor's introduction

This case study concerns job interviews in which the interviewers are Australian and the candidates Chinese. The focus is on interviewer competency; but there is also the suggestion that candidates in general should be responsive to cultural differences in nonverbal communication between themselves and their interviewers, to improve their chances of being selected. In everyday life, the meaning of words is generated contextually and depends on their use,[1] and culture is part of the context.

Unfortunately, cultural differences between interviewers and candidates can result in discriminatory hiring practices. Employees' rights in many countries are set out in various legal documents such as the UK Equality Act 2010; and employers cannot discriminate on the basis of "protected characteristics" that include race, gender, disability and sexual orientation.

Nevertheless, a 2012 report in the *Guardian*,[2] for instance, on job applicants of ethnic minority – including black, Pakistani and Bangladeshi female workers – found racial discrimination and other barriers at the recruitment stage; and that many job applicants of ethnic minority had changed their name or appearance to try to overcome prejudices – and when they did, their scope for getting a job increased.

These examples demonstrate the importance of the case study that follows, of a method called the "structured selection interview" (SSI) that contains psychometric properties. Hilary Osborne[3] reported for *The Guardian* in 2014 that the Co-op Bank's disgraced former chairman, Paul Flowers, landed the job because he did better in psychometric tests than rival candidates. Osborne suggested this element of the recruitment process should be investigated and asked, what exactly are these tests – or, rather, questionnaires.

They are designed to discover what kind of person candidates are, in ways they wouldn't necessarily admit to in interview, with questions designed to expose how they behave and what motivates them; to pick up on any inconsistencies and make it difficult for them to put on an act, there is a built-in "lie scale." Osborne notes that such questionnaires need to be part of a process; and this is confirmed by the following case study that goes beyond usual interview methods to examine the role of culture in the contexts of construction of questions and form of answers.

John Langshaw Austin[4] extended an analysis of contextual meaning to formulate what has become known as speech act theory. He argued that statements and words do not only describe a situation or state a fact, but also perform a certain action by themselves. For instance, the sentence "Please sit down" – for example, as the opening of a job interview – is a request, but Austin suggests that it is more; it does things on its own. Depending on the context and its use, this sentence can have different functions such as a welcome or a warning. Therefore, Austin makes a distinction between "utterance-as-description" and "utterance-as-action" and divides speech acts into three categories: what is said; what the speaker actually intended to say; and what happens as a consequence.

For instance, the sentence "Tell us something about yourself" – commonly said in a job interview – is the actual utterance. The speaker's intention may be genuine interest or a test of some kind. The consequence may be that the hearer relaxes or feels under pressure, depending on how the request is interpreted.

Geertz[5] defines culture as "webs of significance" spun between people through their actions and interactions, and this is the foundation of subjective understanding and cultural identity.[6]

Therefore, meaning is not created in a void; it is structured and sustained by the socio-cultural influences and the environment within which it is generated. Thus, "Please sit down" may have opposite meanings in different settings – a welcome in a domestic environment but a warning of interrogation in the context of a job interview. Wittgenstein[7] emphasizes the importance of context and culture in determining meaning and states that "the speaking of language is part of an activity or of a life-form"[8] and that meaning is deeply rooted in the value system in one's life or "language game." By this argument, candidates need to know the culture-generated rules of the game.

This case study makes plain how problems that foreign job applicants experience may not be related to their lack of understanding but rather misinterpretation of cultural expectations of employer-applicant roles within job interviews. Job interviews should not be static in construction,[9] just as culture is not static; because professional communication nowadays in Australia, as elsewhere, is usually across as well as within discourse systems. Shared knowledge of context is needed.

Erving Goffman[10] may be considered one of the greatest sociologists of the latter half of the 20th century, thanks to his metaphor of life as theatre. He elucidated how individuals and collectives work together to construct a common understanding and representation of "reality." In Goffman's theory, not individuals but "teams" are responsible for cooperatively creating and constituting a particular impression of reality or a particular experience, much like the presentation of a theatre play; and a job interview is a good example. It is like a piece of theatre in which candidates adopt the roles of competent, knowledgeable, honest and professional individuals in order to persuade their interviewers to appoint them. Moreover, their role will be repositioned and reframed, for example, from that of a competent accountant to that of an experienced manager, depending on the nature of the job for which they are being interviewed.

Goffman suggests that "scripts" are vital to interpersonal communication. Many everyday "routine" interactions are "scripted." For instance, asking an acquaintance or a colleague "How are you?" usually solicits a response of "Fine thank you, and yourself?" rather than a detailed and sincere answer about the other person's feelings, health or well-being. This is a routine so familiar that it is performed almost automatically.

Such scripts offer people convenient solutions to social expectations and norms; and there are fairly standard "scripts" for job interviews. Moreover, individuals form first impressions based on people's appearance and on what they wear. Therefore, wardrobe is important in presenting interviewers' and candidates' respective roles and status in the "episode" of life "drama" being played at the time. For example, jeans and a T-shirt are not usually acceptable wear for either role.

Stage and sets constitute part of the context for interaction. If used effectively, they can help convince the "other" to adopt the version of reality that the "team" would like to convey. For instance, for a job interview, a courtroom-like setting in which candidates sit in front of a panel of judges conveys a very different impression from that of an informal room where everybody sits at a round table. Manipulation of scenery, stage and set usually involves a conscious effort to replace the ordinary with the extraordinary and to generate a desired "mood" or "ambience."

The stage is divided into front-stage and back-stage. Front-stage is what the job candidates see, while back-stage provides space for all the support activities including emotional maintenance of interviewers where they can take a break from their role and performance, for instance, by making a cup of coffee in the staff room. They can also use the back-stage for discussions, information sharing, evaluating candidates' performance, providing feedback and so on.

Perception is the internal process by which people select, evaluate and organize the stimuli of the outside world. Individual perceptions are strongly influenced by culture and are an important aspect of intercultural communication – in this case between the culture of the employing organization and the background cultures of the candidates to be interviewed. People from dissimilar cultures usually assign different meanings to the same environmental stimulus (such as objects, events, ideas, signs, symbol and so on), and therefore, they experience and perceive the world differently – as is demonstrated in the case study.

Moreover, people usually think in "schemas," sets of interrelated cognitions that allow them quickly to make sense of the others, of situations, events and places on the basis of limited information. In practice, certain cues activate schemas which then fill in the missing details. Therefore, schemas are preconceptions and general expectations based on a particular system of values, learned through experience and socialization. The more entrenched a schema, the more difficult it is to modify. Hence, schemas play an important functional part in interpreting environmental stimuli. If there are major cultural differences between, say, the schemas of interviewers and job candidates, there will be major differences in interpreting the situation.

Another critically important factor in intercultural communication is nonverbal behaviour, rooted in culture and societal norms and processed on those bases. Given that this process takes place at conscious as well as subconscious levels, nonverbal may be more powerful and influential than verbal communication. It can readily become a source of misunderstanding and even conflict because it has significant variations across cultural boundaries.

After playing a part, professional actors are aware they are no longer "in role"; but personal identity becomes more problematic within the drama of everyday life. Goffman[11] claimed that individuals must decide whether the impression of reality that they project is "true"; and that actors can be "taken in" by their roles. Thus, people who habitually sit in judgment on would-be employees may play the same role in other scenarios where such behaviour would not be appropriate. Candidates who are cast continually as unsatisfactory characters after a number of unsuccessful job interviews may find themselves unintentionally playing the role of a failure in other settings.

Only a relative value should be accorded to the effects of any given performance. Other factors must be taken into account, such as individual differences in identity, values and culture, attitudes and thinking. Every social interaction can be considered as an act of translation, both intra- and inter-cultural. It takes place through the processes of signification and interpretation, verbal and nonverbal, from one person's system of signs, standards and values to those of another.

Abstract:

These case studies explore the influence of cultural attributions on the outcomes of selection interviews by Australian interviewers of Chinese prospective employees. A number of interviews are described, along with the semi-structured debrief interviews with candidates and interviewers. The setting was a large Australian institution.

The results are discussed in terms of attribution theory, while confirming the importance of interviewers' and candidates' skill competency and personality fit in selection interviews. Guidelines are suggested for those who interview candidates from diverse cultures; and for candidates who need to recognize differences in cultural nuances between themselves and their interviewers that might hamper their chances of being selected.

Keywords: abduction, attribution, intercultural selection interview

Introduction

A review of current literature in the area of intercultural communication reveals limited cultural awareness of dominant theories of selection interviews. From a qualitative approach, these case studies demonstrate the impact of bias on the quality of interviews due to cultural misinterpretations. This opens discussion, for both practitioners and academics, on the need to develop cultural awareness in interethnic employee selection and thereby increases its effectiveness and equity.

The structured selection interview (SSI) has been shown to be successful in predicting future job performance. It is widely accepted by academics and professional practitioners across cultural boundaries, but with the result of suppressing discussion of the influence of culture on job interviews. Currently, there are two criterions that make up the SSI – one of competency and the other of personality. "Competency" assesses skills needed to perform the required role; "personality" evaluates suitability of candidates' dispositions for the business and the team.

The following cases serve to introduce a third criterion, that of "culture," thereby enriching the SSI by identifying and dealing with misinterpretations in cross-cultural structured interviews that otherwise would pose distinct threats to the ability of the interviewer to hire effectively and equitably. These 11 cases comprise live selection interviews and debriefing sessions with interviewers and candidates. There were a total of 11 live interviews, 11 candidates debriefs and 12 interviewers debrief. Finally, based on the findings, suggestions are offered to improve widespread use of the SSI across cultural boundaries.

Case presentation

Background

A structured behavioural selection (SBS) interview is an assessment method designed to measure job-related competencies of candidates by systematically inquiring about their behaviour in past experiences and/or their proposed behaviour in hypothetical situations.

Interviewers are trained in SBS methods, and generally speaking, these structured interviews ensure candidates have equal opportunities to provide information and are assessed accurately and consistently. They are popular because interviewers find them more personal than other assessment methods.

Other benefits of SBS interviews are:

• they can evaluate competencies that are difficult to measure using other assessment methods (e.g., interpersonal skills);
• all candidates are asked the same predetermined questions in the same order; and
• all responses are evaluated using the same rating scale and standards for acceptable answers.

Thus, they consist of aligning interview objectives with relevant job criteria (e.g., knowledge, skills and abilities) in cross-cultural settings where interviewers and candidates are from different cultural backgrounds. Each candidate is asked pre-selected questions based on behavioural factors, irrelevant information is disregarded and detailed notes taken.

Eight of the interviewers in this case study were third generation Australians (i.e., born in Australia with both parents also born in Australia) and four were first generation (born overseas but living in Australia). The first generation Australians comprised one Lebanese-born person, one Indian born in Fiji, one Caucasian each born in England and in New Zealand.

The candidate interviews consisted of a mixture of one-on-one and panels (two interviewers per panel maximum). Sometimes an interviewer participated in more than one candidate interview. In all, there were three or four data items in each set, that is, the live job interview, the candidate debrief and one or two interviewer debrief(s). One interviewer declined to participate in the debrief interview.

The candidates were from the ethnic Chinese race. Race is taken to refer to physical appearance such as the colour of the skin, eyes, hair, also bone/jaw structure and so on. Ethnicity is assumed to refer to cultural factors such as culture, ancestry, language and beliefs.

The ten candidates in the study were first generation Australians (eight from China, one each from Cambodia and Malaysia) and one was a second generation Australian. The lack of a comparison or control group for this research was an issue; and further studies should include members of other collectivistic societies such as those of Korea and Japan. Another limiting factor was that not all participants were proficient in the English language. This is a problem with all research in English, as noted, for example, by Squires.[12] Mitigating this limitation in this research was the fact that the researcher and the transcriber had Chinese backgrounds, and therefore understanding some of the candidates' "broken English" was not an issue.

The sample size was small. Mintzberg [13]is one of the many theorists who acknowledge that qualitative studies using small sample sizes can provide a rich and deep understanding of the studied phenomena. Yet, they mean that results are not widely generalizable and the conclusions must be further tested. Moreover, researchers and theories are not culture-free; through interpretation, data become exposed to researchers' cultural assumptions. Cultural theories should therefore be used to limit these effects by taking into account the background of the researchers as well as the place where the theories were devised.

Table 2.1 provides a summary of the types of interview and the participants.

Table 2.1   Summary of cases of live intercultural SBS interviews

Case	SBS interview	Interview type	Interviewer	Candidate
1	S01	Panel	MA(1), MB(1)	C01(1)
2	S02	Panel	MA(1), MB(1)	C02(1)
3	S03	One-on-one	MC(1)	C03(1)
4	S04	One-on-one	MC(1)	C04(1)
5	S05	Panel	MD(2), ME(1)	C05(1)
6	S06	One-on-one	MF(2)	C06(1)
7	S07	Panel	MG(1), MH(2)	C07(2)
8	S08	One-on-one	MI(2)	C08(1)
9	S09	Panel	MJ(2), MX(n.a.)	C09(1)
10	S10	Panel	MK(2), ML(1)	C10(1)
11	S11	Panel	ML(1), MM(2)	C11(1)

Note: Participants' ages are indicated in parentheses: n.a. = not available; (1) = 21–30 years old; (2) = 31 years old and above.

Debriefing the participants

These semi-structured sessions were in two parts. The first contained general questions, and the second focused on cultural aspects of the participants' experiences.

Organizations are understandably sensitive to this kind of research because of the potential to reveal any behaviour by interviewers in their employ that might suggest prejudice or discrimination. Therefore, following literature suggestions by Gao,[14] the HR executive of the financial institution that provided the interviewers was invited to refine the development of the key questions. For the first part of the interview, these questions included:

- When the interview was over, how did you feel it went?
- What were your concerns before you conducted the interview?
- What stood out for you about the interview?

Culture was not discussed unless the participants mentioned it. Any cultural concepts that emerged from the first part were explored further in the second part by amending and/or framing new interviewing questions.

The second part of the interview contained questions that explored the experience of culture. Even though the participants seemed reasonably relaxed at this stage, great care was still taken to ensure that the questions were asked in a sensitive manner, and any signs of participant discomfort were noted. The questions pertaining to culture included:

- How did you feel about interviewing/being interviewed by someone from another culture?
- Were there any responses/questions from candidates/interviewers that you thought were culturally based?
- Research tells us that cultural values can influence your perceptions of candidates/interviewers in job interviews. Do you feel that this has impacted on your interview experience?
- Research tells us that work values are different for people from different cultures. What are some work values that are important to you?
- Research tells us that cultural cues such as race, accent and name can influence interviewers'/candidates' perceptions of candidates/interviewers in job interviews. Do you think this has influenced your experience of the interview?
- Research tells us that cultural stereotypes can influence job interviews. Do you think this has influenced your experience as an interviewer/candidate?
- How would you describe your culture?
- How would you describe the culture of the candidate(s)//interviewers you interviewed?
- What do you think culture is?
- What do you think are some ways people from different races, ethnicities and nationalities respond differently to the same interview questions?
- What do you think should be critical factors in an effective cross-cultural job interview?
- As the interviewer/candidate, what did the outcome of the interview mean to you?
- How did you feel about the environment in which the interview took place?
- Is there any question that I have not asked which you think I should have asked?

Procedures

The study began with identifying the criteria for suitability of a respondent organization to provide a sufficient number of live SBS interviews and to attract interviewers and candidates over a 12- to 18-month period. The largest of the Australian financial services organizations immediately became the primary target group. The key issues anticipated were to protect:

• the reputation of the organization;
• the integrity of the selection employment process; and
• the privacy of the participants.

Since job interviews may be high-stress events, particularly for the candidates, it was decided to audiotape rather than videotape the interviews and subsequent debriefs. At the conclusion of each interview, the researchers retrieved the relevant audiotape and collected the consent forms. The firm's HR executive had advised that all other documents (e.g., resumes) were to go through the firm for delivery to the researchers. Each document was coded to protect participants' privacy. Coding had the added advantage of identifying all documents relating to a particular participant. Identifiers such as names and contact details were deleted.

After the candidates had been informed of the outcome from their job application, the researcher arranged to meet with each of them for a follow-up debriefing session.

A general inductive approach was used for these sessions, using NVivo, together with thematic analysis, to sense the dynamics of intercultural SBS interviews and to understand their critical themes. NVivo is an online platform for analyzing all forms of unstructured data. Qualitative research is particularly suitable when relatively little is known about a subject – in this case, the influence of culture and cultural competence on intercultural interviews.

The interviews were recorded live, as were the debriefing sessions with the participants, using a digital audio recorder. Transcriptions resulted in 546 single-spaced pages and 230,109 words. Double-checking ensured accuracy. Any identifiers (such as names of the organizations and participants) were replaced by appropriate codes to preserve confidentiality and privacy of all concerned.

The transcripts yielded rich data for thematic analysis of verbal, vocal and nonverbal characteristics, which would not be possible in a quantitative study. In addition, field notes were made of the selection and debriefing interviews. They described events leading up to and surrounding the data collection, and included supplementary information arising from conversations with members of the participating financial institution. Observation notes were made also about the selection and debriefing interviews.

In total, 34 field notes were generated. Coding, aided by NVivo, began with reading interviewers' and candidates' transcripts to determine the perceptions of the interviewers and the candidates. Each perception was coded as:

- positive or negative (neutral perceptions are coded as negative);
- cause of positive or negative perceptions (factors that caused the perception were noted in the heading of each code); and
- whether the code was attributed to the candidate or not (i.e., internal or external cause).

Inductive qualitative approach

This study adopted a qualitative approach to understanding the dynamics between Chinese candidates and non-Chinese interviewers.

Qualitative research assumes an interpretive paradigm of the world by which people use their subjective experiences to create and sustain social reality.[15] Aims in this case were:

- to study the texts and conversations of the relevant communication;
- to read the interpretations that gave them meaning; and
- to study the context and situation that influenced interpretation.[16]

One of the main tasks of qualitative research is to capture and interpret accurately the meanings of phenomena (in this case, selection interviews) as they occur in their social context.[17] A control group is not necessary in such non-randomized studies. Emerging factors and descriptions enable the development and formulation of new theories, because of the interpretive and subjective nature of qualitative research.

Thematic analysis versus content analysis

Braun and Clarke[18] argue that thematic analysis is recognized as a generic coding process as well as a qualitative method in its own right. As a generic coding process, factors or patterns are allowed to emerge from an interview or across a data set, which is known as the classical bottom-up inductive thematic analysis method.[19]

A top-down approach, which is based on the researcher's interest, is also possible. This alternative approach is used when known themes from prior research act as concepts in the data analysis. However, prevalence of data for a particular theme does not presuppose its importance. It must be relevant and contribute to the research question. In this case, interviewers' perceptions of candidates' qualities, and the factors (internal or external to the candidates) that led to their attributions, were set up as codes prior to open coding of the relevant data.

Job interviews are usually considered successful when the candidate is offered and has accepted the position: but in the context of this research, interview outcomes were deemed to be successful if candidates were invited for another interview; on the assumption that they were worth further consideration. Unsuccessful outcomes meant that the candidates were eliminated outright. Comparison of successful and unsuccessful interviews allows for identification of critical factors in intercultural SBS interviews and their outcomes.

One candidate received an offer and accepted it; three candidates were invited for another round of interviews; and seven candidates were unsuccessful.

Initial coding resulted in 46 factors. All the coding references were reviewed against their respective codes, that is, factors, to ensure that each code name clearly reflected the content of the references, and that the codes were clearly distinct from each other. In achieving these aims, a few codes were merged, renamed or split and new codes created. The thematic analysis revealed 37 factors influencing the intercultural SBS interviews shown in Table 2.2.

Table 2.2 Relative strengths of factors influencing perceptions based on coding references for each subcharacteristic

	No. of references
CRITICAL FACTOR	
01. Verbal	158
STRONG FACTORS	
02. Cultural savvy	85
03. Interviewers' behaviours	79
04. Career alignment	74
05. English language	70
MODERATE FACTORS	
06. Interview efficacy	60
07. Customer service and sales	52
08. Work experience	48
09. Impressions	45
10. Nonverbal	45
11. Two-way interaction	43

Continued

Table 2.2   Continued

	No. of references
12. Meaning of work	41
13. Interviewers' question quality	37
WEAK FACTORS	
14. Work ethics	28
15. Pre-interview conditions	28
16. Interview preparation	27
17. Physical environment	27
18. Candidates' questions	25
19. Interview experience	23
20. Accent	20
21. Interviewers' cultural background	19
22. Extroversion	17
23. Education	14
24. Candidate pool	14
25. Age	14
26. Cross-cultural communication	14
27. Hours and locations	12
28. Job type and complexity	8
29. Cultural exposure	8
30. Relationship with peers	7
31. Coping with pressure	4
32. Atmosphere	4
33. Relationship with manager	3
34. Interviewers' panel	2
35. Parenthood	2
36. Luck	1
37. Gender	1

The study found that thirty-seven factors influencing intercultural selection interviews can be categorized into nine overarching themes, made up of five internal and four external themes. Communication and culture were predominant. These themes and their respective factors are listed here. The first five themes are internal and the rest are external. The strength-order of the factors and their respective number of coding references are in brackets. For example, candidates' questions were the 18th most prevalent factor, with 25 coding references.

Theme 1: Communication theme
    Factor 1: Candidates' questions (18, 25)
    Factor 2: Impressions (9, 45)
    Factor 3: Nonverbal (10, 45)
    Factor 4: Verbal (1, 158)
    Factor 5: Two-way interaction (11, 43)

Theme 2: Professional assets
   Factor 1: Career alignment (4, 74)
   Factor 2: Education (23, 14)
   Factor 3: Meaning of work (12, 41)
   Factor 4: Work experience (8, 48)
Theme 3: Knowledge, skill and ability (KSA) theme
   Factor 1: Coping with pressure (31, 4)
   Factor 2: Customer service and sales (7, 52)
   Factor 3: Relationship with manager (33, 3)
   Factor 4: Relationship with peers (30,7)
Theme 4: Interview readiness
   Factor 1: Interview efficacy (6, 60)
   Factor 2: Interview experience (19, 23)
   Factor 3: Interview preparation (16, 27)
Theme 5: Personality theme
   Factor 1: Extroversion (22, 17)
   Factor 2: Work ethics (14, 28)
Theme 6: Cultural theme
   Factor 1: Accent (20, 20)
   Factor 2: Cross-cultural communication (26, 14)
   Factor 3: Cultural exposure (29, 8)
   Factor 4: Cultural savvy (2, 85)
   Factor 5: English language (5, 70)
   Factor 6: Interviewers' cultural background (21, 19)
Theme 7: Interviewing theme
   Factor 1: Interviewers' behaviours (3, 79)
   Factor 2: Interviewers' panel (34, 2)
   Factor 3: Interviewers' question quality (13, 37)
Theme 8: Situational theme
   Factor 1: Atmosphere (32, 4)
   Factor 2: Candidate pool (24, 14)
   Factor 3: Hours and location (27, 12)
   Factor 4: Job type and complexity (28,8)
   Factor 5: Luck (36, 1)
   Factor 6: Physical environment (17, 27)
   Factor 7: Pre-interview conditions (15, 28)
Theme 9: Social theme
   Factor 1: Age (25, 14)
   Factor 2: Gender (37, 1)
   Factor 3: Parenthood (35, 2)

These frequencies of the nine themes mentioned by the interviewers and candidates are summarized in Table 2.3.

Table 2.3   Themes influencing interviewers' and candidates' perceptions

Themes	Interviewers' perceptions (in %)	Candidates' perceptions (in %)
1. Communication theme	36.27	7.87
2. Professional assets theme	19.69	8.59
3. KSA theme	15.95	1.18
4. Cultural factors	14.14	34.00
5. Personality theme	4.05	0.58
6. Situational theme	3.44	12.87
7. Interview readiness theme	3.17	13.10
8. Interviewing theme	2.17	20.71
9. Social theme	1.12	1.10

Outcomes

An analysis of the data by themes and participants' perceptions reveals:

- the prevalence of certain themes over others in the perceptions of candidates' performances in the interviews; and
- the different ways in which the themes influence the interviewers and the candidates.

Table 2.3 lists the themes in the order of the strength of their influence on the interviewers' perceptions according to their prevalence in percentages. NVivo calculated the percentages based on the amount of text in each theme relative to the interviewers' and the candidates' respective overall amounts of text across all the themes. The percentages for the nine themes in the interviewers' column should equal 100%, subject to rounding, and the same holds for the candidates' column.

NVivo was utilized for the thematic analysis. Initial open coding using induction and abduction analyses of the data items resulted in 228 codes. Very early on, the factors were divided into categories or themes that matched and reflected factors from the literature on intercultural communication. Eventually, new factors based on emerging patterns in the data were added to the growing list of themes or factors.

In the end, as new codes emerged and similar codes merged, a hierarchy of factors denoted as trees were developed that encompassed all the codes emerging from the data consisting of 9 themes and 37 factors. The queries function in NVivo was helpful in examining, exploring and pinpointing the factors and strengths of the factors that emerged from the data.

Matrix coding was used because the outputs provided instant statistical information that indicated the relative prevalence of the factors present, especially the "coding references" and "percentages" options. Coding references specified the number of data extracts contained in each code, and percentages stipulated the relative amount of text in the selected codes. The prevalence of the factors is graded as follows:

1. Critical factor – more than 100 coding references
2. Strong factor – 70–99 coding references
3. Moderate factor – 30–69 coding references
4. Weak factor – less than 30 coding references

Table 2.4 shows the relative strengths of the various factors influencing the participants.

Table 2.4   Factors influencing interviewers and candidates

Factors	Interviewers	Candidates	Differences
CRITICAL FACTOR			
01. Verbal	123	35	88
STRONG FACTORS			
02. Cultural savvy	32	53	–21
03. Interviewers' behaviours	10	69	–59
04. Career alignment	59	15	44
05. English language	46	24	22
MODERATE FACTORS			
06. Interview efficacy	24	36	–12
07. Customer service and sales	48	4	44
08. Work experience	28	20	8
09. Impressions	45	0	45
10. Nonverbal	40	5	35
11. Two-way interaction	36	7	29
12. Meaning of work	29	12	17
13. Interviewers' question quality	4	33	–29
WEAK FACTORS			
14. Work ethics	26	2	24
15. Pre-interview conditions	2	26	–24
16. Interview preparation	7	20	–13
17. Physical environment	1	26	–25
18. Candidates' questions	25	0	25
19. Interview experience	4	19	–15
20. Accent	19	1	18

Continued

Table 2.4 Continued

Factors	Interviewers	Candidates	Differences
21. Interviewers' cultural background	1	18	–17
22. Extroversion	15	2	13
23. Education	8	6	2
24. Candidate pool	10	4	6
25. Age	9	5	4
26. Cross-cultural communication	10	4	6
27. Hours and locations	4	8	–4
28. Job type and complexity	6	2	4
29. Cultural exposure	4	4	0
30. Relationship with peers	7	0	7
31. Coping with pressure	4	0	4
32. Atmosphere	0	4	–4
33. Relationship with manager	3	0	3
34. Interviewers' panel	0	2	–2
35. Parenthood	2	0	2
36. Luck	0	1	–1
37. Gender	1	0	1

The initial coding resulted in 46 factors. Next, all the coding references were reviewed against their respective codes to ensure that each code name clearly reflected the content of the references and that the codes were clearly distinct from one another. As a result, a few codes were merged, resulting in 37 factors that were believed to influence perceptions. The use of coding references made it convenient to pick up relevant emphases in the successful interviews in relation to the unsuccessful ones.

The verbal factor (or quality of verbal expression) was the critical factor, containing 158 coding references. Four strong factors appeared, namely, cultural competence (85 coding references), interviewers' behaviours (70), career alignment (74) and English language (70).

The next set of eight moderate factors consisted of interview efficacy (60), customer service and sales (52), work experience (48), impressions (45), nonverbal (45), two-way interaction (43), meaning of work (41) and interviewers' question quality (37).

The remaining factors were considered weak: work ethics (28), pre-interview conditions (28), interview preparation (27), physical environment (27), candidate's questions (25), interview experience (23), accent (20), interviewers' cultural background (19), extroversion (17), education (14), candidate pool (14), age (14), cross-cultural communication (14), hours and locations (12), job type and complexity (8), cultural exposure (8), relationship with peers (7), coping with pressure (4), atmosphere (4), relationship with manager (3), interviewers' panel (2), parenthood (2), luck (1) and gender (1). These factors needed to be categorized into the interviewers' and candidates' positive and negative perceptions and whether the attributions were internal or external.

Verbal, as an internally attributed factor, is by far the most influential factor for the perceptions of the interviewers and candidates. For example, this factor influenced the interviewers positively (58 coding references) and negatively (66) very strongly, and to a lesser extent on the positive (20) and negative (15) perceptions of the candidates. This finding meant that even though both the parties acknowledged that the verbal factor was significant, the interviewers placed more emphasis on it than the candidates.

The verbal factor consists of several characteristics: the degree to which the interviewers' questions were answered; speaking styles, particularly culturally sensitive speaking styles; interview types, particularly behavioural interview techniques; and promoting oneself for the role. Given that it is beyond the scope of this study to include the other factors, only the verbal factor is presented.

Discussion

The aim of the study was to contribute to the development of intercultural selection theories, while also providing evidence of practical value for improving interview procedures.

The findings seem to indicate that in the case of intercultural interviews, the SBS interview may not be as robust as many researchers claim. Hence, further research is warranted to examine its intercultural validity.

The outcome of this research is highly relevant to current business practice, as businesses need effective selection procedures in order to identify the right people for their organizations. To this extent, the results of this study might be generalized to all organizations in Australia that might attract Chinese job candidates; and may benefit interview processes for minority groups elsewhere. It is also relevant to future academic research, highlighting the need for a better understanding of the various factors impacting on intercultural selection procedures.

The main result of the study for both interviewers and candidates is its support of the contention that the strongest cultural influence on the outcomes of intercultural SBS interviews is communication style and is the primary determinant of success in employment interviews, as argued, for example, by Young and Kacmar, and Daly *et al.*[20] Effective communication style is not only highly sought-after in the workplace but also has significant influence on interviewers' perceptions of candidates' qualities.

These findings support those of other researchers. For example, Young and Kacmar[21] pinpoint specific verbal behaviour by candidates that appear to influence interviewers' ratings of their knowledge, skills, ability and personality, and hence on hiring outcomes. Moreover, research undertaken by O'Grady and Millen,[22] Hough and Oswald and Latham and Millman[23] supports the findings of this study – that the impact of culture in the conduct of SBS interviews is significant.

Culture influences selection criteria and related behavioural indicators, which makes it a very important theme for interview outcomes. It is the most significant external theme to influence interviewers' perceptions of candidates and is an external factor that can influence the employment interview and mediate its outcomes.

The study shows that both interviewers and candidates in general understood the purpose of a structured behavioural selection interview; and that successful candidates needed to demonstrate qualities that pleasantly surprised their interviewers regarding job-related matters, as well as to act in culturally appropriate ways. However, the critical factor in all SBS interviews is that the quality of candidates' behavioural responses determines interviewers' level of trust; and the candidates in this case study found their interviews challenging. They underestimated the influence of their culture-based behaviour on the perceptions of their interviewers.

During the debriefing sessions, these candidates often attributed the challenging nature of the interviews to their lack of interview experience in general, as well as the SBS interview in particular. The successful candidate in the study, C10, stated that the SBS interview is a form of "cheating," because extensive interview experience, preparation and practice are sufficient to beat the interviewers at their own game. This suggests that the behavioural interview method may not be as robust as many researchers claim.

The study confirms the influence of "culture talk" in job interviews and challenges present literature assumptions about the impartiality of the SBS technique. For example, Motowidlo *et al.*[24] argue that valid judgments are possible from information about interviewees' past behaviour even without access to nonverbal cues in the interview itself. However, cultural implications of body language suggest the existence of differing cultural worlds, therefore accurate interpretation, say, of a "soft" handshake becomes the joint responsibility of interviewer and candidate.

Similarly, cultural differences reshape meanings of "effectiveness" and "equity" in structured interviews across cultures. Moreover, lack of cultural awareness in conflict handling can lead to misinterpretations of candidates' behaviour and may result in interviewers' decisions on hiring that are both wrong and unfair.

The study shows that communication emerges as a significant influence in interview outcomes as stated by Kacmar and others[25] who have shown that verbal communication influences interviewers' perceptions of candidates' personalities and knowledge, skill and ability (KSA). This study shows that communication also influences interviewers' perceptions of candidates' professional assets.

These various perceptions are among the variables that have an ultimate bearing on interview outcomes. A second group of variables, the influence of which is brought out by this study, comprises the external themes of culture, interviewing factors, situational factors, interview readiness and demographics factors. This study's analysis shows that while interviewers attribute many perceptions, particularly negative ones, to candidates' internal characteristics, the candidates themselves attribute many perceptions about themselves, particularly negative ones, to external causes. Attributions appear to be a strong mediating influence on the selection interview outcomes. The model that emanates from this analysis and reflects these findings is shown in Figure 2.2.

SBS interviews are intended to identify candidates with behavioural traits and characteristics essential for success in a particular job, but everybody's behaviour is culturally based, and though candidates from cultures other than those of the interviewers may possess the required traits, they may not be observable. For example, Hofstede's cultural characteristics of collectivism and femininity (quality of life) in a candidate may not appear as positives to interviewers whose culture values the characteristics of individualism and masculinity.[26]

The Chinese candidates in the study were observed to have difficulties in identifying specific past incidents in which they displayed particular behaviour; nor were they good at talking about themselves and their achievements and skills. Their non-Chinese interviewers were looking for personal accounts of strengths and limitations, but Chinese generally are taught to avoid self-aggrandizement which hinders them from revealing their true skills and capabilities at the SBS interview.

In the SBS framework, there is no permissible deviation from behavioural traits pre-identified as required for the job. Thus, SBS interviews are not designed to allow for recognition of cultural nuances and their impact on candidates' behaviour. Hence, one of the recommendations of this study is that it is vital to have an expert who has cross-cultural competency on the panel when candidates from other cultures are being interviewed.

Another key finding from the study is the prevalence of attribution by interviewers and candidates – something that has not been studied in a cross-cultural setting before. The pervasive influence of culture on attribution in SBS interviews was evident in the way the interviewers attributed many more of their perceptions of candidates to personality rather than to external factors such as cultural background, while candidates' awareness of how the interview was progressing was based mostly on external factors such as interviewers' responses. Hence, this demonstrates that attributions in intercultural interviews can be influenced by culture.

"Fundamental attribution error"[27] is the phenomenon of ignoring or underestimating situational factors and consists of a "tendency to attribute one's own behaviour to the situation and others" behaviour to their "character."[28] This case analysis shows that "fundamental attribution error" is prevalent in intercultural SBS interviews. This means that interviewers' perceptions of candidates' suitability for the vacant role are based on cultural differences as opposed to person-job and person-organization fits. In the pursuit of these "fits," interviewers may in effect discriminate unintentionally against candidates on the grounds of culture.

Table 2.5 shows that the non-Chinese, local, Australian interviewers from individualistic Australia attributed 78.86% of their perceptions to internal factors. All the candidates, who attributed more of their perceptions to external factors (69.72%), came from the collectivist Chinese culture.

Table 2.5   Participants' attribution of perceptions (in %)

	Interviewers	Candidates
negative, external	10.10	53.97
negative, internal	40.29	13.37
positive, external	10.99	15.57
positive, internal	38.62	17.08

Further, there are substantial differences in how interviewers and candidates attributed their respective positive and negative perceptions. The most significant difference is among the negative attributions to external causes. While interviewers attributed only 10.10% of their negative perceptions to external causes, candidates attributed 53.97%, a significant difference of 43.87%. Candidates primarily attributed negative perceptions externally – to interviewers' cultural backgrounds and to pre-interview conditions. The interviewers primarily attributed their negative perceptions externally to candidates' lack of English-language proficiency, their behaviour, and the candidate pool.

A lesser but no less significant difference of 26.92% exists between the attributions of negative perceptions to internal causes, that is, 40.29% for interviewers versus 13.37% for candidates. Interviewers primarily attributed negative perceptions internally to verbal factors, interview preparation, work experience and career alignment. Candidates primarily attributed negative perceptions internally, though also to verbal factors, career alignment, and customer service and sales.

A similar difference of 21.54% exists between the attributions of positive perceptions to internal causes, that is, 38.62% for interviewers versus 17.08% for candidates. Interviewers primarily attributed positive perceptions to internal factors – verbal, customer service and sales, career alignment and candidates' questions. Candidates primarily attributed positive perceptions to internal factors – interview efficacy, interview experience and the verbal factor.

Communication skill is critical in assessing candidates person-job fit (through KSA evaluation), person-organization fit (through personality evaluation) and person-career fit (through professional assets evaluation). These perceptions of fit are influenced by cultural, interviewing, situational, interview readiness and demographics themes, as well as attribution in intercultural selection interviews. These are all influences on interviewers' hiring decisions.

The phenomenon of attribution is important because culture is an external factor influencing the perception of candidate fit. Culture-based factors cause non-Chinese interviewers and Chinese candidates to view their strengths and weaknesses in different ways, that is, what is considered strength to Chinese (e.g., modesty) may be considered weakness to the non-Chinese.

Culture also predisposes non-Chinese interviewers and Chinese candidates to attribute perceptions in different ways, that is, the non-Chinese interviewers tended to attribute candidates' behaviour to internal factors, while the candidates tended to attribute the same behaviour to external factors. To the extent that culture-based attributions influence perceptions of candidates' strengths and weaknesses, they should be adjusted to reflect more accurately the true strengths and weaknesses of the candidates. Failure to do so results in unfair employment and discrimination.

The contributions of this chapter to the literature can be seen by comparing the proposed conceptual framework (Figure 2.1) with the emerging outcomes model (Figure 2.2). First, communication is an important variable influencing selection interview outcomes; however, this importance is lost when communication is hidden away as part of the competency factors in the conceptual model.

The emerging model gives appropriate regard to the critical role that communication plays in the selection interview. Second, KSA, which makes up a large part of the competency factors, plays a mediating role in the new model and not a direct role as suggested in the conceptual model.

Third, personality, situational and demographics factors do not directly influence selection interview outcomes as suggested by the conceptual framework. Instead, according to the emerging outcomes model, these factors, including culture and the interviewing factors, interview readiness and professional assets, mediate interview outcomes. Fourth, perceptions, not biases, play an important mediating role in outcomes.

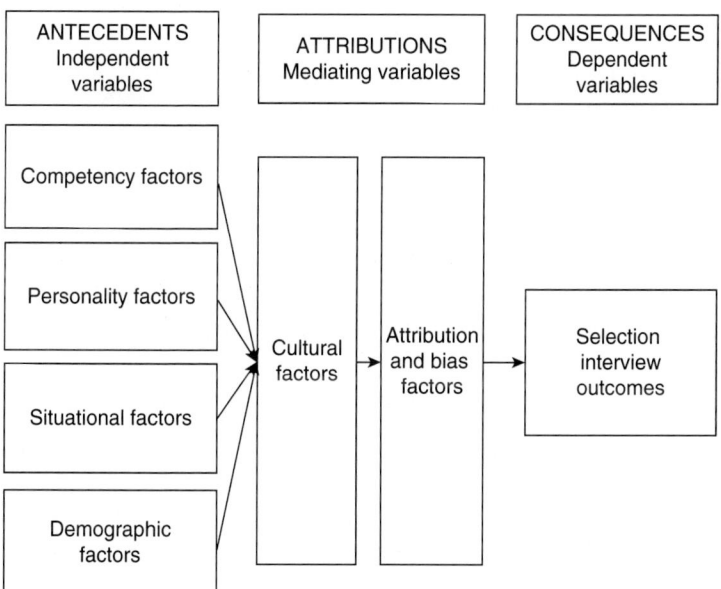

Figure 2.1 Conceptual model of intercultural selection interview
Source: Author.

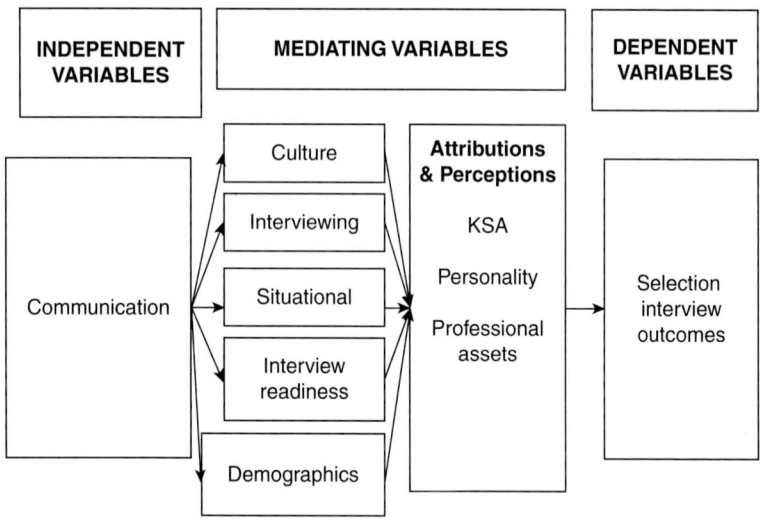

Figure 2.2   Emerging outcomes model
Source: Author.

In conclusion, studies focused on the psychometric properties, discrimination and communication in the intercultural interview and using quantitative methods overlook the influence of culture in the selection interview process. This qualitative study has unearthed the impact of cultural differences in the SBS interview process and illuminated what the HR executive of the financial organization has called "the elephant in the room" in the structured behavioural selection interview.

To sum up, this study has found that culture mediates the outcomes of structured behavioural selection interviews in intercultural selections. A key research finding has been that the influence of culture is often overlooked by non-Chinese interviewers' intent on seeking job and organization fits. Chinese candidates, on the other hand, are very aware of the influence of culture, subtly becoming conscious of differences in expectations between the interviewers and themselves.

This chapter has shown that culture, embedded in communication, influences selection interview outcomes, and that these influences are strongly manifested in the case of the verbal and two-way interaction factors in communication. In addition, culture has a strong mediating influence on outcomes via the perceptions of interviewers, which distort their attributions of the following factors: KSA, professional assets, personality, interview readiness and interviewing.

Another key research finding of this study has been the prevalence of the phenomenon of attribution in interviews, something which has not been examined before. The perceptions of non-Chinese interviewers and Chinese candidates are influenced by the same themes, but the degrees of influence are different. Interviewers are influenced largely by internal themes while candidates are significantly influenced by external themes. Interviewers are most influenced by the internal themes of communication, professional assets and KSA. Candidates are most influenced by the external themes of culture and interviewing and the internal theme of interview readiness.

The pervasive influence of culture in the selection interview is therefore evident in two ways. First, there is a tendency for the Chinese candidates to attribute more perceptions to external factors than to internal factors. Second, the actual causes of the positive and negative perceptions of non-Chinese interviewers and Chinese candidates differ.

The final key research finding of this research is that the structured behavioural interview may not be a suitable tool for intercultural selection. Because of the direct and indirect influence of culture, structured behavioural selection interviews may not be as robust as many researchers claim. They are susceptible to cultural influences and may need to be modified accordingly for the purposes of intercultural selection. Extensive experience, preparation and practise are required to ensure that candidates can beat the interviewers at their game.

Summing up, the contribution of these case studies to relevant literature is that they confirm the presence of "culture talk" between interview parties and demonstrate how it affects the quality of the interviews.

Implications for practitioners

Very little research has been carried out on actual communication practices in intercultural communication as a form of social interaction,[29] particularly concerning the question of how participants of different cultures perceive and attribute a candidates' performance in a selection interview. There are differences in the attributions made by the interviewers and candidates in these interviews. Reconciling the differences would help bridge the gap between the interviewers and candidates. This would require that the interviewers and candidates be aware of the different causes of their perceptions in interviews.

The literature has identified many factors that are influencing interviewers' perceptions of candidates in interviews. The literature, however, does not identify and separate the factors and their characteristics into those that have a greater tendency to positively influence the interviewer and those that tend to negatively influence the interviewer. Furthermore, the factors that are influencing the candidates' positively and negatively have not been identified.

Most of the factors being studied are internal and focused on the candidates' personalities and skill fits. Relatively little attention has been given to the external factors, which largely remain to be investigated. Moreover, the degree to which attributions occur in intercultural interviews has not been explored in the literature.

Implications for organization policy

Two issues arising from this research have important implications for organization policy. The first is the revelation of the importance of career fit, which goes above and beyond person-job fit and person-organization fit in selection decisions. The second is the influence of culture on the behavioural interview that has implications for the training of interviewers and the interview panel.

Implications for government policies

Job selection practices can be discriminatory, making it difficult for new settlers to become employed.[30] This study shows that a lack of cultural awareness and sensitivity has a critical impact on interview outcomes. Diversity characterizes the cultural landscape of Australia and its workforce. The benefits of a diverse workforce – possessing the many different skills that Australia needs – continue to elude many employers, with the result that many skilled immigrants with a high level of English continue to be underemployed.[31]

The present study has shown that there are significant cultural differences that pose challenges to interviewers and candidates in selection interviews. The government needs to provide the resources to train organizations and incoming migrants on the challenges of interpersonal communication, not just in selection interviews but also in the workplace generally.

The study has shown that English-language proficiency is only one aspect of this training need. Cultural awareness, knowledge and sensitivity are also core needs. The selection interview is a key situation where interpersonal interaction and communication are crucial.

Notes

1. Peter Buzzi and Claudia Megele, 2011, "Honne and tatemae; a world dominated by a 'game of masks,'" in Elizabeth Christopher (ed.), *Communication across cultures* (UK: Palgrave Macmillan).
2. Philip Landau, 7 December 2012, "Fighting discrimination at job interview," http://www.theguardian.com/.
3. Hilary Osborne, 30 January 2014, "Psychometric tests in job interviews: what are they looking for?" http://www.theguardian.com/.
4. J.L. Austin, 1962. *How to do things with words* (Cambridge, MA: Harvard University Press).
5. Clifford Geertz, 1993 [1973], *The interpretation of cultures: selected essays* (London: Fontana Press).
6. A. Jansson, 2002, "The mediatization of consumption: toward an analytical framework of image culture," *Journal of Consumer Culture*, 2(1), 5–31.
7. L. Wittgenstein, 1953/2001. Philosophical investigations (G. E. M. Anscombe, trans.) (3rd ed.) (Malden, MA: Blackwell Publishers).
8. Ibid., 10.
9. Helen Deresky and Elizabeth Christopher, 2012, *International management; Managing cultural diversity* (Australia: Pearson), chapter 1.
10. E. Goffman, 1959, *The presentation of self in everyday life* (New York: Doubleday).
11. Ibid.
12 A. Squires, 2009, "Methodological challenges in cross-language qualitative research: a research review," *International Journal of Nursing Studies*, 46(2), 277–287.
13 H. Mintzberg, 1979, "An emerging strategy of 'direct' research." *Administrative Sciences Quarterly*, 24(4), 582–589.
14 H. Gao, 2005, "The invisible handshake: interpreting the job-seeking communication of foreign-born Chinese in the United States," PhD dissertation, University of South Florida, USA.
15. G. Morgan, 1980, "Paradigms, metaphors, and puzzle solving in organization communication," *Administrative Science Quarterly*, 25, 608–621.
16. S. Ting-Toomey, 1984, "Qualitative research: an overview,." in W.B. Gudykunst and Y.Y. Kim (eds), *Methods for intercultural communication research* (Sage Publications), 169–184.
17. C. Marshall and G.B. Rossman, 1989, *Designing qualitative research* (Sage Publications).
18. V. Braun and V. Clarke, 2006, "Using thematic analysis in psychology," *Qualitative Research in Psychology*, 3, 77–101. doi: 10.1191/1478088706qp063oa.
19. G.A. Bowen, 2006, "Grounded theory and sensitizing concepts," *International Journal of Qualitative Methods*, 5, 1–9.
20. A.M. Young and K.M. Kacmar, 1998, "ABCs of the interview: the role of affective, behavioral, and cognitive responses by applicants in the employment interview," *International Journal of Selection and Assessment*, 6, 211–221. doi: 10.1111/1468-2389.00092. A.J. Daly, M.C. Barker and P. McCarthy, 2005, "Preferences in recruitment and selection in a sample of Australian organizations," *International Journal of Organizational Behaviour*, 9, 581–593.
21. Young and Kacmar, 1998.

22. C. O'Grady and M. Millen, 1994, *Finding common ground: intercultural communication strategies for job seekers* (Sydney: Macquarie University).
23. L.M. Hough and F.L. Oswald, 2000, "Personnel selection: looking toward the future – remembering the past," *Annual Review of Psychology*, 51, 631–664. doi: 10.1146/annurev.psych.51.1.631. G.P. Latham and Z. Millman, 2002, "Context of the employment interview," in J.F. Gubrium and J.A. Holstein (eds), *Handbook of interview research: context and method* (Sage Publications), 473–496.
24. Stephan J. Motowidlo, Gary W. Carter, Marvin D. Dunnette, Nancy Tippins, Steve Werner, Jenifer R. Burnett and Mary Jo Vaughan, 1992, "Studies of the structured behavioral interview," *Journal of Applied Psychology*, 77(5), October, 571–587. http://dx.doi.org/10.1037/0021-9010.77.5.571.
25. K. Michele Kacmar and Wayne A. Hochwarter, "The interview as a communication event: A field examination of demographic effects on interview outcomes," *International Journal of Business Communication*, July 1995 vol. 32(3) pp. 207–232; A. M. Young and K. M. Kacmar, 1998, "ABCs of the interview: The role of affective, behavioural and cognitive responses by applicants in the employment interview," *International Journal of Selection and Assessment*, 6, 211–221.
26. Geert Hofstede, 2001, *Culture's consequences: comparing values, behaviors, institutions and organizations across nations* (SAGE Publications).
27. R. Shirazi and A. Biel, 2005, "Internal-external causal attributions and perceived government responsibility for need provision: a 14-culture study," *Journal of Cross-Cultural Psychology*, 36, 96–116. doi: 10.1177/0022022104271428.
28. R.M. Kanter and R.I. Corn, 1994, "Do cultural differences make a business difference? Contextual factors affecting cross-cultural relationship success," *Journal of Management Development*, 13, 5–23. doi: 10.1108/02621719410050219
29. Donal Carbaugh, 2007, "Cultural discourse analysis: communication practices and intercultural encounters," *Journal of Intercultural Communication Research*, 36, 3, 167–182.
30. David S. Gill, 2007, *Employee selection and work engagement: do recruitment and selection practices influence work engagement?* (ProQuest).
31. A.J. Daly, M.C. Barker and P. McCarthy, 2005, "Preferences in recruitment and selection in a sample of Australian organizations," *International Journal of Organizational Behaviour*, 9, 581–593.

References

J.L. Austin, 1962, *How to do things with words* (Cambridge, MA: Harvard University Press).
G.A. Bowen, 2006, "Grounded theory and sensitizing concepts," *International Journal of Qualitative Methods*, 5, 1–9.
V. Braun and V. Clarke, 2006, "Using thematic analysis in psychology." *Qualitative Research in Psychology*, 3, 77–101. doi: 10.1191/1478088706qp063oa
P. Buzzi and C. Megele, 2011, "Honne and tatemae: a world dominated by a 'game of masks,'" in Elizabeth Christopher (ed.), *Communication across cultures* (UK: Palgrave Macmillan).
D. Carbaugh, 2007, "Cultural discourse analysis: communication practices and intercultural encounters," *Journal of Intercultural Communication Research*, 36(3), 167–182.

Choon Hwa Lim (2012) "The mediating role of culture in structured behavioural selection interviews," PhD thesis, Macquarie University.

Choon Hwa Lim, E. Zhuravleva and M. Chavan, 2011. "Tripping over the culture talk in the structured selection interview process," in BAM (British Academy of Management), 25th conference on building and sustaining high performance organisations in a challenging environment. Birmingham: Aston University. 12–15 September 2011.

A.J. Daly, M.C. Barker and P. McCarthy, 2005, "Preferences in recruitment and selection in a sample of Australian organizations," *International Journal of Organizational Behaviour*, 9, 581–593.

H. Deresky and E. Christopher, 2012, *International management: managing cultural diversity* (Australia: Pearson), chapter 1.

H. Gao, 2005, "The invisible handshake: interpreting the job-seeking communication of foreign-born Chinese in the United States," PhD dissertation, University of South Florida, USA.

C. Geertz, 1993 [1973], *The interpretation of cultures: selected essays* (London: Fontana Press).

D.S. Gill, 2007, *Employee selection and work engagement: Do recruitment and selection practices influence work engagement?* (ProQuest)

E. Goffman, 1959, *The presentation of self in everyday life* (New York: Doubleday).

G. Hofstede, 2001, *Culture's consequences: comparing values, behaviors, institutions and organizations across nations* (Thousand Oaks CA: SAGE Publications).

L.M. Hough and F.L. Oswald, 2000, "Personnel selection: looking toward the future – remembering the past." *Annual Review of Psychology*, 51, 631–664. doi: 10.1146/annurev.psych.51.1.631.

A. Jansson, 2002, "The mediatization of consumption: toward an analytical framework of image culture," *Journal of Consumer Culture*, 2(1): 5–31.

R.M. Kanter and R.I. Corn, 1994, "Do cultural differences make a business difference? Contextual factors affecting cross-cultural relationship success," *Journal of Management Development*, 13, 5–23. doi: 10.1108/02621719410050219.

P. Landau, 7 December 2012, "Fighting discrimination at job interview," http://www.theguardian.com/.

G.P. Latham and Z. Millman, 2002, "Context of the employment interview," in J.F. Gubrium and J.A. Holstein (eds), *Handbook of interview research: context and method* (Sage Publications).

C. Marshall and G.B. Rossman, 1989, *Designing qualitative research* (Sage Publications).

G. McDonald, 2000, "Cross-cultural methodological issues in ethical research," *Journal of Business Ethics*, 27(1/2), 89–104.

H. Mintzberg, 1979, "An emerging strategy of 'direct' research." *Administrative Sciences Quarterly*, 24(4), 582–589.

G. Morgan, 1980, "Paradigms, metaphors, and puzzle solving in organization communication," *Administrative Science Quarterly*, 25, 608–621.

S.J. Motowidlo, G.W. Carter, M.D. Dunnette, N. Tippins, S. Werner, J.R Burnett and M. Jo Vaughan, October 1992, "Studies of the structured behavioral interview," *Journal of Applied Psychology*, 77(5), 571–587. http://dx.doi.org/10.1037/0021-9010.77.5.571.

C. O'Grady and M. Millen, 1994, *Finding common ground: cross-cultural communication strategies for job seekers* (Sydney, National Centre for English Language Teaching and Research, Macquarie University).

H. Osborne, 30 January 2014, "Psychometric tests in job interviews: what are they looking for?" http://www.theguardian.com/.

M.Q. Patton, 2002, *Qualitative research & evaluation methods*, 3rd edition. (Thousand Oaks CA: Sage Publications).

R. Shirazi and A. Biel, 2005, "Internal-external causal attributions and perceived government responsibility for need provision: a 14-culture study," *Journal of Cross-Cultural Psychology*, 36, 96–116. doi: 10.1177/0022022104271428.

A. Squires, 2009, "Methodological challenges in cross-language qualitative research: a research review," *International Journal of Nursing Studies*, 46(2), 277–287.

S. Ting-Toomey, 1984, "Qualitative research: an overview," in W.B. Gudykunst and Y.Y. Kim (eds), *Methods for intercultural communication research* (Sage Publications), 169–184.

L. Wittgenstein, 1953/2001. *Philosophical investigations*, 3rd edition, G.E.M. Anscombe, trans. (Malden, MA: Blackwell Publishers).

A.M. Young and K.M. Kacmar, 1998. "ABCs of the interview: the role of affective, behavioral, and cognitive responses by applicants in the employment interview," *International Journal of Selection and Assessment*, 6, 211–221. doi: 10.1111/1468-2389.00092.

3
Communication Competence in Health Care: The Case of the Cross-Cultural Caregivers

Somayeh Alizadeh and Meena Chavan

Editor's introduction

The authors of this case study point out that more and more people live in a multicultural environment today, which means that many health practitioners have to interact with people from different cultures.

It is true also that health care is now a global industry. To take just one example, an inaugural conference was held in Singapore in May 2014, the International Conference on Humanitarian Medical Missions Volunteers Beyond Borders. It was dedicated to all medical volunteers working across and beyond borders; with the aim of drawing attention to the scope of humanitarian activities across all medical disciplines. A second conference was held in November of the same year.

Médecins Sans Frontières (MSF)[1] is an international, independent, medical humanitarian organization that delivers emergency aid to people affected by armed conflict, epidemics, natural disasters and exclusion from health care. It offers assistance to people based on need, irrespective of race, religion, gender or political affiliation.

In 2009, the Committee on Understanding and Eliminating Racial and Ethnic Disparities in Health Care[2] reported that racial and ethnic disparities in health care reflect access to care; and that even after all other factors have been taken into account, race and ethnicity remain significant predictors of the quality of health care received. The report offers recommendations for improvements in medical care financing, allocation of care, availability of language translation, community-based care and other arenas. The committee responsible for the report emphasizes the potential of cross-cultural education to improve provider-patient communication and explains how to integrate cross-cultural learning within the health professions.

Findings such as these illustrate the importance of case studies such as this, by Chavan and Alizadeh, that offer some culture-based reasons why intercultural communication may break down between patients and care givers.

It is pertinent to add that Lindstrom's study (Volume 2, Chapter 1) of a tobacco control programme in the US includes the information that because of community diversity, a county health department in Oklahoma was rightly concerned that generic anti-smoking messages would fail to persuade, or might even offend, important cultural segments of the intended audience. This is yet another example of the complexities – even the minefields – of health care provision to members of multicultural societies.

Abstract:

Health care sectors in many countries are challenged by growing cultural diversity and problems with interactions between overseas patients and local clinicians. This report is of predicaments in the multicultural context of Australia. Through interviews with patients from diverse ethnic origins, it identifies the impact of caregivers' cultural competence on the quality of care and level of patient satisfaction. The study reveals that cultural dissimilarities can affect patients' perceptions of health care in negative ways; but communication competence helps providers to bridge the cultural distance between them and their patients and enhances the quality of care.

Keywords: health care, intercultural communication competence, patient satisfaction

Introduction

Access to health care is a human right, and good health is the most important worldwide social goal.[3] To provide superior medical services and remain competitive, health sectors should not only keep up with the latest equipment and treatment techniques, but also be able to address challenges such as ageing populations, demographic differences, increasing demand and a variety of expectations amongst diverse clients.[4]

Coping with these challenges may be more difficult when there is cultural diversity between patients and health professionals. Australia has become the second most multicultural country in the world, with its population estimated to be 23,571,600 as of 21 August 2014. More than 200 languages are spoken at home and some of the 83 ethnic groups in Australia are from Africa, Asia, India, Latin America, the Middle East, Pakistan and western, central and eastern Europe.[5] Moreover, due to government policy to promote the entry of skilled workers and the migration of health workers from different countries to Australia, one-third of medical workers are foreign-born.[6]

Diversity of patients and health practitioners may cause problems with intercultural interactions in medical institutions. Culturally different patients have different expectations of health care, and providers may fail to recognize and cater to them.[7] Additionally, dosage errors may occur when providers fail to consider different responses to some medications, due to ethnicity differences. The following cases illustrate some negative impacts on health care quality and patient satisfaction as a result of breakdowns in cross-cultural communication between patients and medical staff and how cultural competence enhances both quality of care and patient satisfaction.

The study was undertaken as a qualitative, exploratory, first part of a two-pronged research project to measure the impacts of cultural dissimilarity and cultural competence on quality of care and patient satisfaction. To date, there has been very little empirical work in these areas,[8] but without evidence it is difficult to convince health care managers to invest time and money on promoting cultural competence training, techniques and practices.

Moreover measuring patients' satisfaction is crucial. Satisfied patients are more likely to follow medical instructions and attain desirable health outcomes,[9] and patient satisfaction is an important factor in patient retention and financial benefits for the relevant institution. Many researchers consider perceived service quality to be one of the major antecedents of patient satisfaction.[10]

Case presentation

On the principle that detailed understanding can only be established by talking directly with people and allowing them to tell their stories,[11] this was a qualitative study of how cultural and linguistic barriers might hinder delivery of high-quality care; and it explored providers' competence in mitigating cultural issues.

Forty semi-structured interviews were conducted with patients from diverse ethnic origins who live in Australia; they included Chinese,

Vietnamese, Arabs, Persians, Indians, Afghans, Malaysians, Indonesians and white Australians. Seventeen examples are provided in this report. The interviews were conducted in English, and some patients with lower levels of proficiency were accompanied by family members as interpreters to answer questions and share stories.

The participants were asked to be specific about perceived poor- and high-quality services received during recent visits to clinics or hospitals. They were asked explicitly whether cultural dissimilarity with their health care providers was a source of misunderstanding or conflict and, if so, how the providers had managed it.

Case #1 An Australian woman in her mid-thirties

The woman in question was suspicious of the technical expertise of "foreign doctors" due to what she claimed is the lower quality of medical education in less developed countries. She said she had received poor-quality care from Asian doctors because of their formal manners and lack of full explanation of her symptoms. She attributed this to Asian culture, where it is not customary, she said, to have long, friendly conversations with strangers.

Case #2 An Australian man in his late forties

He claimed to have received poor service from a non-native, English-speaking doctor, who repeatedly asked him for clarification about his symptoms. The patient doubted whether the doctor could understand his answers. He distrusted the doctor's diagnosis and found the visit useless.

Case #3 An Iranian woman in her late forties

She usually visits an Iranian Australian doctor who gives her holistic advice. This doctor knows the kind of food she eats and its effects on her system; she trusts her diagnoses. In addition to medical treatment, this patient usually receives dietary advice tailored to her as a middle-aged Iranian. For example, she was advised to eat low-fat yogurt to prevent diarrhoea while on a course of antibiotics. She said she has never been given this kind of supplementary dietary advice by any non-Iranian doctor.

Case #4 An Afghan man in his early sixties

He believed that female doctors are less knowledgeable than their male counterparts, until he was treated by an Iranian female doctor with an excellent bedside manner. She understands his dialect (some Afghans speak Farsi like Iranians, but with different dialect), and he does not need help communicating with her. The doctor calls him "my father" and tells him that God will help him recover soon. Like him, she is a practicing Muslim (she wears a head scarf), and this comforts him even more. He trusts her and follows her advice and has achieved good results so far.

Case #5 A Chinese woman in her late twenties

She is usually less satisfied and more stressed visiting non-Chinese doctors. She finds it hard to describe her symptoms in English. She tries to find appropriate terms from the Internet before visiting a local doctor; but she either uses words that are too technical or too close to slang to be understood, and her heavy accent is also a handicap. She is anxious because she thinks she is tiring the doctor and keeping other patients waiting. Due to this frustration, she often leaves out relevant information about her symptoms.

Case #6 An Arab woman in her mid-thirties

This patient recalled how happy she was to be looked after by an Egyptian doctor during her labour. Despite the rest of the hospital staff being nice, she was very stressed and was comforted when she found someone speaking her own language and familiar with her home country. This made her feel relaxed, especially since she has no family with her in Australia.

Case #7 An Iranian woman in her late thirties

During her previous pregnancy in her home country, she received excellent care from an African nurse. In Australia, when her new baby was born, she was stressed because she could speak little English and her teenage daughter had to act as an interpreter. Also, she was not familiar with Australian medical procedures.

However, the Australian nurse said she understood the patient, as a Muslim, might have some religious and cultural concerns and took time to explore these. She asked about the patient's previous labours and Iranian delivery practices and described potential differences in Australia. This encouraged the patient to disclose her fears and to feel at ease.

Case #8 A Malaysian woman in her late twenties

She had visited a medical specialist on several occasions and found him to be culturally competent and familiar with Muslims' religious preferences.

He asked her permission before examining her and assured her that the medicine he prescribed did not contain alcohol or gelatine.

This patient had had a negative experience with another doctor, who prescribed medicine that contained pork gelatine without asking her if she had any concerns, and she did not take it.

Case #9 An Arab woman in her late twenties

She believes that non-Muslim doctors cannot help Muslim patients because they are not familiar with Islamic practices. She said that, for instance, they tend routinely to ban patients from fasting during pregnancy, yet she is not aware that fasting is actually harmful for the baby. Although in Islamic countries pregnant women are exempt from fasting, this patient – like many Muslim women – chooses to fast during Ramadan and did so during this pregnancy. However, after a while, she became unwell and began to eat again. She kept all this information from the non-Muslim doctor because she feared he would admonish her. She said she would have been more candid if the doctor had been aware that her pregnancy was during the period of Ramadan and discussed the issue of fasting with her. In that case, she might have maintained better health.

Case #10 An Australian woman in her late thirties

A non-Australian doctor diagnosed her as suffering from thalassemia, an inherited blood disorder in which the body makes an abnormal form of haemoglobin, the protein in red blood cells that carries oxygen, and leads to anaemia. Treatment may involve regular blood transfusions and folate supplements.

In fear of such treatment and suspicious of the accuracy of the diagnosis, she got a second opinion from an Australian doctor. This doctor told her that thalassemia occurs most often in people from Southeast Asia, the Middle East, China and in those of African descent, though one form of the illness can be found in people of Mediterranean origin. Since this Australian patient's forebears, many generations ago, were from Scotland, and there was no family history of the disorder, the diagnosis seemed doubtful and the patient was treated for mild anaemia, with complete success.

Case #11 An Iranian woman in her early thirties

In Iran, she suffered for years due to ovarian cysts and had three ultrasounds over a three-year period, also taking medication prescribed by a specialist. In Australia, she asked a local doctor to carry out another ultrasound. The doctor refused, severely criticized the Iranian doctor for ordering the procedure so frequently, and was unwilling to prescribe the same medication as before. The patient complained that lack of it might affect her fertility, but instead of explaining his decision the doctor told her that her case was not serious and that she should not make such a fuss about it.

She said issues concerning fertility are very important to many Iranian women as they want to have only one child, but not until they are in their mid-thirties. Therefore, they need to be sure their reproductive systems remain healthy. She did not trust the Australian doctor and during a visit to Iran visited her specialist, who gave her the required reassurance.

Case #12 A Fijian man in his mid-forties

He suffered from gout. He was prescribed some tablets by an Australian doctor, but could still barely walk after taking them. He returned to the doctor and asked for the pills he had been given in Fiji. The doctor refused but did not explain why. The patient visited another Australian doctor, with the same result. He believes Australian doctors do not understand that different types of people need different medication. His wife had the same problem, that the type and dose of antibiotics prescribed by Australian doctors were not as effective as those given by doctors in Fiji for similar conditions.

Case #13 An Iranian woman in her late thirties

She had a bad experience during her labour. The Australian doctor assumed she did not need information about hospital procedures since this was not her first pregnancy; but her first baby was born in Iran, where procedures are different. For example, she had assumed pregnant women are immediately admitted into hospital when their waters break. This is common in Iran, but in Australia, women are asked to wait until labour begins. Besides, instead of receiving an enema, as is routine in Iran, the nurse closed the patient's rectum with her fingers, which caused her huge physical distress.

Case #14 An Iranian woman in her late thirties

Though she is Muslim, when she gave birth, she was happy with a non-Muslim nurse who was sympathetic to her specific concerns. For example, the nurse warned her she might be examined by a male doctor, but explained that being touched by a man is acceptable for medical purposes. The patient was still worried about this, but pleased that the nurse discussed her concerns in a respectful way.

Case #15 A Chinese man in his late twenties

He was very happy with an Australian doctor who was familiar with Chinese culture, had twice visited China and could speak a little Mandarin. The doctor asked him about his diet and whether he was taking any Chinese herbal medicine. The patient said none of the doctors he had visited previously in Australia had asked him such specific questions, and he had not felt comfortable when consulting them. This doctor took time to involve him in discussion of his symptoms, even though his English is not good.

Case #16 An Arab woman in her mid-thirties

She had to spend ten days in hospital, and though she received acceptable service, she was embarrassed because she was given no time to cover her head before a male doctor arrived. The staff was aware she was a practicing Muslim, and she was annoyed that they did not give her the common courtesy of an early warning. She would have been happier if they could have been more respectful and had taken her religion into consideration.

Case #17 A Malaysian woman in her late twenties

She received good quality care during her labour at the hospital. However, both she and her husband felt uncomfortable about asking for the placenta after the birth. They were afraid of being despised by the Caucasian staff, but their culture requires burying a baby's placenta after birth. The staff had no knowledge of this ritual, and therefore did not mention it. The couple would have been grateful for an opportunity to discuss the matter when the wife was first admitted.

Outcomes

Since the majority of the health workers in Australia are from the country's mainstream culture,[12] members of ethnic minorities are more likely to be affected by cultural differences. However, this study shows patients from the ethnic majority also have issues when interacting with overseas-trained or non-Australian providers. Findings also show that cultural difference is only one of two major factors in patient dissatisfaction; the other is perceived lack of providers' medical knowledge.

Cultural competence

Participants described clinicians as culturally competent when they are aware that patients of different backgrounds may have different religious and cultural concerns and may follow different treatment practices. They speak fluent English, are experienced in understanding foreign accents, build a relationship with patients and explore cultural differences patiently, respectfully and without interruption, by asking them detailed questions about their particular needs and encouraging them to express their concerns. They also ask patients about the medical instructions they were given in their countries for similar health conditions and are familiar with treatment options. They explain negative consequences of medication overuse and the advantages of proposed alterations. Accordingly, patients are more likely to be convinced that the diagnosis and the instructions are reliable.

Cultural and technical knowledge

When patients feel providers are knowledgeable about their particular issues, they feel more comfortable talking to them and are more likely to trust their advice. This applies not only to providers' medical knowledge but also to their awareness of patients' religious values, preferred communication styles and preferences for care.

Cultural knowledge helps providers guess at what is being concealed from them, and so they can refer tactfully to personal issues and encourage patients to reveal more information.

All participants stressed that high-quality care cannot be delivered by health workers who lack medical proficiency, no matter how good their cultural and communication skills. A number of participants shared stories about receiving wrong diagnoses and ineffective advice from doctors of their own ethnic backgrounds but continued to visit them for months because they could not speak English well and no other doctors were available nearby who could speak their language.

In general, these cases provide evidence that cultural differences between patients and health care providers may interfere with effective intercultural communication. On the other hand, similarities are likely to result in better care outcomes. Misunderstandings seem to occur in general for the following reasons:

Prejudice

For example, Australian patients' distrust regarding the technical competence of medical staff from developing countries. They believe such providers are more likely to make wrong diagnoses and prefer, on principle, to seek treatment from providers of their own background.

On the other hand, some immigrant patients stated that though Australian doctors may have better theoretical knowledge, they may not be as experienced as their own local doctors in dealing with the variety and type of medical problems and diseases that are common overseas but not in Australia. One example relates to fasting during pregnancy, when the Arab patient was doubtful whether the Australian doctor could provide her with proper advice.

Language barriers

Both Australian and immigrant patients experienced encounters in which they did not receive quality care due to language barriers. Non-native, English-speaking providers appear sometimes to have difficulty understanding Australian patients (particularly those with strong Australian English accents) and as a result may not provide them with the most suitable treatment. On the other hand, Australian doctors sometimes misunderstand patients' English if they use unfamiliar words and speak with strong foreign accents.

Language barriers appear to constitute a more serious issue for non-native English speaking patients than the other way about. This was a matter of concern not only for less educated patients or patients with a poor level of English proficiency, but also for educated patients and for those who could speak fluent English. There are many different ways of describing symptoms and types of pain in different languages, and these patients could not always find equivalent words and expressions in English.

Furthermore, compared with English speakers, non-English-speaking patients are less able to understand different accents. Some respondents complained that usually they cannot understand everything doctors tell them in consultation, not only those with an Australian accent but also those with non-native accents that are different from their own. Nevertheless, they usually pretend to understand because they don't want to be looked down on or to exhaust their providers.

Communication styles

Patients' perception of health care quality is affected negatively by different communication styles and expectations of level of formality during clinical interactions. Some Australian participants complained about the inability of some immigrant providers to build a relaxed doctor-patient relationship. For instance, they claimed that Asian doctors are less likely to make friendly conversation and explain reasons for, and details of, proposed treatment. Similar claims were made by some non-Australian patients, especially Middle Easterners and Indians. They felt they did not receive enough information and emotional support from those doctors.

Values and treatment preferences

A number of immigrant participants admitted they do not always take Australian doctors fully into their confidence. They may not reveal their beliefs about illness, their treatment preferences, medication habits and ideas about causes of their problems because they do not want to be criticized.

Some treatment preferences, derived from their cultural backgrounds, concerned types and doses of particular drugs and the use of diagnostic imaging. Some medical practices, common in some countries, are not acceptable under the Australian health care system, and this affects relevant patients' perception of providers' knowledge and damages relationships with them, especially when patients are harshly criticized by Australian providers for their stated treatment preferences.

Cultural competence and quality of care

Patients judge the cultural competence of health care providers on their cross-cultural knowledge and skills, their functional and technical expertise in treatment outcomes as well as quality of service. Thus cultural competence by care providers results in patients' perception of high-quality service and vice versa.

Overview

There have been a number of studies of intercultural communication and cultural competence within the Australian health care system.[13] Chenowethm *et al.*[14] have studied cultural diversity as impacting significantly on nursing care quality. They have identified cultural insensitivity in care practices that lead to poor-quality outcomes for health consumers and their families.

They suggest that nurses should pay attention to interpersonal relationships and develop respect for patients' value systems and ways of being, in order to protect their rights and to avoid a tendency to stereotype individuals from particular cultures. They add that expertise of qualified nurses from different cultures can greatly assist this process.

Murray and Skull[15] discuss the problem that refugees and asylum seekers face a number of barriers to accessing health care and improved health status in Australia. These include language difficulties, financial need and unemployment, cultural differences, legal barriers and a health workforce with generally low awareness of issues specific to refugees. They add that, importantly, current Australian government migration and settlement policy impacts also on access to health and health status.

An adequate understanding of these hurdles to health is a prerequisite for health providers and health service managers if they are to tailor health care and services appropriately.

Manderson and Pascale[16] describe how immigrants position their differences in health care settings. Westerman[17] has studied the role played by cultural differences in engagement of Indigenous clients in mental health services; and Small et al.[18] researched the role of culture and communication in Vietnamese, Turkish and Filipino women's experiences of giving birth in Australia.

Of course, applications of theories of intercultural communication to cultural diversity in health care are not limited to Australia. In the online International Encyclopaedia of Communication, Watson[19] has contributed a chapter on intercultural communication in health care; and there are many national studies. For example, Schouten and Meeuwesen[20] found major differences in the Netherlands in doctor–patient communication as a consequence of patients' ethnic backgrounds. They found that doctors behave less affectively when interacting with ethnic minority patients compared to white patients and that the former are less verbally expressive; they seem to be less assertive and affective during medical encounters than white patients.

Tjale and de Villiers[21] examined cultural issues in health and health care in Southern Africa and found that spirituality, economics, politics and kinship are among the cultural factors in transcultural nursing. They described cultural competence as an area of health care that incorporates the values, beliefs and lifestyle choices of patients in order to provide culturally congruent, competent and compassionate care.

In the US, Johnson et al.[22] conducted a cross-sectional telephone survey of 6,299 white, African-American, Hispanic and Asian adults. They found that demographics, source of care and patient–physician communication explain most racial and ethnic differences in patient perceptions of cultural competence in care givers. However, the differences are not fully explained by these factors, and further research is needed to examine sources of cultural bias in the US medical system.

Anderson et al.[23] found that culturally competent health care systems, which provide culturally and linguistically appropriate services, have the potential to reduce racial and ethnic health disparities. When clients do not understand what their health care providers are telling them, and providers either do not speak the client's language or are insensitive to cultural differences, the quality of health care can be compromised.

These researchers reviewed five interventions to improve cultural competence in health care systems:

1. Programmes to recruit and retain staff members who reflect the cultural diversity of the community served
2. Use of interpreter services or bilingual providers for clients with limited English proficiency
3. Cultural competency training for health care providers
4. Use of linguistically and culturally appropriate health education materials
5. Culturally specific health care settings

Unfortunately, they could not determine the effectiveness of any of these interventions, because there were either too few comparative studies, or they were not pertinent Purnell[24] is one practitioner who has created a model for cultural competence in transcultural health care. It is represented by a series of concentric circles, with the outer ring representing global society. The second ring is labelled "Community," defined as a group of people having a common interest or identity and living in a specified locality. The third ring represents "Family" and is defined as two or more people who are emotionally involved with each other. The fourth ring represents "Person" and is defined as a socio-cultural human being in constant adaptation to the environment.

This 12-step model is used to examine 33 population groups from a health care perspective and to provide understanding of the traditions and customs of their societies, hence a perspective on the implications for patient care.

Summary

In summary, more and more people today are living in a multicultural environment. This means that many health practitioners have to interact with people from different cultures. Good communication is vital to effective health care, so communication problems in intercultural encounters have the potential to result in low levels of patient satisfaction and even patient misdiagnoses. In such encounters, health practitioners not only face the natural barriers of communicating with patients who may be unfamiliar with their medical language, but also may face added challenges when patients have culturally different health belief systems.

Much research into intercultural communication and health care has been anecdotal, as are the aforementioned case studies; but it does seem that when health care professionals achieve good communication skills and intercultural understanding, then intercultural communication competence (ICC) follows. The underlying assumption of ICC is that communication occurs predominantly at interpersonal levels and that cultural sensitivity develops as individuals gain knowledge and appreciation of other cultures.

Notes

1. http://www.msf.org/.
2. Committee on understanding and eliminating racial and ethnic disparities in health care, Board on Health Sciences Policy, Institute of Medicine, 2009, Unequal Treatment: Confronting Racial and Ethnic Disparities in Health Care; National Academies Press.
3. Primary Health care, 1978.
4. M. Zineldin, 2006, "The quality of health care and patient satisfaction: an exploratory investigation of the 5Qs model at some Egyptian and Jordanian medical clinics," *International Journal of Health Care Quality Assurance*, 19(1), 60–92.
5. http://www.buzzle.com/articles/ethnic-groups.html, accessed 22 August 2014.
6. Australian Institute of Health and Welfare, 2009, "Health and community services labour force," http://www.aihw.gov.au/publication-detail/?id=64424 68220.
7. J. Campinha-Bacote, 2002, "The process of cultural competence in the delivery of healthcare services: A model of care," *Journal of Transcultural Nursing*, 13(3), 181–184. P. Sharma, J.L.M. Tam and N. Kim, 2009, "Demystifying intercultural service encounters: toward a comprehensive conceptual framework," *Journal of Service Research*, 12(2), 227–242.
8. See, for example, D.E. Hayes-Bautista, 2003, "Research on culturally competent healthcare systems: less sensit(ivity, more statistics," *American Journal of Preventive Medicine*, 24(3), 8–9. S. Saha *et al.*, 2011, "The role of cultural distance between patient and provider in explaining racial/ethnic disparities in HIV care," *Patient Education and Counselling*, 85(3), e278–e284.
9. A. Castro and E. Ruiz, 2009, "The effects of nurse practitioner cultural competence on Latina patient satisfaction," *Journal of the American Academy of Nurse Practitioners*, 21(5), 278–286.
10. M. Zineldin, 2006, "The quality of health care and patient satisfaction: an exploratory investigation of the 5Qs model at some Egyptian and Jordanian medical clinics," *International Journal of Health Care Quality Assurance*, 19(1), 60–92. T.S. Dagger, J.C. Sweeney and L.W. Johnson, 2007, "A hierarchical model of health service quality: scale development and investigation of an integrated model," *Journal of Service Research*, 10(2), 123–142.
11. J.W. Creswell, 1998, *Qualitative inquiry & research design: choosing among five approaches,*" (Thousand Oaks, CA: SAGE Publications).
12. Australian Institute of Health and Welfare, 2009.

13. See, for example, L. Manderson and P. Allotey, 2003, "Storytelling, marginality, and community in Australia: how immigrants position their difference in health care settings," *Medical Anthropology: Cross-Cultural Studies in Health and Illness*, 22(1), 1–21; published online: 26 October 2010.

14. L. Chenowethm, Y.-H. Jeon, M. Goff and C. Burke, 2006, "Cultural competency and nursing care: an Australian perspective," first published online 23 January 2006; *International Nursing Review*, 53(1), 34–40, March 2006.

15. S.B. Murray and S.A. Skull, 2005, "Hurdles to health: immigrant and refugee health care in Australia," *Australian Health Review* 29(1), 25–29.

16. Manderson and Allotey, "Storytelling, marginality, and community in Australia ," 1–21.

17. T. Westerman, 2004 (guest editorial), "Engagement of Indigenous clients in mental health services: what role do cultural differences play?" *Advances in Mental Health*, Vol. 3, Indigenous Mental Health, 88–93.

18. R. Small, P. Liamputtong Rice, J. Yelland and J. Lumley, 1999, "Mothers in a new country: the role of culture and communication in Vietnamese, Turkish and Filipino women's experiences of giving birth in Australia," *Women & Health*, 28(3), 77–101; published online: 21 October 2009.

19. B.M. Watson, 2008, "Intercultural communication in health-care," *The International Encyclopaedia of Communication* (Blackwell Publishing)

20. B.C Schouten and L. Meeuwesen, December 2006, "Cultural differences in medical communication: a review of the literature," *Patient Education and Counseling*, 64(1–3), 21–34.

21. A. Tjale and L. de Villiers, 2004, *Cultural issues in health and health care: a resource book for Southern Africa* (Cape Town: Juta).

22. R.L. Johnson, S. Saha, J.J. Arbelaez, M.C. Beach and L.A. Cooper, February 2004, "Racial and ethnic differences in patient perceptions of bias and cultural competence in health care," first published online 27 February 2004; *Journal of General Internal Medicine*, 19(2), 101–110.

23. L.M. Anderson, S.C. Scrimshaw, M.T. Fullilove, J.E. Fielding and J. Normand, April 2003, "Culturally competent healthcare systems: a systematic review," *American Journal of Preventive Medicine*, 24(3), Supplement, 68–79.

24. L.D. Purnell, 18 September 2012, *Transcultural health care: A culturally competent approach* (Google eBook; F A Davis Company).

References

L.M. Anderson, S.C. Scrimshaw, M.T. Fullilove, J.E. Fielding and J. Normand, April 2003, "Culturally competent healthcare systems: a systematic review," *American Journal of Preventive Medicine*, 24(3), Supplement, 68–79.

Australian Institute of Health and Welfare, 2009, "Health and community services labour force," available at http://www.aihw.gov.au/publication-detail/?id=6442468220.

J. Campinha-Bacote, 2002, "The process of cultural competence in the delivery of healthcare services: a model of care," *Journal of Transcultural Nursing*, 13(3), 181–184.

A. Castro and E. Ruiz, 2009, "The effects of nurse practitioner cultural competence on Latina patient satisfaction," *Journal of the American Academy of Nurse Practitioners*, 21(5), 278–286.

L. Chenowethm, Y.-H. Jeon, M. Goff and C. Burke, March 2006, "Cultural competency and nursing care: an Australian perspective," first published online 23 January 2006; *International Nursing Review*, 53(1), 34–40.

J.W. Creswell, 1998, *Qualitative inquiry & research design: choosing among five approaches* (Thousand Oaks, CA: SAGE Publications).

T.S. Dagger, J.C. Sweeney and L.W. Johnson, 2007, "A hierarchical model of health service quality: scale development and investigation of an integrated model," *Journal of Service Research*, 10(2), 123–142.

D.E. Hayes-Bautista, 2003, "Research on culturally competent healthcare systems: less sensit(ivity, more statistics," *American Journal of Preventive Medicine*, 24(3), 8–9.

R.L. Johnson, S. Saha, J.J. Arbelaez, M.C. Beach and L.A. Cooper, 2004, "Racial and ethnic differences in patient perceptions of bias and cultural competence in health care," first published online 27 February 2004; *Journal of General Internal Medicine*, 19(2), 101–110, February 2004.

L. Manderson and P. Allotey, 2003, "Storytelling, marginality, and community in Australia: how immigrants position their difference in health care settings," *Medical Anthropology: Cross-Cultural Studies in Health and Illness*, 22(1), 1–21; published online: 26 October 2010.

S.B. Murray and S.A. Skull, 2005, "Hurdles to health: Immigrant and refugee health care in Australia," *Australian Health Review*, 29(1), 25–29.

Primary health care; Report on the international conference on primary health care, Alma-Ata, USSR, 6–12 September 1978; http://whqlibdoc.who.int/publications/9241800011.pdf.

L.D. Purnell, 2012, *Transcultural health care: A culturally competent approach* (Google eBook: F A Davis Company), 18 September 2012.

S. Saha *et al.*, 2011, "The role of cultural distance between patient and provider in explaining racial/ethnic disparities in HIV care," *Patient Education and Counselling*, 85(3), e278–e284.

B.C. Schouten and L. Meeuwesen, December 2006, "Cultural differences in medical communication: a review of the literature," *Patient Education and Counseling*, 64(1–3), 21–34.

P. Sharma, J.L.M. Tam and N. Kim, 2009, "Demystifying intercultural service encounters: toward a comprehensive conceptual framework," *Journal of Service Research*, 12(2), 227–242.

R. Small, P.L. Rice, J. Yelland and J. Lumley, 1999, "Mothers in a new country: the role of culture and communication in Vietnamese, Turkish and Filipino women's experiences of giving birth in Australia," published online: 21 October 200; *Women & Health*, 28(3), 77–101.

A. Tjale and L. De Villiers, 2004, *Cultural issues in health and health care: a resource book for Southern Africa* (Juta and Company Ltd).

B.M. Watson, 2008, "Intercultural communication in health-care," *The International Encyclopaedia of Communication*, Blackwell Publishing.

T. Westerman, 2004 (guest editorial), "Engagement of Indigenous clients in mental health services: what role do cultural differences play?" *Advances in Mental Health*, 3, Indigenous Mental Health, 88–93.

M. Zineldin, 2006, "The quality of health care and patient satisfaction: an exploratory investigation of the 5Qs model at some Egyptian and Jordanian medical clinics," *International Journal of Health Care Quality Assurance*, 19(1), 60–92.

4

Jason and the Jaguar: The Case of the Unmotivated Employee

Elizabeth Christopher

Editor's introduction

This case study is illuminated by a summary of major Western theories of motivation and differences in workplace cultures that require different leadership styles. The leadership behaviour it describes might be usefully applied to other management situations that require workers to be motivated to perform even unwelcome tasks, because they are encouraged to feel part of the firm.

A good example[1] is provided by the UK firm John Lewis Partnership (JLP), whose workforce has a strong vested interest in "going the extra mile" because its members have a stake in the business. In 2007, JLP announced its employees had received 18% of their salary as a bonus – equivalent to nine weeks' pay. The company, an employee-owned organization, had enjoyed such a good year that it could afford to pay out £155 million in bonuses alone.

Motivation can be described as an urge (sometimes irresistible) to do something; or as a drive to achieve certain goals. In terms of management, it means the amount of effort employees are willing to put into work to perform tasks of value to their employers. In this case, Jason seems initially to have lacked sufficient motivation to make a special effort to help his manager out of a difficulty. She found a non-work-related incentive to persuade him to do so; but the result was that he gained a new sense of loyalty to his boss.

David Clarence McClelland,[2] who died in 1998, was a US social psychologist. He developed a model of motivation based on three needs that he believed were shared by all human beings: for power, affiliation and achievement. He argued that although all three are felt by everybody, for most people one is dominant: thus, some people will seek power (control) as their first priority, others will value affiliation (relationships) more than achievement (task) or vice versa.[3] His model was based on Henry Murray's[4] theory of personality, and he applied it to management systems, as co-founder of the McBer Consulting Company, to assist companies to improve their methods of evaluating employees and training managers.

While it would be impertinent to judge Jason's personal motivations in the case that follows, his actions do seem to have been in response to all three of McClelland's identified needs but perhaps mostly to power, that is, his need to control his environment. He was resolute and self-confident in pursuit of his aims and willing to deputize for his leader only when it seemed in his best interest to do so – though he demonstrated affection for his girlfriend and, eventually, loyalty to his manager. Maria's success in motivating him to do what she wanted was due to her recognition that appeal to his enlightened self-interest would be her most effective tactic.

McClelland is only one of many theorists and researchers who have written extensively on practical aspects of motivation in the workplace, for example Chris Argyris,[5] Frederick Herzberg,[6] Rensis Likert,[7] Douglas McGregor,[8] Abraham Maslow,[9] Elton Mayo[10] and Victor Vroom.[11]

Argyris explored the impact of formal organizational structures, control systems and management on individuals. He found that while bureaucratic or pyramidal values tend to lead to mutual mistrust by individuals, humanistic or democratic values tend to lead to more trusting, authentic relationships in which people are treated as human beings. He argued that in such environments both organizational members and the organization itself are given an opportunity to develop to the fullest potential, and there is an attempt to make work exciting and challenging. This case study appears to support his contention.

It conforms also to Herzberg's two-part theory by which it is not the extrinsic factors of the job environment that motivates workers, such as pay and working conditions, but intrinsic factors such as their sense of achievement, recognition and interest. Moreover, Likert found that a participative system works well, in which managers and team members have confidence in each other and motivation is by rewards based on agreed-on goals and cooperative teamwork – as between Jason and Maria.

McGregor proposed an X-Y theory: that there are two fundamental approaches to managing people. Theory X suggests that people in general dislike work and will avoid it if they can; they avoid responsibility and are relatively unambitious; therefore, they must be coerced to work towards organizational objectives. Theory Y suggests that people will apply self-control and self-direction in the pursuit of these goals if they see them as of value. In this case, Maria seems to have applied both theories to her negotiation with Jason.

Maslow argued a hierarchy of five levels of basic human needs: a lower order of physiological (food and shelter) and security motivations and a higher order of relationships, status and self-development. It was to this higher order that Maria seems to have appealed.

Mayo's Hawthorne experiments were conducted between 1927 and 1932 at the Western Electric Hawthorne Works in Chicago. He found that workers increased productivity because of the stimuli of being singled out, involved and made to feel important – as was Jason. Moreover, Jason sought a fair balance between what he put into work for his superior and what he, personally, got out of it; and this behaviour corresponds to Adam's Equity Theory. Similarly, Vroom's Expectancy theory assumes that motivation is based on the three assumptions that the individual will value the offered reward, will feel confident of achieving the set goal and, having achieved it, will receive the desired reward.

Another way of examining leadership styles is to distinguish between "transactional" and "transformational" leadership styles.[12] Transactional leadership is argued to maintain the status quo – that is, to monitor the smooth running of the operation and its members; whereas transformational behaviour is needed to inspire, energize and stimulate team members and to respond effectively to crises.[13] In this case, Maria appears to have changed her behaviour effectively from transactional (i.e., general management of the office) to transformational in order to deal with the crisis caused by Jason's initial refusal.

Finally, some general assumptions about Jason's motivations can be made by applying the cross-cultural research findings of researchers such as Hofstede[14] and Trompenaars.[15] Both find that motivation is situational and many cultural variables affect people's sense of what is attainable, and thus affect motivation.

One example is how much control people believe they have over their environment and their destiny; whether they believe that they can control certain events and not just be at the mercy of external forces.[16] For example, a culture high in individualism, such as that of Australia, suggests people will be motivated by reward systems that offer opportunities for individual advancement and autonomy. These characteristics are part of a working culture of competition, whereas members of cultures high in collectivism, as in Thailand, will be more likely to be motivated to work through appeals to company and group goals: or, as in China, cash in hand to take home to the family.

While it is impossible to generalize from the case of one Australian, Jason's behaviour appears to conform to the aforementioned sociotype[17] of mainstream Australian culture; that is, to a major set of characteristics that tend to be true across a particular group of people, rather than a stereotype, which is a misleading simplification.

Abstract:

This is a case of finding culturally appropriate means to motivate an employee to perform an unwelcome task in an individualistic, democratic work culture with a flat power hierarchy.

The director of a small office in Sydney, Australia, urgently, at short notice, needed an employee to work on a Saturday. His job description did not include working weekends and he refused. Since she could not order him to comply, she had to find a way to persuade him. This leader's methods can be related to David McClelland's theory of motivational needs for affiliation, power and achievement.

Keywords: cultural differences in motivation, employee motivation, leadership

Introduction

Background to the case

This case demonstrates that the phrase "intercultural communication" should be taken to include differences in work cultures. If the described situation had taken place, say, in Thailand or in Turkey rather than in Australia, the CEO would merely have commanded the office manager to work over the weekend, who would have had no choice but to comply if he wanted to keep his job. Readers should find the case useful as an illustration of the need in international management to find culturally appropriate ways to motivate employees.

Case presentation

A few years ago, Maria was in charge of the Sydney office of a Japanese company. The office manager was a young man called Jason. He was a good worker but "typically Australian" in the sense of setting a high value on his own worth, dignity, individual freedom and equality under the law.[18]

One week, Maria received a telephone call from the head office in Kyoto. Apparently, a very senior representative of the company had decided to visit Sydney briefly as part of an Asia-Pacific business trip. He would be in town on a Saturday, arriving early in the morning and departing the same evening.

Maria was aware that Japanese are always conscious of their hierarchical position in any social setting; they act accordingly and expect others to do so.[19] Therefore, this senior representative of the parent company would assume that his arrival would be treated with respect. Moreover, as a member of a collectivist society, he would expect to be taken care of by his loyal staff for the whole period of his brief stay.

Most unfortunately, Maria was due in Melbourne that same weekend to represent the company at a business exhibition and to meet with important clients. It was essential that the firm show its presence there; and nobody could deputize for her.

She explained the situation to Jason and asked him to meet the Japanese executive, Mr. Yamamoto, at the airport and to apologize for her absence with due humility and explain the good reasons for it. Then, he was to show the distinguished visitor around the office, introduce him to the staff, take him to lunch at a fancy restaurant, show him a few Sydney scenic highlights and generally look after him before seeing him off again in the evening.

Jason listened to all this with a blank face, and then said simply: "Look, Maria, you know I don't work on Saturdays."

Highly disconcerted, Maria replied: "Jason, this is exceptional. You know I can't meet Mr. Yamamoto myself, and you know how important it is that he be impressed with our operations here."

"Yes," said Jason. "But I have a new girlfriend. She lives in Brisbane and is coming down to visit me that weekend. There's no way I'm going to disappoint her."

Maria thought of suggesting that he take the girlfriend with him to meet the Japanese visitor, but since she didn't know her, she decided it would be too much of a risk. They seemed to be at stalemate – until she had another idea.

She remembered that in the morning when she arrived for work and parked in her designated car stall, Jason had driven up and parked beside her. He was driving an ancient, Ford, whereas Maria's car was a scarlet E-type Jaguar. He was enchanted, had walked round and round it and asked all kinds of technical questions, most of which she had been unable to answer.

With this in mind, she now said: "Jason, what if we were to exchange cars for that weekend? You would have to explain to your girlfriend about Saturday, but you could ferry the Japanese guy round all day; and then your girlfriend all Sunday?"

He looked at her in frank disbelief. "Do you mean I can drive your car all weekend?"

"Yes. I'll drive your car to the airport and leave it in the long-stay car park. Then I'll bring it back to the office on Monday and we'll exchange back again."

"Wow!" He said slowly. "My girlfriend has friends in Sydney. She could spend that Saturday with them; and we could have a great day on Sunday! Thank you, Maria, I promise to take great car of the Jag; and to give Mr. Yamamoto the time of his life!"

Outcomes

And so it was. The Japanese executive called Maria the week after that momentous Saturday to thank her for his visit, to praise the office setup and staff in general and Jason in particular. Since Jason had reported an "awesome" Sunday with his girlfriend and Maria's weekend in Melbourne had been in its own way equally successful, the story had a happy ending all round.

An interesting endnote was that the whole experience changed Jason's professional relationship with his office manager. Before it, though he had always been an efficient employee, he had not gone beyond the strict terms of his employment. After that Saturday, however, and from then on, he went out of his way to be helpful and supportive.

Notes

Names and minor details of the story presented in this chapter have been changed for the sake of confidentiality.

1. S. Norris, Friday, 30 March 2007, "Cooperatives pay big dividends," http://www.theguardian.com/.
2. D.C. McClelland, 1987, *Human motivation* (CUP Archive).
3. E. Christopher, 2012, *International management: explorations across cultures* (Kogan Page), 118.
4. H.A. Murray, 2007, *Explorations in personality* (Oxford University Press), first published in 1938.
5. C. Argyris, 1964, *Integrating the individual and the organization* (New York: Wiley & Sons).
6. F. Herzberg, 1966, *Work and the nature of man* (New York: World Publishing Co.).

7. R. Likert, 1967, *The human organization* (McGraw Hill).
8. D. McGregor and J. Cutcher-Gershenfeld, 2006, *The human side of enterprise* (McGraw-Hill Professional).
9. A. Maslow, 1954, *Motivation and personality* (New York: Harper).
10. L.F. Urwick (Lundall Fownes), 1960, *The life and work of Elton Mayo* (London: Urwick, Orr and Partners Ltd.).
11. V.H. Vroom, 1994, *Work and motivation* (Wiley).
12. The concepts of transformational and transactional leadership were first discussed by Max Weber in 1947. See J.A. Congera, 1999, "Charismatic and transformational leadership in organizations: an insider's perspective on these developing streams of research," *The Leadership Quarterly*, 10(2), Summer, 145–179.
13. B.M. Bass, 1985, *Leadership and performance beyond expectations* (Free Press).
14. G. Hofstede, 1984, *Culture's consequences: international differences in work-related values* (SAGE Publications).
15. F. Trompenaars and Charles Hampden-Turner, 1997, *Riding the waves of culture: Understanding diversity in global business* (McGraw-Hill).
16. H.M. Lefcourt, 2014, *Locus of control: current trends in theory & research* (Psychology Press).
17. H.C. Triandis, 1981, *Handbook of cross-cultural psychology*, in H.C. Triandis and W.W. Lambert (eds) (Allyn & Bacon, Incorporated).
18. https://www.dfat.gov.au/facts/people_culture.html.
19. http://geert-hofstede.com/japan.html.

References

C. Argyris, 1964, *Integrating the individual and the organization* (New York: Wiley & Sons).
B.M. Bass, 1985, *Leadership and performance beyond expectations* (Free Press).
E. Christopher, 2012, *International management: explorations across cultures* (UK: Kogan Page).
J.A. Congera, 1999, "Charismatic and transformational leadership in organizations: an insider's perspective on these developing streams of research," *The Leadership Quarterly*, 10(2), Summer, 145–179.
F. Herzberg, 1966, *Work and the nature of man* (New York: World Publishing Co.).
G. Hofstede, 1984, *Culture's consequences: international differences in work-related values* (SAGE Publications)
H.M. Lefcourt, 2014, *Locus of control: current trends in theory & research* (Psychology Press).
R. Likert, 1967, *The human organization* (McGraw Hill).
A. Maslow, 1954, *Motivation and personality* (New York: Harper).
D.C. McClelland, 1987, *Human motivation* (CUP Archive).
D. McGregor and J. Cutcher-Gershenfeld, 2006, *The human side of enterprise* (McGraw-Hill Professional).
H.A. Murray, 2007, *Explorations in personality* (Oxford University Press).
H.C. Triandis, 1981, *Handbook of cross-cultural psychology*, H.C. Triandis and W.W. Lambert, editors (Allyn & Bacon, Incorporated).

F. Trompenaars and C. Hampden-Turner, 1997 *Riding the waves of culture: understanding diversity in global business* (McGraw-Hill).

L.F. Urwick (Lundall Fownes), 1960, *The life and work of Elton Mayo* (London: Urwick, Orr and Partners Ltd).

V.H. Vroom, 1994, *Work and motivation* (Wiley).

5

Cross-Cultural Management: Discrepancies between Dealing with Diversity at Corporate and Individual Levels of Employment

Dharm P.S. Bhawuk and Smriti Anand

Editor's introduction

This case presents both the corporate-level perspective and that of an employee. It allows examination of the gap between what Schein[1] describes as the espoused values captured in the policies of an organization and as experienced by employees when such policies are translated into action. Knowing that such a gap exists is the first step toward understanding diversity issues and addressing them.

When organizations make policies to address any issue, especially the sensitive one of diversity, then managers need to keep in mind that the implementation of the strategy is only as strong as the weakest link. Each case of failure becomes much like a legal precedent, and employees refer to it as evidence that the diversity policy is simply window dressing.

This is not a cynical observation. It took the United States more than one hundred years to deal with the issue of race relations, from President Abraham Lincoln's Emancipation Proclamation on 1 January 1863 (the third year of the American Civil War) to the Civil Rights Act that on 2 July 1964 outlawed discrimination based on race, colour, religion, sex or national origin. All diversity effort is about change management, which requires that policies be implemented consistently over many years to engender confidence in all concerned – employees, vendors, customers and so forth – that the organization is serious about bringing about change. This case shows that gaps do exist between corporate policies and how they are meted out to individual employees and managing such gaps is a serious challenge that today's managers are up against.

A critical question is raised in this case: whether flex-time is a time-honoured organizational practice or a fluffy perquisite available at the whim of a manager, possibly to be withdrawn on a short notice. Women and men, though perhaps still primarily women, who want to balance work and family are the targets of this practice. The time needed to nurture children should not be held hostage to the vicissitudes of organizational performance – of employers who say, in effect, if the economy is good and the company is doing well, we will provide flex-time, otherwise not. Flex-time requires commitment and adjustment by everybody in the organization to help those who have a need to work from home for part of the time. There should be no discrimination between different divisions; some people in every unit may need flex-time, and it should be permitted, if the firm is serious about implementing diversity policies.

Another issue in the case is that of performance measurement. Can an employee or manager who consistently performs above average suddenly become a poor performer? Drucker's[2] idea of management by objectives provides a useful tool that could have been used in this case to avoid creating a frustrating situation for a high performer like Jin. None of Jin's managers were willing to sit with her and set mutually acceptable goals and then evaluate her on those objectives. In this case, there is more evidence of application of Theory X management[3] than of management by objectives, since most of Jin's supervisors seem to have assumed she needed coercion, control and punishment, rather than cooperation and collaboration.

Finally, organizations need to recognize that while the legal employment contracts remain largely uniform across the workforce, the psychological contracts[4] (PCs) – reciprocal obligations perceived by the employees – have unique components based on sex/race/ethnicity/culture.[5] This is an important aspect of deep-level diversity[6] in the workplace. For example, coming from a collectivistic[7] society, Jin was trying to form family-like bonds with her employer organization. These bonds made her very loyal, but they also made her feel quite betrayed when a PC breach occurred. Managers need to be trained about cultural differences and their repercussions for the PCs formed by employees, else organizations will keep paying a heavy price.

When human resources, like Jin, are lost to an organization, especially when it has spent thousands of dollars on training them, arguably their immediate managers should be held responsible. If firms were to implement such a proposal, HR personnel would put pressure on line managers to create a positive environment for their people to succeed, rather than being in a hurry to let them go.

Abstract:

This case study captures some of the career issues facing women and members of minority groups in US society. The story is of a high achieving minority woman manager and the way her career advanced and then declined, leading her finally to leave her employment after investing seven years in the organization. The views of senior managers of this organization on its diversity policy are presented; and the case reveals a discrepancy between the handling at corporate and individual levels of minority and women employees.

Keywords: employment careers, workforce diversity, women and minority groups

Introduction

Organizations have spent the past decade developing and implementing diversity strategies to break the glass ceiling and to make the workplace friendly to women and minorities. We present a case study capturing "thick descriptions" of career issues facing minority women in the workplace. We start by sharing the story of a high achieving minority woman manager, how her career evolved from the beginning to the end when she left the organization. She invested seven years in the organization, and just when she thought her career had taken off, she had to leave.

The case is discussed in the context of the description of the diversity policy of the organization, which is presented in the second section of the case. The comparison of the two perspectives, one from below and one from above, should lead to an understanding of how minority issues are visualized and dealt with at the corporate level, and how these policies are delivered at the grass-root level. Recommendations for ways in which managers might deal with diversity in the workplace are given.

Case presentation

A unique case of unrealized potential? Jin's story

Upon completing her graduate degree in mechanical engineering, Jin Liang[8] joined Aventa, a Fortune 100 firm, in January 1997. At Aventa's network group, Jin was responsible for designing communications equipment to be used by the US government. Based on her excellent performance, she was promoted to a lead engineer within 18 months. Jin saw a bright career at the firm, and joined a part-time MBA programme at a prestigious business school.

During this period, Jin had a baby girl. She took maternity leave, and later on continued with her team leader responsibilities. Jin felt that the organization was supportive of her family/school commitments. For example, she could telecommute twice a week or change her work hours to attend MBA classes. Aventa was also paying for Jin's education.

In January 2000, Jin's boss left the firm on a very short notice. Jin took on all his responsibilities and worked some crazy hours for a while. The team members liked as well as respected her. After a few months Jin asked for a promotion, which was granted. She was now managing eight engineers and was responsible for large projects. She was quite happy, but felt that her newly acquired business skills were not being used.

In March 2001, Jin decided to look for another opportunity within Aventa. She still enjoyed the engineering work, but did not want to become an engineering manager. She also felt that as the firm was paying for her MBA, she should try to stay there. She searched for marketing and business development opportunities in different sectors of the firm.

After evaluating all the offers, and balancing them against her family needs, in July 2001, Jin decided to take a product management position in the Consumer Products Group (CPG) of Aventa. Her new responsibilities included managing an MP3 player from concept to launch. She was awarded a promotion and saw great potential in her new job.

Consumer Products Group was the biggest business for Aventa and was not doing too well at the time. The products were too late to market the feature set was not at par with other competing products and Aventa was rapidly losing market share. In October 2001, Jin's team was reorganized, and her job was significantly changed. Jin was asked to manage a product that was soon to be retired. Jin's boss Jack left to manage a PDA (Personal Digital Assistant) team within CPG.

Many people in Jin's current team lost their jobs, and she started worrying about her future. Jack was responsible for bringing her to CPG, and when he asked her to join his new team, she agreed. She felt that Jack valued her skill set, understood her family commitments and would likely provide her with excellent career prospects. In the new team, Jin was responsible for launching a PDA (code name Leopard) in Europe. Leopard's design was already final, and she started working on the market launch process.

In March 2002, CPG had massive workforce reduction, and Jack was one of the first people to be let go. There was no announcement or any kind of communication from upper management. One week after Jack's departure, Jin received an email that Julie (one of Jack's colleagues) would be her new manager. The next day, Julie called Jin and her colleague Eva to her office and announced that she did not have the time to manage anyone, and so unofficially Dave was going to be their manager. So far, Dave had been Jin's colleague; she knew that he was either at her grade level or at most one level up. When she was brought into this team, she was promised a high-flying career, and suddenly all that seemed too far away.

Jin met with her new boss Julie and shared her concerns; she also requested to be a direct report to her, but Julie refused. Jin had a long commute to work, which was why she had arranged to telecommute two days a week. Julie said that she was not happy about Jin's "part-time" work schedule. Jin explained that telecommuting was making her more effective, and she had been successfully using it for past three years. Julie said that circumstances had changed, and everyone ought to be thankful for still having a job. Jin did not like her comments, and asked for a written order before she would stop telecommuting. The Leopard project was cancelled shortly afterwards and Jin was asked to research future applications for PDAs. Aventa had a future application team devoted to this very purpose; Jin's work was essentially duplication of their efforts.

Dave and Julie had known each other for a while; they were both Caucasian and seemed to share a good rapport. They would often meet for lunch, or Dave would accompany Julie to the on-site day care centre to pick up her son. They would have informal discussions about various projects during these meetings, and Jin would be left out. Jin felt that her job was in jeopardy.

Two months later, Jin was asked to start writing specific technical feature descriptions for future products. CPG already had a team for this purpose, but Julie and Dave did not want to communicate with them, so Jin was asked to learn and do this task. Jin felt that again she was duplicating another team's effort, but continued with the project anyway.

By the third quarter of 2002, the workforce reduction initiative was over, and Jin started feeling there was a future for her in CPG. Dave had asked her to attend a weekly meeting on Wednesdays (her telecommute days were Wednesday and Friday), so she started telecommuting only on Fridays. Once she did that, the Wednesday meetings stopped.

Around this time, the CPG marketing team was reorganized once again. The team was split in a matrix organization with two parts – product management and product marketing. Jin was placed in product marketing. It was not clear why people were being placed under one category or the other. Job functionality was not very clear either. She had a new manager Terence, based in Aventa's satellite office in another city. Terence seemed nice, but he made it clear he did not have much time for managing anyone. Jin was officially his direct report, and a dotted line to Julie. Dave and Julie were part of product management team, and Dave reported to Julie. Jin was still working for Dave and Julie; however, now Terence did her official performance evaluations and so on.

Shortly afterwards, Jin was assigned to a new product code named Jaguar. Dave was the product manager and Jin was product-marketing manager. Dave would often not share product related information with her. On being asked he would say that he was not used to managing anyone and just forgot to share information.

Jin still wanted to stay at Aventa, and bought a home close to work. She applied and found another marketing position within CPG organization; however, Terence did not allow her to move. In December 2002, the Jaguar project was cancelled, as the sales teams did not like the product's features. Jin had always expressed concerns about the feature set but was overruled by Dave (product management team had the final decision making power). Shortly afterwards, they were asked to work on an updated version of Jaguar called Murphy; however Jin strongly felt that the feature set was still not good enough. Murphy was being manufactured in Taiwan, and was going to be launched worldwide.

In January 2003, Jin had a performance review and was given average rating. This was a new ranking system, and Terence said it was customary for a new marketing person to be ranked average. In engineering teams, Jin had always been ranked high, but she accepted Terence's reasoning.

In March 2003, Terence moved to a new position and Carl became Jin's manager. Carl had a long-term working relationship with Julie. Carl also made it very clear that things would stay as they were. Jin kept working on the Murphy project and tried to have a better relationship with both Dave and Julie.

In April, Jin and Dave went to various parts of Asia to make pre-launch presentations of their phone. Jin had worked hard on all the presentations; still Dave wanted to be the only presenter. Jin objected and insisted on presenting a fair share. Even in Asia, Dave excluded her from some meetings.

Jin was now also working on another older product whose marketing manager had moved on to another position. This product was being very poorly received in the market and Julie was its product manager. Jin's manager Carl advised her to spend very little time on this product as it was soon to be taken off the market.

In June 2003, Jin had a performance review with Carl, and she was informed that Julie was unhappy with her performance. This was surprising because Jin had already had a performance review with Dave where he had expressed satisfaction with her performance. She had tried several times to meet with Julie for a performance review, but Julie was always unavailable. Carl said that Julie had not mentioned any specifics.

Jin requested Julie to give her detailed feedback, and after many requests, was allowed 15 minutes of her time. Julie again said that Jin was not meeting her expectations. She did not give Jin any concrete information to work with. She mentioned some other managers who were working on completely different products (different launch regions, price segment and feature sets) and said Jin was not as good. Jin could not see a basis for comparison, and they did not reach any decision. Julie also indicated some unhappiness over Jin's time allocation towards her product and Jin's telecommute (one day per week). Julie mentioned that Dave was unhappy with Jin's performance as well.

Jin's performance rating remained average, but now she felt worried. So far she had been hoping to move from average to high rating, and suddenly without any reason it seemed that she was actually going to be pushed further down. After this meeting with Julie, Jin was not informed about product meetings on many occasions, and was sometimes asked to make a presentation in these meetings. If she were not prepared, Carl would email and complain or do so in person.

Jin was working long hours, especially making long conference calls in the evening with the team in Asia, and started feeling that there was no point in continuing. Going to work was becoming painful, because every day there was some unpleasantness. Julie would often impose her ideas on Jin, or shoot down Jin's ideas in a meeting. On some days, Julie would send work to Jin around 4 p.m. and ask her to finish it right away (Jin's typical work hours were 6:30 a.m. to 4 p.m., and conference calls from 8 p.m. to around 11 p.m.).

Meanwhile, the sales team again declined to take Murphy, as the feature set was still not competitive enough. Dave had arranged a conference call with them without informing Jin, and so she was not part of this decision, even though she was the product's marketing manager. This incident helped her make up her mind. She complained to Carl about this information hiding and all the other instances.

In September 2003, Jin met with her department's HR person Tanya and told her she was under considerable stress due to team conflicts and wanted to seek her advice. Tanya first suggested that the stress might be due to personal issues, such as time management, childcare arrangements, marital issues and so on. When Jin insisted that there were no personal issues, Tanya asked her to file an official complaint and explained how that would initiate a long process of inquiry before reaching any conclusions. Jin did not feel up to it. She asked if HR could help her move to another position, but was told that was not possible. Tanya offered in-house counselling for stress relief to Jin, which she refused.

Jin met with Carl and informed him of her decision to leave. He said that he felt Julie was unfair but there was not much that he could do. Before leaving, Jin decided to meet Carrie (Carl's boss) and Kevin (head of product marketing). Carrie said that she had already met with Julie and was convinced that Jin was a poor performer and was blaming Julie unfairly. Carrie was sceptical that in such bad economy someone would leave a well-paying job due to stress. She suggested that Jin was trying to leave Aventa after getting paid for her MBA (she had graduated in March 2003) and that the company would definitely try to get its money back.

Kevin suspected that Jin was unhappy with marketing as a career, rather than with her team. He asked her to reconsider her decision as Aventa had invested heavily in her, but she told him about her interactions so far with Carl and Carrie. Kevin asked her to somehow fix things. Jin could not see any support from any direction and left Aventa in November 2003.

Diversity management at Aventa: the corporate perspective

Aventa started its diversity effort in the 1990s. They rejected the bottom-up approach and preferred to take the top-down route to diversity management. The champion of diversity management at Aventa was its CEO and that facilitated the top-down approach.

Factors that led to the development and implementation of diversity programme

Historically, at Aventa, EEO/AA has been looked upon as the cost of doing business with the government. Diversity was not recognized as a business issue and was viewed more as a constraint imposed from the external environment in the context of EEO/AA. The organization went through a paradigm shift, in the 1990s, in recognizing diversity issue as an internal concern, a business issue rather than something external to the organization. There were two reasons for Aventa to consider diversity as an internal business issue.

First, the workforce demographics are constantly changing. African-Americans and Hispanics population growth is four and seven times that of Caucasian Americans, which leaves firms no choice but to hire from these minority populations. Projections of labour force also show that there will be a shortage of technical people in the future and that would create a need to integrate minorities and women in the Aventa workforce. Aventa approached this scenario by preparing itself to answer the question that these minority workers would ask in the future: "Where are people like me in your hierarchy?"

The second reason for Aventa to attend to the issue of diversity was the fact that in the 1990s excessive turnover among women was reported in the US media. Many of these women were becoming self-employed entrepreneurs. Aventa anticipated that these women would not like to do business with any organization that they suspect might indulge in discrimination against women.

Aventa had not felt any market pressure from suppliers, clients or shareholders to attend to diversity issues. Unlike some organizations, it had not felt any legal pressure either. Aventa was addressing the diversity issue purely on a proactive basis to better prepare itself for the global market place.

Outcomes

How did Aventa implement diversity efforts?

Aventa took a "changing corporate culture or organizational development" approach to managing diversity – the workforce is diverse and so the management needs to be diverse too. If management is diverse, they believe there would not be any problem handling a diverse workforce. They operationalized diversity management through succession planning and were working at breaking the "glass ceiling."

Aventa had seven Business Units (BUs) and the presidents of each of these units had been made accountable for the implementation of the diversity efforts to reach parity goals. The goals were given to the BU presidents in the early 1990s. Since there were not many minority individuals at the vice-president (VP) level, Aventa set a goal of promoting *at least* three women and two minority individuals to the position of vice-president each year starting in the early 1990s and planned to continue with this process for the next five years. The BU presidents were responsible for identifying, from among minorities, capable individuals, including women (and white men), who could become VPs and then groom them to take that position in about three years. For director, manager and beginner positions, Aventa set a goal to match the national census, that is, to have, in specific functional areas, as many managers and directors as the average national percentage of that ethnic group.

The evaluation of this programme in the first five years showed that in the first two years they came close to achieving parity goals for the organization (goals missed by only 1.6% and 2.6% for the two years, respectively). However, on the whole, Aventa had done very well in breaking the glass ceiling. It had 2 women and 6 minority people as vice-presidents in the early 1990s and 16 women and 26 minority people as vice-presidents by mid-1990s. The increase in women and minority individuals in senior management also showed a percentage increase.

It is important to note that the increase in vice-presidents was not in the traditional areas of human resource management, but in important and critical functional areas. In Aventa, women and minority individuals occupied such key positions as head of software engineering for one of the BUs, head of robotics, general manager of the paging international network, general manager within the consumer products organization, vice-president of labour law and so on.

Aventa's diversity efforts had brought it recognition from various quarters. Catalyst, the renowned women's advocacy organization, awarded it the Catalyst Award in the mid-1990s. It also received other prestigious awards. Aventa was ranked within the top 20 companies among the 100 best companies to work for in the US. Aventa used these awards as an indicator of its success in implementing diversity efforts.

How did Aventa integrate corporate and BU diversities efforts?

The corporate office was responsible for formulating the strategy, which was communicated to the BUs. The first leg of the diversity efforts involved the CEO communicating "Management Accountability," that is, the CEO told the presidents of the BU what was to be done, why it was to be done and how the presidents were accountable. The CEO was assisted by the vice-president of diversity in formulating the strategy.

The BU presidents were accountable for "Internal Readiness." They were responsible for finding out where the barriers to diversity were in their units, what strategy they would need to take to eliminate those barriers, how the president would communicate about this to others in his or her unit and how she or he could make it clear that it was a strategic and not a tactical issue. In short, the presidents were responsible for preparing their units to be ready to handle diversity issues effectively by breaking the glass ceiling.

The third leg of Aventa's diversity efforts involved managing "Community Relations." Aventa was striving to build a strong partnership with community organizations. Unlike in the past when it fended off community organizations by giving them donations, it was now closely networking with them. Aventa worked closely with organizations like the Urban League for Blacks, La Raza and Catalyst (women's advocacy). This allowed the organization to gain the confidence of different communities.

Each BU has an EEO/AA unit and the VP of diversity meet with them twice a year. This is called the Chairman's AA Committee, and it helps keep the communication lines active between the corporate office and the BUs at the grass-root level. At the time this case study was made, there were 24 people working in the area of diversity, serving 56,000 employees.

Appendix 1: Organizational Chart July 2001 – March 2002

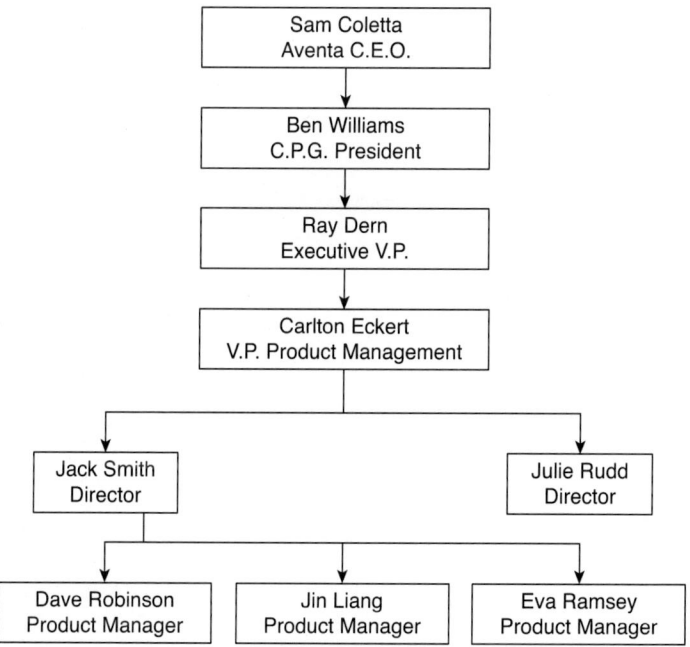

Figure A1.5.1 Organizational chart: July 2001–March 2002
Source: Author.

Appendix 2: Organizational Chart October 2002 – March 2003

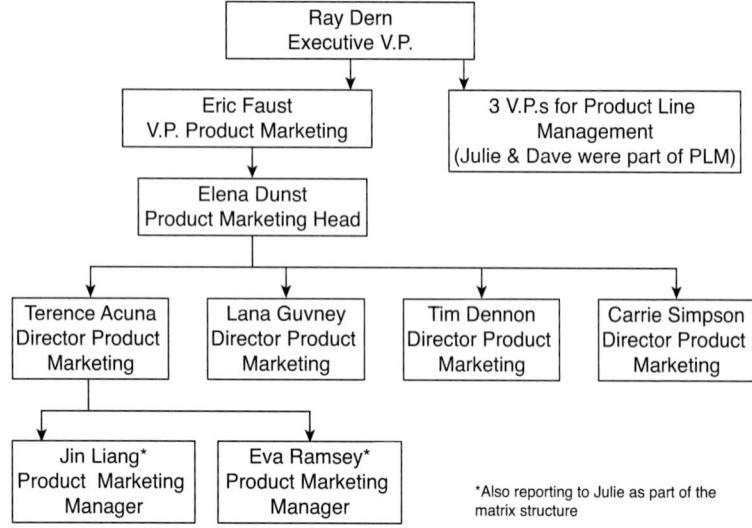

Figure A2.5.1   Organizational chart: October 2002–March 2003

Source: Author.

Appendix 3: Organizational Chart March 2003 – November 2003

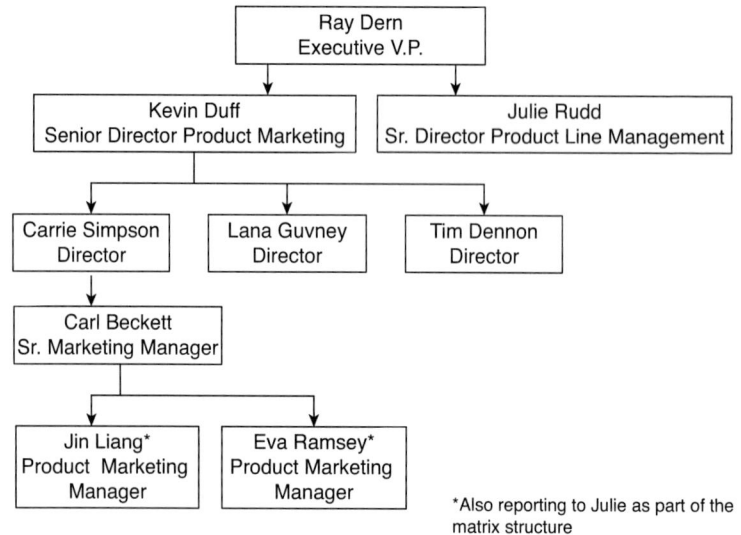

Figure A3.5.1   Organizational chart: March 2003–November 2003

Source: Author.

Notes

1. E.H. Schein, 2010, *Organizational culture and leadership* (4e, Jossey-Bass).
2. Peter Drucker, 2013, *People and performance* (Google eBook; Routledge).
3. Douglas McGregor, 1987, *The human side of enterprise* (Penguin).
4. D.M. Rousseau, 1995, *Psychological contracts in organizations: Understanding written and unwritten agreements* (Sage Publications).
5. D.C. Thomas, K. Au and E.C. Ravlin, 2003, "Cultural variation and the psychological contract," *Journal of Organizational Behavior*, 24(5), 451–471.
6. D.A. Harrison, K.H. Price and M.P. Bell, 1998, "Beyond relational demography: Time and the effects of surface-and deep-level diversity on work group cohesion," *Academy of Management Journal*, 41(1), 96–107.
7. H.C. Triandis, 1994, *Culture and social behavior* (McGraw-Hill Book Company).
8. All names of people and companies in this case are fictitious.

References

Peter Drucker, 2013, *People and performance* (Google eBook: Routledge).

D.A. Harrison, K.H. Price and M.P. Bell, 1998, "Beyond relational demography: Time and the effects of surface-and deep-level diversity on work group cohesion," *Academy of Management Journal*, 41(1), 96–107.

Douglas McGregor, 1987, *The human side of enterprise* (Penguin).

D.M. Rousseau, 1995, *Psychological contracts in organizations: Understanding written and unwritten agreements* (Sage Publications).

E.H. Schein, 2010, *Organizational culture and leadership* (4e, Jossey-Bass).

D.C. Thomas, K. Au and E.C. Ravlin, 2003, "Cultural variation and the psychological contract," *Journal of Organizational Behavior*, 24(5), 451–471.

H.C. Triandis, 1994, *Culture and social behavior* (McGraw-Hill Book Company).

6
The Challenge of Building Professional Relations across Cultures: Chinese Officials in America

Jiayi Wang and Helen Spencer-Oatey

Editor's introduction

This meticulously detailed description and its analysis require almost no introduction; effectively, they speak for themselves. This case study is relevant to all business and government cross-cultural meetings. It has always been advisable to understand the cultural factors in international negotiations but Richard Lewis[1] is only one of many writers who have been arguing for decades that negotiation is becoming a science, dominated by the USA. Lewis writes that anyone who has mediated, for instance, at a Japanese-US joint venture knows that the moment intercultural factors enter the arena, the landscape can change completely.

In the current climate (in which, e.g., the leaders of Germany, France and Russia are holding talks to help end the conflict in eastern Ukraine[2]), appreciating cultural bias is essential. Lewis suggests that three key reasons are:

1. There is a tendency to assert cultural values more powerfully when negotiating parties are under pressure.
2. Under globalization, Westerners are being forced into understanding different negotiation mind-sets.
3. Relationship skills – including negotiation – are overtaking linear task-oriented skills (like production, logistics and IT) as the main driver of competitive edge.

As the case study illustrates, cultural preparation to understand different worlds is central to successful international strategy and tactics. Perhaps also it is worth noting that the authors' analysis relies most heavily on the work of two theorists, Fons Trompenaars and Charles Hampden-Turner,[3] and on the writings of Harry Triandis.[4]

Trompenaars and Hampden-Turner classified cultures along a mix of behavioural and value patterns, and their research focuses on the cultural dimensions of business executives. They identified seven culture-based value orientations:

1. Universalism versus particularism (rules should be the same for everybody vs circumstances alter cases)
2. Communitarianism versus individualism (we vs I)
3. Neutral versus emotional (outward control of emotional display vs show feelings freely)
4. Defuse versus specific (direct vs implicit)
5. Achievement versus ascription (what you are vs who you are)
6. Human-time relationship: synchronous vs sequential (more than one activity at a time vs one thing at a time)
7. Human-nature relationship: internal versus external control (self-reliance vs external constraints)

Wang and Spencer-Oatey refer to the Chinese officials in their case study as owning a particularist (relationship-based) preference, whereas their US counterparts were more universalist (rule-based) in general. It seems that business representatives and government officials from universalistic cultures negotiating with their Chinese counterparts must recognize that relationships matter and take time to develop; they form the basis of trust that is necessary to do business. In a particularistic culture, contracts are only a rough guideline or approximation.

In 1999, Triandis[5] discussed some of the limitations of social psychology research. Based on his previous studies, he argued that much of the focus of research by social psychologists reflects Euro-American concerns and are therefore of limited generality. He suggested such limitations would be remedied by increased attention to cross-cultural studies, because many of the key constructs of the discipline, such as self and conformity, are culture-bound. This is one of the reasons why the following case study is so useful with its cultural insights to Chinese interactions with westerners.

Abstract:

This case study explores the ways in which Chinese government officials interpreted American professionals' hosting behaviours during a three-week delegation visit to the USA. Drawing on video recordings of the delegation's intercultural interactions and spontaneous comments made during evening reflection and planning meetings, the study describes a number of incidents that the delegates experienced as surprising or annoying in some way and the key strategies they used for handling them. Also, the study examines the types of hosting behaviour to which the delegation members were particularly "face sensitive" and notes that, interestingly, the Chinese and American officials often had different interpretations of the same interactions.

Keywords: American, Chinese, government officials, hosting, professional relations

Introduction

Professional communication across cultures is of growing importance in today's globalizing world, and this entails the management of professional relations. Cultural guidebooks may provide lists of dos and don'ts or try to describe concepts that are particularly important to a given cultural group. However, such accounts tend to be superficial and generalized while case studies can provide rich and nuanced insights.

This case study examines how members of a Chinese ministerial delegation built and managed relations with their American hosts during a three-week official visit to the USA. It focuses particularly on hosting issues. This kind of professional interaction, which involved government officials from both the USA and China, has rarely been studied before, not least because it is so difficult to gain access to examples. Moreover, this longitudinal study illuminates how the Chinese officials adjusted their relevant perceptions, behaviours and strategies over time.

Readers will be able to obtain valuable insights from the analysis of this authentic case, helping raise their awareness of the complex factors and multiple perspectives involved in building professional relations across cultures through managing hosting arrangements.

Case presentation

The Chinese Ministry of X[6] has a long-term relationship with its American counterpart, the US Department of X (American Government Department, abbreviated as AGD). Both sides had agreed on the schedule in advance.

The delegation visited six major American cities during their three-week visit, and the Chinese officials had twenty-six meetings with twenty-three American organizations (see Table 6.1). The overall host was the American Government Department. Among these exchanges, seventeen meetings were video recorded completely, four meetings and one banquet were video recorded in part with supplementary audio recordings and at five meetings recordings were not allowed due to the nature of the American government organizations.

Table 6.1 American hosting agencies

No	American organizations	Abbreviations
1	University	
2	Federal Organization 1 (national, equivalent to central)	FO1
3	Federal Government Organization 1	FGO1
4	Federal Government Organization 2	FGO2
5	Non-profit NGO 1	NGO1
6	Federal Organization 2	FO2
7	Private Firm	
8	Federal Government Organization 3	FGO3
9	State Government Organization 1	SGO1
0	Non-profit NGO 2	NGO2
1	Professional Association 1	PA1
2	State Government Organization 2	SGO2
3	Federal Government Organization 4	FGO4
4	Federal Government Organization 5	FGO5
5	Volunteering Organization 1	VO1
6	Professional Association 2	PA2
17	Division A, the American Government Department (AGD)	
18	Division B, the American Government Department (AGD)	
9	Federal Organization 3	FO3
20	Division C, the American Government Department (AGD)	
21	Federal Organization 4	FO4
22	Federal Organization 5	FO5
23	Professional Association 3	PA3

Source: Authors' own.

Typically, members of high-level official delegations, usually leaders from various departments, do not have much contact with each other before their trips. After returning home, they frequently only hold one formal internal meeting to summarize and reflect on their intercultural experiences, though during their trip they might discuss informally some matters that arise.

This delegation differed from most others in this regard. The head of the delegation (HOD) was already a leader of the other delegates in their daily work, and perhaps because of this, he formally dedicated a considerable amount of time during the trip to an internal meeting in the evening of every working day after and/or before special events. The evening reflection and planning meetings aimed to report, share and understand in a timely and efficient manner any issues arising in their intercultural contact with their American counterparts.

Hosting emerged as a central theme in the Chinese officials' relational reflections and planning, and four aspects of hosting were regularly commented on: welcomes, opening of formal meetings, rescheduling, and banquets and entertainment.

Welcome for the visiting officials

The officials were welcomed in a similar way most of the time. They were greeted by the Americans from the hosting agency at the gate of the building and then escorted all the way to the meeting room. Interestingly, they had problems with how they were treated at the security checks and this issue caused heated discussion at the evening meetings.

At almost all the government buildings, the delegation had to go through security checks. While these procedures might vary from place to place due to the nature of the organizations, they were particularly upset by the strict security checks when they visited two federal government organizations (FGO1 and FGO2) in the afternoon of Day 4.

The delegation felt that they lost face when asked to take off their belts at the checkpoint. As a matter of fact, the Chinese officials went through similarly stringent procedures at the airports, but they did not feel uncomfortable because their identity at that time was temporary, as passengers. Like everybody else at an airport, they took off their shoes and removed their belts. However, when they had to pass through the same procedures at the entrance to the government buildings, all the Chinese delegates, in suits and ties, were extremely annoyed at having to hold their trousers by hand to pass through the security gate. They saw themselves as visiting officials, and they complained to each other in Chinese in the presence of the Americans.

In the evening, the HOD drew attention to this incident, asking the group not to associate it with strong feelings of face loss.

Data extract 1: EM comment

> *When visiting a government agency like this afternoon, we must abide by their regulations, such as removing belts and not bringing any electronic devices into the X government organisations. Don't feel a huge loss of face when being asked to remove the belts according to their requirements. Pay attention to our image.*

The HOD's pacification seemed to work, as the group did not complain about the security check any more in the following evening meetings.

Opening a formal meeting

In addition to how they were welcomed, the ways in which the Americans opened the meetings also drew these officials' attention. On most occasions, it was the first time the Americans were meeting the Chinese visitors. The majority of the American hosts, especially officials, opened the meeting very formally, by, for example, giving a welcome speech and asking the delegation to give a return speech. Yet one American professional, Professional 7 (P7), director of a federal project, surprised the group by mentioning his grandchildren.

At the beginning of the morning meeting, the chairperson Director Jackson introduced P7 by reading out his bio, "P7 is... to work on the Y project here and across the nation and to spend time with his grandchildren", and to bring in a personalized connection, added that his grandchildren were lovely. P7 then started the meeting by talking about his grandchildren.

Data extract 2: Video recording

1	P7:	It is a great honour for me to be here and to be able to talk to
2		a group of officials... who are working on the issues of X in
3		China. To further emphasize Director Jackson's comments
4		on the last sentence of my bio, it was an honour enough for
►5		me to leave my two grandchildren in City B[7] so that I can be
6		with you today to do this. My wife and I just brought them
7		back with us from State J for a visit, a four-year grandson
8		who is very energetic (2) and an eight-year granddaughter.
9		Anyway, thank you very much for inviting me. If you don't
10		mind, I'm actually gonna take off my jacket to join you in
11		greater comfort. Welcome to the State weather!
12		

P7 made a straightforward informal request to take off his jacket (see lines 10–11). It was extremely hot in early August in this state. Although the air conditioner was working on full power in the meeting room, P7 was still sweating. He seemed to be trying to pitch the supposedly formal meeting as an informal interaction. He started smiling as soon as he mentioned his grandchildren, but the Chinese officials did not give any reaction.

If we take these officials' non-reaction (as captured in the video data) at its face value, it suggests that such a style for opening a meeting did not work its magic. However, P7's opening strategy, in fact, stimulated heated discussion at the evening meeting among the delegates who seemed to have hidden their feelings by keeping silent and showing blank faces at the daytime meeting. The group were actually "surprised" (DHOD, EM comment) or even "shocked" (HOD, EM comment) by his openness, as DHOD commented in detail.

Data extract 3: EM comment

> *I was shocked because we will never use our family members as an opening for a formal meeting with people we don't know or foreign guests. Yes, I talk about my grandson all day along, but I only talk about it to you. I would not talk to Americans about that.*

The DHOD's remarks explained the group's experiences and reactions: they would never use their families as an opening of such formal intercultural meetings.

Nevertheless, this breach of expectations was not interpreted negatively. In fact, P7's mentioning of family drew the distance closer and the delegation believed that it had contributed to a closer relationship between the Chinese delegation and the American professional. This implies that "Do in Rome as Romans do" might not be the golden rule that prevails in all contexts.

Additionally, this episode also sheds some light on the dynamic balance between formality and informality. While a meeting might be deemed as formal, certain elements of informality can contribute to the relational atmosphere of the event.

Rescheduling

As the schedule was agreed on by both sides in advance, the Chinese officials normally followed it. On Day 14, a Friday, the delegation left City A for City C early in the morning. They had two blocks of meetings that day. In the morning, they went to a powerful professional association (Professional Association 2, PA2) to meet with several divisions of that organization. In the afternoon, they went to an influential volunteering organization (Volunteering Organization 1, VO1).

When they arrived in City C after more than two hours' drive from City A in the morning, they felt very tired because they went to visit PA2 straightaway. Therefore, at the end of the first meeting with PA2, the HOD made a request to reschedule the remaining meetings with the other divisions of PA2, "Can you rearrange the rest of today's meetings?" To the Chinese group's shock, the American director categorically refused the request by saying "No, we can't because it is at such short notice." In the Chinese delegation's eyes, the American's manner of refusal led to a plunge in relationship quality and a big loss of face for the Chinese group.

While the Chinese officials were upset by the relational slump, they did try to make sense of the American's "blunt" refusal.

Data extract 4: EM comment

HOD:	I asked the director of PA2 to change the schedule for the rest of the meetings with the other divisions. She was not very polite to refuse us directly.
D10:	We were shocked at that moment. She didn't ask the other divisions and just refused our request abruptly. "No, we can't because it is at such short notice."
D15:	It was a dramatic turn. The first meeting with the international division went very well. We had built good relations. A smooth meeting plus a carefully chosen gift increased both sides' face. We also joked about the iced beer they offered. The atmosphere, like our face, had gradually climbed up to a higher level, reaching the climax when she joked about the iced beer. Till that moment, I rated PA2 as the best individual hosting agency. However, she suddenly refused our request so firmly. Everything began to fall down. All the efforts that morning till that moment were almost in vain. Our relations fell down to the level at the starting point.
D3:	That's true. They were definitely impolite. She didn't want to know our reason for rescheduling at all. She didn't ask, did she?
D4:	No. We just asked tentatively because we did not want to put pressure on them. Nor did we expect that she would respond without any leeway. At least she should say, "OK. I'm afraid that I have to ask the other divisions you are going to meet" and it would be an ideal opportunity for her to show the host's care for the guests by asking us why we wanted to change the schedule.
DHOD:	That's correct. We didn't give her the compelling reason that we were so exhausted. We were only making a tentative request whilst withholding the strong argument. It was already a concession and we were putting ourselves in their shoes. Otherwise, we would tell her about our long journey and previous intensive activities. If I were the host, I would put the guest's needs first. The primary goal of us hosting foreign visitors at home is to meet their needs as much as possible. We won't refuse such a request. Moreover, we'll do our utmost to make the arrangement before giving them a definite answer "no."
HOD:	We had also lost a bit of our face.

As this extract shows, the group viewed their head's bald-on-record request to reschedule the other meetings without presenting the reasons as considerate, and interpreted the American director's refusal negatively. Clearly, the way in which the American director dealt with the officials' request for rescheduling had a far-reaching implication on the Chinese relational interpretations.

Banquets and entertainment

Interestingly, banquets and entertainment played an equally, if not more, important role in the Chinese officials' efforts to maintain 'face' within the relationship with their US counterparts, and to evaluate it, than did the more formal meetings. Thus their interpretations of banquets and social dinners offered some illuminating insights.

Overall, they thought that the banquets hosted by the Americans were not as successful as a social dinner in City A, because the relational atmosphere was relatively cold, whereas at the social dinner, everything seemed to have fallen into place. This dinner was initiated by the Chinese officials, and it took place at a popular Taiwanese restaurant. It was filled with enthusiastic toasts and lively chat, and everybody ended up in a happy mood.

Data extract 5: EM comment by the DHOD

> *[The Americans] seemed to enjoy the Chinese dinner with forks and spoons and of course our good liquor. The two young Americans were the target of our toasts so they were almost drunk with red face in the end, but they enjoyed it. It was interesting. Originally the HOD and I were thinking of asking them to drink a little bit at first, but the two young men finished the liquor in one shot. They were so straightforward. We appreciated their warm response. Then every one of us began to propose more toasts to them. For the ladies we were much softer. I think everyone had a good time at the dinner. The food was delicious. The Chinese liquor was wonderful. And we chatted with each other animatedly. Although there was no separate room in the restaurant, the screen helped us to have a private space with three tables close enough to liven things up. This absolutely showed our heartfelt personal thanks to the American officers who accompany us every day. So we prepared special gifts for them all – delicately carved combs made of peach wood for the ladies and silk ties for the men. They loved them so much. In addition to the deepening relations with the American side in general, we succeeded in pushing our personal relations with the individual American officials who serve us up to a new height. Director Jackson said he would really like to see us again in future and our delegates*

all warmly invited them to China. This dinner worked better than daily business activities for us to have closer relations. A dinner like this enables us to understand each other more deeply than seeing each other at the meetings for ten days.

As can be seen from this comment, the Chinese officials' relational concerns went well beyond meetings. The key terms here are "toasts" and "social talk," which may have contributed to their relations with the Americans in the banquet context. Contrary to their preferred emotional concealment in the meeting contexts, they seemed to favour emotional display at the banquets and social dinners. Conviviality was perceived as the key.

In short, the Chinese officials were face-sensitive to various aspects of how they were hosted during their delegation visit. The aspects that they touched upon included the ways in which they were welcomed, the opening of formal meetings, rescheduling, and banquets and entertainment. The Americans' hosting behaviours became a prominent theme in their interpretations with regards to building professional relations across cultures.

Outcomes

The Americans' hosting behaviour to which the Chinese officials were particularly "face sensitive" during this trip yielded both positive and problematic outcomes for the building of professional relations across cultures.

Problematic outcomes

The Chinese participants noted that the Americans' hosting behaviour as regards welcomes, rescheduling and banquets had a comparatively problematic impact on relations.

Welcomes for the visiting officials

As can be seen from the security check incident, the group reckoned that, as senior visiting foreign officials, they could have skipped some of the procedures such as removing their belts in the reception halls of the federal government buildings. According to them, the American hosts' failure to simplify the security check processes for them was regarded as synonymous with failing to respect and play out the hierarchical difference between them as senior visiting officials and the other visitors in general. This was probably why they felt so negative about the hosting behaviour that made them lose face and thereby impeded relations as the lack of distinction in treatment was equated with a lack of status differentiation. Echoing Bond and Hwang's[8] essence of Chinese society, that is, "harmony-within-hierarchy," this again manifested the importance of hierarchy. Reflection of hierarchy seemed to be taken as the principal norm by the Chinese officials in hosting contexts.

From another perspective, it seems that the Chinese and the American officials had different expectations concerning the treatment of visiting foreign officials. Consistent with previous studies of business people,[9] the Chinese officials had a particularist (relationship-based) preference whereas their American counterparts were more universalist (rule-based) in general. Chinese delegations tend to expect special treatment "based on a logic of the heart and human friendship."[10] In other words, the host's consideration (or considerateness) carries greater weight than conforming to the rules in such circumstances. For most Chinese, there is a tradition of adding a human touch to reason and law in the legal system[11] whereby laws and rules could be modified in particular situations. This is reflected in the word order in the popular Chinese saying "emotion, reason and law" [情、理、法].[12] For the Americans, however, the reverse order seemed to be true, that is, "law, reason and emotion" [法、理、情]. Such divergence might be traced back to the relative particularist orientation of Confucianism[13] and the ideal of universalism upheld by Plato and Aristotle.

There are pros and cons for both particularists and universalists. While people may think their ways of doing things are the best, we could not simply assume that one orientation is necessarily superior to the other. The universalist American officials' strictly enforcing the procedures ensured equality and equity, but implied a lack of flexibility and consideration for the guests. The particularist Chinese officials, however, might break the rules for visiting foreign counterparts, which demonstrates their flexibility and thoughtfulness as hosts, yet at the expense of equality for all.

This dilemma is not easy to solve. In the business contexts, Trompenaars and Hampden-Turner[14] suggest continuously improving universal rules to cover more particular situations and to make them more humane. In official intercultural interaction, this is not highly relevant, yet, as the authors have said, particularism and universalism are actually a matter of degree. It is worthwhile to open our minds to understand and learn from the other side.

Rescheduling

As can be seen from the delegates' extended discussions regarding the request for rescheduling, the American host's response to the Chinese delegation's request marked a plunge in relations.

While making and handling such a request in intercultural contexts can be a minefield for a host, this may become "an ideal opportunity" for the host to show his or her "concern for the guests by asking why" (D4, EM comment). The host may draw closer to the guests, if the request is managed properly by taking into account both the sociolinguistic and pragmatic differences and the different norms of hosting which professionals are often unaware of. The main norm in the requesting contexts for the Chinese officials seemed to be considerateness.

In this case, the HOD's bald-on-record request and the American director's direct refusal may reveal some conventionalized sociolinguistic and pragmatic differences as regards requests and rejections. First, the group viewed their head's request without any justification/explanation as considerate by "not presenting the compelling reasons" (DHOD, EM comment) to "put pressure" (D4, EM comment) on the American host. Consistent with Lee-Wong's[15] findings of the Chinese preference for bald-on-record requests, this interpretation at the first glance seemingly violates the general tendency described in the Chinese cultural script of requesting: off-record hinting.[16]

However, this longitudinal study helps reveal that the Chinese had been avoiding making any request[17] to the Americans, direct or indirect. This request was, in fact, the only formal one they made during their entire stay in the US. The "deviant" case could be explained by the exceptional situation whereby the Chinese did not have the luxury of time to hint implicitly. In other words, this is consistent with the other researchers' generalizations that Chinese people probably are less direct and explicit than westerners,[18] and so they usually avoid making any verbal requests. It is just that when "squeezed," they may bounce to being equally or even more direct than Americans. This confirms the necessity of studying politeness as a social phenomenon[19] and beyond lexico-grammatical[20] forms.

Second, the American director's refusal of this request gave rise to the group's strong reaction, even though it followed the standard Anglo-American script, that is, direct refusal plus an excuse. It indeed sounded "offensively" blunt to Chinese ears,[21] because the delegation did not "expect that she would respond without any leeway," and they assumed that she would at least say, "OK, I'm afraid that I have to ask the other divisions you are going to meet" (D4, EM comment). This supports the general warning of "never say no" to Chinese.[22] As this case shows, it may lead to dangerous misunderstanding.

Banquets

The group reiterated the relational significance of banquets hosted by the Americans in the evening meetings, and they spent considerable time on planning and reflection before and after each of the events. For example, the first farewell banquet took place in the banquet hall of a business Golf Club when their stay in City A came to an end. Present at the formal banquet were the heads of the American agencies, governmental and non-governmental, whom they had visited in the first two weeks. The evening before the banquet, the HOD explicitly highlighted its relational implication:

> *Our stay in City A is coming to an end. Therefore at tomorrow's lunch banquet, we must push our relations to a new climax. We already knew all the leaders. Propose more toasts and enliven the atmosphere. This lunch banquet marks the closing of the first phase of our trip, and its significance is self-evident. Propose more toasts and develop our relations with the American side. (EM comment)*

Clearly, the Chinese officials took the banquet seriously because of its huge relational significance. Proposing "more toasts" to the hosts and "enliven[ing] the atmosphere" to develop relations with the Americans were repeated over and over again in the group's strategic planning of this kind of events.

Despite their careful planning, nearly all the formal banquets held by the Americans seemed to fall short of the group's expectations. The main reason seemed to be that as hosts, the Americans did not play their "due"' role in lifting the relational atmosphere.

Let us take the reflection on the first farewell banquet as an example. All the participants sat at tables of six–seven, and there were six tables altogether, three on each side of the aisle which led to the podium at the front of the hall. So every Chinese delegate was sitting next to at least one American leader, and since additional interpreters were provided, each table had at least one interpreter. On behalf of all the hosting agencies in the first two weeks, the American Director of the International Office, Director Jackson, kicked off the banquet by making a brief speech and proposing a toast, but he did not go to other tables for further toasting. Feeling obliged not to outperform the hosts, the HOD also did not go beyond doing what Director Jackson did, and so there were no toasts back and forth that could have quickly lifted the atmosphere. The group believed that the banquet could have been better with things like liquor and more toasts, but since the Americans were the hosts, the Chinese could hardly do anything to improve it.

This was true with the other banquets. The group expected the official farewell banquet to be a jolly, warm and exciting event where people talked animatedly, celebrating the conclusion of the trip and looking into the future, and so on and so forth. Conviviality emerged as the principal norm in the banquet contexts for the Chinese officials.

In short, the problematic outcomes revealed that the Chinese officials and the American hosts had different norms and expectations, with different conventions applied in different contexts.

Positive outcomes

Despite all these problems, there were aspects of hosting that had a positive impact on relations which the Chinese officials regularly commented on: opening of formal meetings and social dinners.

Opening of formal meetings

As can be seen from Data extract 2, although the American director P7's mentioning of his grandchildren breached the Chinese norms of opening a formal meeting, that is, do not mention family in formal meetings, the Chinese delegates spoke highly of this strategy, because "[s]incerity and warmth are the most important" for bilateral relations and "[a]nything else is secondary" (DHOD, EM comment). So the host speaking in this way signalled that "we are treating you as very important people" and highlighted the importance of the principle of warmth in meeting contexts for positive Chinese evaluations.

Social dinners

Unlike the formal banquets hosted by the Americans, the social dinner at a local Taiwanese restaurant to which the Chinese officials invited some of the Americans yielded positive relational outcomes, because as hosts of this particular event, the Chinese officials successfully lifted the relational atmosphere through dining, wining and talking. Conviviality was achieved.

Clearly, concerns over banquets and entertainment were embedded in the building of professional relations. The findings suggest that the Chinese officials attached equal or even greater importance to banquets than to meetings. The banquets and the social dinner were held in

consistently high regard by the Chinese officials. In professional intercultural interaction, Chinese professionals at large tend to place great
emphasis on social events.[23] While emotional display in the presence of
intercultural interactants is discouraged, the banquet can be a formal-
ized event for showing emotions. The key Chinese elements of a good
banquet and/or social dinner include wining, talking and an animated
atmosphere. To make these events successful, the Chinese may expect
the hosts to have toasts and go around from table to table, which might
be less common in the West.

In conclusion, despite all the details of arranging practicalities, as we
can see from the case study, the Chinese officials had different expectations of hosting behaviour, and there were different norms applied to
different contexts.

What could have been done differently and why

While these aspects of hosting seemed to be trivial, their relational implications could be huge. In this case study, both sides only talked about the
overall schedule before the visit (e.g., Day 1 noon, Welcome banquet);
more detailed practical arrangements could have been communicated.
If the hosts could have provided more details such as "warnings" about
the essential security check processes at certain government buildings,
on the one hand, the Chinese officials may have interpreted this as a
sign that "the hosts are very considerate" and that "they are treating
us as very important people"; on the other hand, this could have better
prepared the Chinese officials for the trip as well.

How to tackle such problems in the future

If you are going to host Chinese officials, there are several things that
you can take away from this case study. First, given the impact of hosting
behaviour on professional relationships, it is advisable to provide the
visiting Chinese officials with more details of the practical arrangements
in advance, and, if necessary, discuss them with the Chinese side before
the trip.

Second, you need to be aware that you may have different norms and
expectations for hosting. Even though you do not necessarily have to
change your behaviour, it will be helpful if you can tell the visiting officials that you are aware of their norms and explain the differences to
help them to foresee the differences or even the "difficulties" they might
encounter. Such pre-warnings may minimize or even turn around the
negative impact unexpected events may have on the building of professional relations across cultures.

We have learned that in professional intercultural interaction with Chinese, it is important for non-Chinese not to underestimate the value of social activities and to be aware of the potential differences in this area. For some Chinese professionals, a host's handling of banquets can be a significant aspect of a guest's relational evaluation of hosting. For example, if you are hosting a banquet for visiting Chinese officials, it might be useful if you, as the host, could acknowledge the differences by just adding a few more sentences when proposing the toast to all the guests at the beginning of the banquet: "I know in China a good host should have toasts and go around. Actually I was rather impressed when I was in China. Yet I'm afraid it is less common here, so please bear with us." By doing so, you may reverse the impact of having a "cold" start, and if the visiting officials have a laugh at what you have said, this could make a "warm" start and contribute to the relational atmosphere.

Conclusion

In intercultural interaction, a good understanding of the other side's norms and principles can be extremely useful for avoiding misunderstanding and miscommunication, and although different principles tend to be stressed in different contexts by different cultural groups, contexts can actually become an integral part of the conventionalized formulae.[24] For example, the Chinese officials seemed to prefer emotional concealment in the presence of their intercultural interactants in intercultural meeting contexts. Conversely, conviviality and emotional display in banquet settings were stressed. Overall, both the broader hosting principles such as warmth, conviviality and considerateness as well as the specific contexts need to be taken into account. Since the normative differences in hosting are often highlighted in the handling of details, a host in intercultural encounters may follow the advice of thinking globally and acting locally, and keep in mind that hosting can be hugely significant for the guest's relational evaluation of the host and for the building of professional relations across cultures.

Notes

1. R.D. Lewis, 1996, *When cultures collide: managing successfully across cultures* (National Book Network).
2. N. Allen and J. Winch, 6 February 2015, "Ukraine crisis: Angela Merkel and Francois Hollande fly to Russia for peace talks," http://www.telegraph.co.uk/.
3. F. Trompenaars and C. Hampden-Turner, 2005, *Riding the waves of culture: understanding cultural diversity in business* (Nicholas Brealey Publishing).

4. H. Triandis, 2001, "Individualism and collectivism: past, present, and future," in D.R. Matsumoto (ed.), *The handbook of culture and psychology* (Oxford University Press), 35–50.
5. H.C. Triandis, 1999, "Cross-cultural psychology," *Asian Journal of Social Psychology*, 2, 127–143.
6. The name of the ministry has been anonymized.
7. The states and cities have been anonymized by giving each an alphabet code.
8. M.H. Bond and Hwang Kwang-Kuo, 1986, *The psychology of the Chinese people* (Oxford University Press).
9. Trompenaars and Hampden-Turner, *Riding the waves of culture*.
10. Ibid.
11. Xianbi Huang, 2008, "Guanxi networks and job searches in China's emerging labour market: a qualitative investigation," *Work, Employment & Society*, 22(3), 467–484.
12. B. Ziporyn, 2008, "Form, Principle, Pattern, or Coherence? Li in Chinese Philosophy," *Philosophy Compass*, 3(3), 401–422.
13. J. Ock Yum, 1988, "The impact of Confucianism on interpersonal relationships and communication patterns in East Asia," in L.A. Samovar and R.E. Porter (eds), *Intercultural communication: a reader*, 8th ed. (Wadsworth Publishing Company), vol. 55, 374–388.
14. Trompenaars and Hampden-Turner, *Riding the waves of culture*
15. Song Mei Lee-Wong, 1994, "Imperatives in requests: direct or impolite-observations from Chinese," *Pragmatics*, 4(4).
16. A. Wierzbicka, 1996, "Contrastive sociolinguistics and the theory of 'cultural scripts': Chinese vs English," in M. Hellinger and U. Ammon (eds), *Contributions to the Sociology of Language* (Mouton de Gruyter), vol. 71, 313–344.
17. G.T. Bilbow, 1995, "Requesting strategies in the cross-cultural business meeting," *Pragmatics*, 5(1), 45–56.
18. See, for example, Ge Gao and S. Ting-Toomey, 1998, *Communicating effectively with the Chinese* (Sage). Triandis, "Individualism and collectivism," 35–50.
19. Bilbow, "Requesting strategies in the cross-cultural business meeting."
20. J. Culpeper, 2011, *Impoliteness: using language to cause offence* (Cambridge University Press).
21. Wierzbicka, "Contrastive sociolinguistics."
22. T. Fang, 2012, "Yin Yang: a new perspective on culture," *Management and Organization Review*, 8(1), 25–50.
23. Hong Seng Woo and C. Prud'homme, 1999, "Cultural characteristics prevalent in the Chinese negotiation process," *European Business Review*, 99(5), 313–322.
24. J. Culpeper, 2012, "(Im)politeness: three issues," *Journal of Pragmatics*, 44(9), 1128–1133.

References

G.T. Bilbow, 1995, "Requesting strategies in the cross-cultural business meeting," *Pragmatics*, 5(1), 45–56.

M.H. Bond and Kwang-Kuo Hwang, 1986, *The psychology of the Chinese people* (Oxford University Press).

J. Culpeper, 2011, *Impoliteness: using language to cause offence* (Cambridge University Press).

J. Culpeper, 2012, "(Im)politeness: three issues," *Journal of Pragmatics*, 44(9), 1128–1133.

T. Fang, 2012, "Yin Yang: a new perspective on culture," *Management and Organization Review*, 8(1), 25–50.

Ge Gao and S .Ting-Toomey, 1998, *Communicating effectively with the Chinese* (Sage).

Hong Seng Woo and C. Prud'homme, 1999, "Cultural characteristics prevalent in the Chinese negotiation process," *European Business Review*, 99(5), 313–322.

S. Mei Lee-Wong, 1994, "Imperatives in requests: direct or impolite-observations from Chinese," *Pragmatics*, 4(4).

H .Triandis, 2001, "Individualism and collectivism: past, present, and future," in D.R. Matsumoto (ed.), *The handbook of culture and psychology* (Oxford University Press), 35–50.

F. Trompenaars and C. Hampden-Turner, 2005, *Riding the waves of culture: understanding cultural diversity in business* (Nicholas Brealey Publishing).

A.Wierzbicka, 1996, "Contrastive sociolinguistics and the theory of 'cultural scripts': Chinese vs English," in M. Hellinger and U. Ammon (eds), *Contributions to the sociology of language* (Mouton de Gruyter), vol. 71, 313–344.

Xianbi Huang, 2008, "Guanxi networks and job searches in China's emerging labour market: a qualitative investigation," *Work, Employment & Society*, 22(3), 467–484.

J.O. Yum, 1988, "The impact of Confucianism on interpersonal relationships and communication patterns in East Asia," in L.A. Samovar and R.E. Porter (eds), *Intercultural communication: a reader*, 8th edition (Wadsworth Publishing Company), vol. 55, 374–388.

B. Ziporyn, 2008, "Form, Principle, pattern, or coherence? Li in Chinese philosophy," *Philosophy Compass*, 3(3), 401–422.

7

Disattending Customer Dissatisfaction on Facebook: A Case Study of a Slovenian Public Transport Company

Rosina Márquez-Reiter, Sara Orthaber and Dániel Z. Kádár

Editor's introduction

In an increasingly mobile and social world, the marketing battle is going digital. A good example was advertising for the 2014 Brazil World Cup.[1] Traditional media sectors, including TV and radio, enjoyed their usual advertising revenue but the real winners, in terms of direction of marketing resources and effort, were social media such as Twitter, YouTube and Facebook.

The unusual case study in this chapter examines the love-hate relationship between corporate users of these media and their subscribers. They have made it possible for firms to promote products and services to hundreds, hundreds of thousands and even millions of would-be customers. As a corollary, the effects of consumer-to-consumer feedback, positive and negative, have become a critical factor in the marketplace.

Mangold and Faulds[2] are only two of many writers on the topic. They argue that social media represent a hybrid strain of promotional activity because not only do they enable companies to "talk" to their customers but also customers can "talk" directly to one another. The content, timing and frequency of these conversations are outside advertisers' direct control – in contrast to the traditional integrated marketing set-up.

Therefore, administrators of commercial sites in social media must learn to shape consumer discussions to be favourable to their firms' performance goals and to deal with negative responses, some examples of which are described and discussed in the following case study.

Abstract:

Drawing on data from the Facebook page of a Slovenian public transport company, the case study examines customers' responses to the company's marketing status updates and the way they are responded to or not by the page moderator. Discussion of the case includes a comment that complaints made by telephone, unlike those online, do not permit company agents to ignore them. The study examines the ways in which administrators respond to customers' comments and how customers react and observes how open-comment platforms such as Facebook may allow expressions of public dissatisfaction to affect corporate strategy.

Keywords: administrator response, commercial promotions, customer feedback, Facebook

Introduction

Corporate Facebook pages

As a social media platform, Facebook is used strategically by companies for promotional purposes, including building rapport with (potential) customers. This is because the medium enables direct communication with an unlimited number of users provided they subscribe to the page by clicking the "like" and "follow" buttons.

On Facebook, users look for entertainment, knowledge sharing and updating. Researchers such as Champoux et al.[3] have investigated how companies try to avoid overt product-pushing or aggressive selling. Typically, they post informal, positive topics to ease communication, increase their "visibility" and exploit what scholars such as Lee and Walther and Jang[4] term as interactive and participatory affordances of such websites to create a virtual community by fostering topical discussions. They provide opportunities for subscribers to contribute to administrators' newsfeed updates, including photographs and videos, by responding to the content or by "liking" it.

When administrators update the company's page, the items immediately pop up in subscribers' newsfeeds, inviting them to comment on any post published, at any time, as often as they wish.

Kerbrat-Orecchioni[5] has pointed out that the process is one of continuous, essentially polylogal, interaction, in that they involve a potentially infinite number of participants and the activities are never finally closed unless the post is deleted by the producer (i.e., the page moderator).

The construction of messages is separate from their transmission, but the medium also allows interactions in real time: what Meredith[6]

describes as a form of *quasi*-asynchronous communication, by which the participants are not (necessarily) simultaneously online; nor can they see what others are writing. Posted messages may not receive, nor be expected to receive, an immediate response. Subscribers can type their message below the status update in the "write a comment" box. These posts are then visible to all those categorized by Goffman[7] as ratified recipients who are entitled to add further comments. He divided listener roles into those of "ratified" (addressed and unaddressed recipients) and "unratified" hearers (bystanders, overhearers and eavesdroppers) to aid analysis of multi-party verbal encounters.

However, there are different levels of social media participation, since it takes place in asymmetrical interpersonal settings. On the one hand, administrators animate the "voices" of their companies and can address or ignore subscribers' comments (and therefore their ratified status). On the other hand, input is by individual commentators representing only themselves. Nevertheless, as writers such as Gibson, Hutchby and Herring have noted,[8] participatory websites such as Facebook allow these individuals to complement or, contrary to the projected expectation of a particular type of response (cf. Licoppe),[9] undermine company messages. More importantly, as the present case study shows, it is the promotional messages, and in particular what Maynard and Hudak[10] term as interactional disattentiveness the customers receive from the page moderator, that generate customers' moaning. Such disattentiveness is effected by means of sequential deletion or by the page moderator's warding off responsibility for the complaints, thus preventing customers from seeking redressive action despite the fact that the technological affordances of Facebook allow it.

Case presentation

This case study examines customers' responses to a company's Facebook updates and the ways in which these responses are dealt with by the page administrator. It draws on publicly available data from the Facebook page of a Slovenian public transport company called Grem z vlakom (I'm going by train).

The company joined Facebook on 10 May 2010 and currently has nearly 33,000 subscribers, who can follow its online activities. The company's page is administered by a woman who remains anonymous, but for the purpose of the case is referred to here as Maria. She publishes updates and responds to customers' queries. Formal complaints are rarely dealt with online, but forwarded to the relevant department and thus taken offline.

The company's main purpose for Facebook is to attract travellers, particularly of the younger generations, who travel by train on a daily basis or during the holidays.[11] To this end, the company occasionally raffles small prizes such as train ticket discounts or theatre and concert tickets, not only to create a fun "social" atmosphere, but more importantly to appear as a modern organization that is passionate about its customers. However, as Example 1 shows, even the announcement of raffles can trigger customer moaning (i.e., a grumble in general rather than of a specific problem (cf. Edwards).[12]

For the purpose of this case study, Maria's activities were monitored over a period of 16 months (from January 2012 to November 2014) to examine the company's practice of posting status updates. During this period, she posted 274 updates, that is, approximately 2 per week. Of these, 161 were commented on by at least one subscriber (in 5 instances, the update yielded no "likes" or comments). Maria responded to 64/161, sometimes more than once. She did so either by providing a general response or addressing individual commentators by tagging them in the post (when this function is used, commentators receive notification of a reply).

As Table 7.1 shows, the interactions chosen for this case study were selected from a corpus of 58 updates that evoked negative comments by at least two subscribers. Of the 58, the most "liked" and/or commented-on topics included a weather forecast, a train package for an upcoming sports event, a typo and wrong factual information in an update, and using increased VAT on fuel prices to attract new customers. Recently Maria removed 22 updates from the wall, along with subscribers' comments, and permanently deleted two posts. All updates comprised a photograph, typically a train, and were accompanied by a short message (e.g., Examples 2 and 3). The photographs can now only be found in one of the company's many Facebook albums.

Table 7.1   Descriptive statistical information on the selected Facebook posts

Data collection period	January 2012–November 2014
Dataset	58 status updates
Max. no. of comments per update	24
Max. no. of "likes" per update	430
Min. response time (subscriber)	1 minute
Min. response time (administrator, Maria)	1 minute
Max. response time (subscriber)	1 month
Max. response time (when a response is provided) (Maria)	20 hours
Total no. of posts by subscribers	358
Total no. of posts by Maria	31

Source: Authors' own.

The number of "likes" varied dramatically from update to update – though it is interesting to note that subscribers who posted negative comments to the company's updates may also "like" the update. The item that evoked 430 "likes" (typically they range between 5 and 20) announced generous government subsidies for train fares for students and pupils. This suggests that the update reached its target audience of young people and provides evidence for the success of the company strategy for Facebook.

It is important to note here that the company provides a cheap form of public transport on an outdated state-owned infrastructure. Given that its services yield little or no profit, it relies heavily on state funding. Due to the ongoing economic crisis in Slovenia, all investments in the outdated infrastructure and rail fleet such as onboard wireless internet access, online ticketing or self-service ticket machines have been postponed year on year.

The vast majority of subscribers' comments are posted within a few hours of the relevant update, with very few being added over the following two or more days. This suggests that moans are triggered by the pop-up of updates in their newsfeeds when subscribers log in to Facebook, and they seize the opportunity immediately to voice their feelings. However, the fact that a few comments are posted days later shows that this type of communication allows for posts that may sit unread for long periods. Moreover, the fact that subscribers published over 350 comments, of which Maria replied to only 31, confirms that the Facebook medium allows its users to post remarks that will never receive a response.

The following are three representational examples of polylogal or "multi-participant" interactions[13] between Maria and subscribers, in which they respond to her updates.

Example 1: promotion of a concert

On 19 May 2014, at 13:47, Maria posted a promotional message announcing an upcoming raffle for concert tickets. The offer yielded 14: likes" and 2 comments by two different subscribers.

13:47 Maria	Naj vam na ta lep sončen začetek delovnega tedna zaupamo, da se nam v kratkem obeta koncert znane slovenske glasbene rock skupine, ki bo na skrivni lokaciji za omejeno število naših uporabnikov.
Like 👍[14]	*On this sunny beginning of the working week let us tell you that shortly there will be a concert of a well-known Slovenian rock band which will be at a secret location for a limited number of our users.*

14:55	Maja Novak	Glede na pogostost in hitrost vasih vlakov, smo vsi vasi uporabniki omejeni.
Like 🖒¹		*Based on the frequency and speed of your trains, we as your users are all stupid/limited*
15:00	Maria	Maja Novak, gre za koncert, kjer bo manjše število povabljenih in to so naši uporabniki, torej v določenem številu …
		Maja Novak, it's about a concert, to which a small number will be invited and these are our users, that is, a certain number of them …
21 May 2014		
23:58	Peter Horvat	Brez veze. V Koper vozi le tovorni vlak. Da potovanje s kolesom je misija nemogoče.
		Whatever. Only a freight train runs to Koper. Yes travelling with a bike is mission impossible.

Following the ritual of online interaction,[14] Maria starts a chat by initiating a topic without a prior greeting, thus inviting ratified recipients to expand on it. She not only starts a discussion or chat, but also projects expectation of a particular type of response.[15]

An hour later, the first subscriber, Maja Novak, responds (her post was "liked" by one subscriber who did not participate in this thread). She draws attention to the lack of service concerning frequency and speed of trains. She thus engages in moaning. She then deliberately misinterprets Maria's phrase "limited number of users" as an implication that she and her fellow followers are "stupid." Her irony might be considered offensive by other unaddressed recipients, though most likely was meant to entertain. It is in keeping with the findings of this case study – and those of other researcher such as Lee[16] – that in public online environments such as Facebook, users feel highly motivated to "come across" as witty and creative.

It is pertinent to note, however, that in this setting a first subscriber's negative response is likely to trigger a chain of moans. Also, as noted by Collins,[17] Facebook has a history of ritualistic (i.e., established or conventional) moans that operate as "flaming" (inflammatory) invitations that incite others to participate.

To prevent this kind of escalation, five minutes later, Maria responds to Maja Novak by addressing her directly and creating sequential deletion. In other words, she is disattending the moan but repairing any damage it might have caused by repeating the invitation. There is little research on repair in online interaction, although Schönfeldt and Golato[18] suggest that "interlocutors adapt the basic repair mechanisms which are available in ordinary conversation to the technical specificities of chat communication."

Maria also resists the attempted change of subject by explaining to Maja what the original update was about, implicitly reprimanding her and evoking some notion of accountability for her behaviour. She does not receive an uptake from Maja Novak, which suggests Maja's moan was a ritual invitation; she does not intend to engage with Maria, but rather expects the support of other subscribers in their joining the ritual.

Accordingly, Peter Horvat adds a comment two days later in which he provides a negative assessment of Maria's offer ("Whatever"). He then moans – in ritual agreement with Maja – about the lack of passenger trains to a desired destination and the inability to carry a bicycle. Thus, he aligns with Maja and – as argued, for example, by Edwards[19] – such alignment legitimizes her action. Peter displays understanding of Facebook as a medium to lodge complaints, albeit without explicitly holding the company accountable. Neither he nor Maja addresses the topic proposed by Maria but shift from it by moaning about something else, that is, the company's services.

Maria has responded to Maja by preventing her moan to develop into a complaint and to gain control over the interaction; but she refuses altogether to respond to Peter. There is no dialogue; rather there are two monologues or singles, representing an attempt to promote a concert and to disallow the subscribers' moans from developing into fully fledged complaints.

The next example shows how, despite producing singles only, correspondents can support each other's moans.

Example 2: a leap into the railway history

On 31 August 2014, at 8:40, Maria shared a picture of a train, published by a member of another Facebook public group called Railway Enthusiasts. She posted it to the company's page, where as well as 24 "likes," it received 6 comments. She added a message: "A leap into railway history" followed by three dots, that is, a discourse marker frequently used in computer-mediated communication. Rooksby[20] suggests that this represents a pause for thought and an invitation for others to comment.

8:40	Maria	Grem z vlakom Skok v železniško zgodovino ... *Leap into the railway history ...*
Like 👍 24		
8:54	Nikola Petric	Ko bo ukinjena Gomuljka v rednem prometu. Eno dajte v muzej *When Gomulka is withdrawn from its everyday use. Put one in a museum*

9:19	Anja Kosic	Od jutar pa spet gomuljka pelje na sikt bomo mal mokri
		Tomorrow with Gomulka again to work we'll be a bit wet
9:23	Mitja Kos	ali pa v sedanjost
		or to the present
10:45	Klemen Pozar	vam ni treba skakat v zgodovino, ste tam že ves čas!
		No need to jump to the past, you're still there!
19:17	Marko Potocnik	Gomulke so samo še staro železo vam na sž to še ni jasno a vas ni sram da tole sploh vozi

Like 👍 2

		Gomulkas are nothing but scrap iron you just don't get it at sž[21] aren't you ashamed that this is in use?
1 Sep	Damjan Donko	ja da vozi će že vozi bi za gomilko moral veljati vsaj 50%
14:26		*well if it has to be used a discount of 50% at least should apply for Gomulka*

Following Maria's post, four subscribers comment on it within the first two hours. The first, Nikola Petric, names the type of train in the picture. By displaying knowledge that this type of trains are still used on a regular basis, he challenges Maria's expertise as claimed implicitly by her phrase "a leap into the railway history."

Similarly to Maja Novak's utterance in the previous example, Nikola's post seems to operate as an online flame to fire a chain of ritual moans. About 25 minutes later, the next subscriber complains about outdated trains with no air-conditioning. The third commentator, by using the conjunction "or," inverts the sense of Maria's original message and thus ritually aligns himself with the previous correspondents. The next contributor also undermines Maria's description of the train by moaning that the company still lives in the past, implying a dissonance between her version and the reality.

On the same day, several hours later, Marko Potocnik focuses on the picture rather than on the accompanying text and moans about the absurdity of these trains. His reaction is provocative, as evident from his negative assessment. He displays anger and annoyance through choice of lexical terms, for example, "scrap iron." Although finally he uses interrogative syntax, he does not appear to expect a response from Maria; he seems merely to be reacting to her post. She is anonymous, so he addresses her formally in the second-person plural, but refers to the company by its informal abbreviation "sž." His choice of grammar distances him from Maria but implies familiarity with the company. The next day the sixth commentator, Damjan Donko, adds his support to Marko's comments.

Unlike in the previous example, Maria does not reply to any of these contributors. This might be interpreted as a routine rejection of subscribers' misgivings; though it would appear to be important to address them, since the negativity of the exchange has been so clearly "visible." The commentators demonstrate mutual opposition to Maria's post from its first appearance, displaying knowledge that such trains still run in Slovenia. They challenge her domain of knowledge by what Bruxelles and Kerbrat-Orecchioni[22] have described as an unspoken coalition, or temporary alliance, against her. Their common interest, however, is not only to back each other, but more importantly to point to the discrepancy between the content of the posts and the reality of their experience, that is, that the train in the picture is not a historical curiosity but a feature of the present.

Example 3: join me?

This focuses on customers' reactions to the company's marketing strategy to lure them to switch from other forms of transports to trains.

In the height of summer, on 7 August 2012, at 7:19 a.m., Maria posted a photograph of an attractive young businessman resting and listening to music on his tablet. The message was in the first-person singular: "It is so nice when on my way to work I can listen to my favourite music and take a nap. Join me?" With an invitation and an emoticon "smiley" at the end, Maria encourages recipients to respond.

7.19	Maria	Tako prijetno je, ko na poti v službo lahko med poslušanjem svoje najljubše glasbe še malo zadremam. Se mi pridružiš? ☺
Like 👍 89		*It is so nice when on my way to work I can listen to my favourite music and take a nap. Join me?* ☺
7:32	Miha Novak	Mislim, da tale fotografija ni nastala na dolenjski liniji, kjer so potniki brez klime pri +35 prisiljeni na vožnjo pri odprtih oknih.
Like 👍 7		*I think this photo was not taken on the route towards Dolenjska region, where the passengers at + 35 without the air conditioning are forced to ride with the windows wide open.*
7:34	Mojca Kovac	Se popolnoma strinjam s predhodnikom. Zadeva ni nič boljša na drugih progah SZ.
Like 👍 3		*I agree completely with the above. The situation on other routes is no better.*
7:39	Iva Medved	Upam, da enkrat v zelo bližnji prihodnosti namestite brezžični internet ...
Like 👍 1		*I hope that in the very near future you'll install wireless ...*
8:08	Maria	S to fotografijo smo želeli malo polepšati današnje jutro, predvsem damam ;) Kar se pa neklimatiziranih vlakov tiče pa je dejstvo, da tudi mi za vas, naše zveste potnike želeli imeti nove, udobne, klimatizirane vlake, a o večjih investicijah odloča naš lastnik. Verjetno vam gremo že na živce, ker se nenehno ponavljamo. No,
bi		

do konca leta imamo sicer v načrtu še nekaj prenov dizel motornih garnitur, aktivnosti o novih voznih sredstvih pa potekajo. Zato vas prosimo za razumevanje in potrpljenje v teh najbolj vročih mesecih.

With this photograph we wanted to make your morning nicer, especially the ladies'. As far as trains with no air conditioning go it's a fact that we would also like for our loyal customers to have new, comfortable, air-conditioned trains, but our owner is in charge of all major investments. We're probably starting to get on your nerves, because we keep repeating ourselves. Anyway, by the end of the year we plan to refurbish a few diesel motor trains, activities about new fleet are in progress. We would like to ask for your understanding and patience during these hot months.

About ten minutes after the post, the first subscriber, Miha Novak, responds. By commenting on where the photograph was *not* taken, he signals a complaint. He draws attention to the poorly equipped trains that run on his route. In doing so, he not only reveals the discrepancy between the photographic representation and the reality of trains on a specific route, but signals the relevance of his grievance.

Two minutes later, Mojca Kovac endorses the message and becomes an ally. By accepting Miha's flaming invitation to take part in the ritual, but by arguing that the situation is not better elsewhere, she pursues and expands on the prior commentator's moaning, in a chain of complaining and arguing of a kind identified by Dersley.[23] She thus collaborates with Miha to change the topic.

Not more than five minutes later, the third commentator, Iva Medved, shifts away from both topics as she emphasizes lack of internet access onboard the trains, hence making the moaning even broader – that is, it is clear at this stage that the aim of all three commentators is not to resolve a particular problem but rather to build solidarity. Iva's moan was also triggered by the photograph, that is, the tablet the man is using to listen to the music.

About half an hour later, Maria responds by providing an explanation for the choice of photograph. She uses the first-person plural, and adds a "wink" emoticon, described by Meredith[24] as a compensation for prosodic or nonverbal communication, thus reorienting to the topic at hand. To save the face of the company, she shifts responsibility to the owners, that is, the state, thus distancing the company from the poor condition of the trains, to prevent the moans from developing into complaints.

According to Sigman's[25] analysis of the discontinuous aspects of continuous social relationships, Maria's behaviour is retrospective, in that she acknowledges commentators' previous interactional contributions, but at the same time prospective, in that she attempts to prevent further moans by asking for subscribers' understanding. She does so by providing what Ide[26] calls a *quasi*-apology with which she reveals that her shifting of responsibility is a tactic she has used before.

Maria then lists some changes planned by the company. She does so to initiate topic change, most likely with the object of blocking negative response from the commentors as well as to prevent further moans from others. She uses the discourse particle "anyway" to close the previous topic; and by initiating a new one, she effectively discounts the moaning already under way.

Outcomes

This case study was made because over the past decade, Facebook has expanded from being a popular medium by which to interact with friends to a state-of-the-art platform for companies to promote themselves and receive feedback. It allows customers to voice grievances even if these are never responded to, and it empowers them to associate with each other and create alliances against relevant companies. However, the small number of ratified recipients who moan about promotional messages suggests that such power is not always realized, because of the ways in which the companies' page administrators react.

Analysis focuses on customers' negative responses to a transport company's marketing updates and promotional messages in the form of pop-ups in newsfeeds. The study reveals that Facebook administrators such as Maria can prevent moans from developing into complaints by sequential deletion (as in Example 1). That is, she creates a sequence in which she refrains from replying to the previous message, in effect "deleting" that contribution, with the objective of preventing the moans from developing into complaints: thus, she gains control over the unfolding of the interaction. Alternately, she may refuse to reply at all (as in Examples 1 and 2) or may shift responsibility to a third party – in this case the state of Slovenia, the company's owner (as in Example 3).

The case data support other findings (such as those of Orthaber and Márquez-Reiter[27]) that technologically mediated interaction does not trigger remedial action – unlike telephoned complaints that have to receive a response. Nevertheless, subscribers still continue to use Facebook to voice their feelings about corporate postings that appear in their newsfeed when they log in, especially when they read marketing information that does not accord with their personal experience of the advertiser's services. However, owing to lack of response – that might evoke requests for remedial action – subscribers fail to follow up on their initial moaning. Nor do they seem to hold page administrators accountable for lack of reaction.

The argument of the case is that avoidance of corporate responsibility is only possible because of the asynchronous aspect of Facebook as a form of communication. Messages can be posted that may remain unread or never responded to. Administrators thus have the power to disattend the legitimate status of those who moan – although if the number of moaners should reach a critical mass, it would impact negatively on the image of the relevant company.

Discussion of the case contends (as does Kádár,[28] for example) that the way in which customers (real and potential) express their dissatisfaction with the moderator's behaviour represents a form of ritual complaining in that their anger effectively is an expression of solidarity with fellow customers (see Table 7.1, page 111). It is interesting to note that over three months of the period of the case study (from August to November 2014) the administrator deleted a number of company posts from the Facebook wall after commentators had voiced negative feelings towards them.

The case study supports the findings of researchers such as Jucker and Taavitsainen[29] in that it illustrates that ritual chains of dissatisfaction are forged when a customer makes a "flaming" comment, that is, one that conveys a (c)overt insult to the service provider – and other customers join in. Thus, the phenomenon of "moaning" studied in this case has potential to operate as an invitation to fellow customers. This is because a moan represents a general problem, rather than an isolated incident to be resolved by the moderator or by the impoverished state-owned company.

It is interesting to note in this case that of comments posted to 150 status updates, 85% were "singles" (single contributions). On the one hand, this suggests that engaging in a discussion with the company does not seem to be the commentators' primary goal, but rather that their reaction is triggered by the pop-up of updates in their newsfeed. It provides them with an opportunity to voice their feelings without explicit demand that something should be done.

On the other hand, it suggests that users understand and accept that, in Facebook, topics can be left unfinished; and also that commentators may endorse and provide support for each other's moans by tying their comments to those of the previous correspondent either explicitly (as in Example 3, l. 6–7); by increment (as in Example 1, l. 10–11; Example 2, l. 8); or they "like" each other's entries (see the number of "likes" below each commentator's name in the examples). They exploit the medium by forming alliances against the company administrator (Maria in this case) to moan about the given topic.

Case analysis further shows that ratified recipients know how to exploit the medium as a public, open-comment platform by supporting each other's moans in spite of Maria's attempts to disattend them. This is in tune with previous findings, such as those of Neurauter-Kessels,[30] that in online interaction users not only feel less accountable for their behaviour and less at risk of losing public "face," but are also more honest; while Maria, though personally anonymous, is much more exposed in her role as the administrator of the page – as is its owner, the company.

Regardless of what the company actually has to offer, Maria's task is to present it in a positive light, for instance, by advertising special offers. However, the company suffers from financial struggles, outdated infrastructure and train fleet, all of which impact on service delivery and customer satisfaction. Its social media strategy is weak because it cannot provide the services it offers; and Maria has the almost impossible task representing an outdated business system as "modern." For example, to maintain a positive company image, she has to resort to removing negative information altogether from the company's profile.

Nevertheless, Maria's lack of attention to customer comments operates as an act of (self-sensed) power rather than inability to suggest practical solutions. Maria's destructive ritual of recurrently ignoring others derives from her role as institutional representatives of a state-owned public utility that enjoys the monopoly of the service it offers, yet is not accountable to its users. Tension thus arises within a two-fold ritual practice between three parties, as illustrated by Figure 7.1. The wide rectangle illustrates that both administrator/company and customers interact via the same medium. The company, a 'silent partner', uses Facebook to increase visibility and association with its customers indirectly, as indicated by the dotted arrow, because its intentions are mediated/communicated by the administrator (Maria).

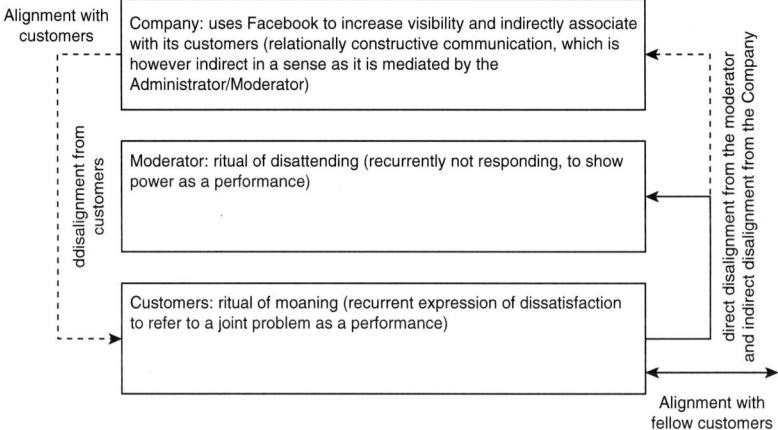

Figure 7.1 Ritual practices in operation in the studied setting
Source: Author.

Analysis shows it is the discrepancy between the infrastructural services and the pseudo-modern customer service that triggers the moaning. This mismatch appears to reach a level at which nearly every moderator's communicative attempt on Facebook is challenged by at least some of its subscribers, thus exposing the sensitivities and risks of online communication between companies and customers.

The behaviour of both Maria and customers challenges the supposedly harmonious relationship between clients and service providers. Maria's challenge is less obvious, given that the organization's norms bind its representative to restrain from any open form of aggression. Nevertheless, ignoring customers' misgivings results in the deterioration of their business relationship. Though Maria may attempt to reverse negative impact by seeking alignment with customers (see Example 3), such attempts are doomed to some extent to fail, because the basic strategy of routinely disattending customers' moans inherently violates their right to be treated properly. Moreover, as Richins[31] points out, moaning has the potential to strengthen the relationship between fellow customers, especially when considering that a complaint is more likely to be more effective if made by a group rather than by an isolated individual.

On a theoretical level, the study draws attention to the importance of using what Kádár[32] describes as relational ritual frameworks to study customer (and service provider) behaviour.

From a purely "rational" point of view, moaning is an "irrational" activity as it does not help customers to resolve pertaining problems with a service provider. However, it would be an error to regard the phenomenon of moaning simply as a let-off-steam type of behaviour. As this study has demonstrated, it has the potential to trigger ritual participation.

From a purely rational point of view, moaning is irrational in that it does not help customers to resolve problems with their service providers. However, it would be an error to regard moaning simply as "letting off steam." As this study has demonstrated, it has a potential to trigger ritual participation.

In the data, there is no evidence that moaning, even if it becomes a chain of ritual complaints, changes service providers' behaviour; yet joint complaining in online forums – perhaps even more than individual complaints – has the potential to trigger changes if the number of complainants reaches a critical amount. This is illustrated, for example, by a June 2014 report[33] that social media leave companies and brands very vulnerable. The report compares everybody being able to post what they want to a fire hose being open. Referring specifically to Twitter, the report states that "one too many negative tweets can seriously tarnish a brand's image" and that companies are responsive to complaints because "they don't want them going viral." Thus, ritual moaning has an important role to play and cannot be ignored in business and organization studies.

Summary

In summary, the company in this case uses Facebook as a platform to connect with numerous (potential) customers by seeking association with them and increasing its visibility. Customers, on other hand, avail themselves of this opportunity to associate with others to highlight their misgivings. The ritual of disattending customers' grievances is a noteworthy phenomenon that needs to be further explored as it can reveal information about the service providers' culture(s) and the broader cultural setting in which an organization is situated.

Finally, it is pertinent to note that in the data studied, the company is present only in an indirect way. Clashes and related ritual behaviour take place between customers and moderators – this shows the important role that moderators such as Maria play in the corporate Facebook drama.

Notes

The data for this study were taken from an open public platform visible to anyone without prior approval by the administrator(s) and therefore does not contain any privileged information. This social networking site also does not have any rules about soliciting research participants. The name of the company page is not provided in the chapter and names of all participants have been altered. In addition, to further secure anonymity, dates of publication have been removed and times of postings changed.

1. M. Sweney, Monday, 9 June 2014, "Social media set to be advertising winners at the Brazil World Cup," http://www.theguardian.com/.
2. W. Glynn Mangold, D.J. Faulds, 2009, "Social media: the new hybrid element of the promotion mix," *Business Horizons*, 52(4), July–August, 357–365; Elsevier.
3. V. Champoux, J. Dugree and L. McGlynn, 2012, "Corporate Facebook pages: when 'fans' attack," *Journal of Business Strategy*, 22(2), 22–30.
4. C.K.M Lee, 2011, "Micro-blogging and status updates on Facebook: texts and practices," in C. Thurlow and K. Mroczek (eds), *Digital discourse: language in the new media* (New York: Oxford University Press), 110–130. J.B. Walther and J. Jang, 2012, "Communication processes in participatory websites," *Journal of Computer Mediated Communication*, 18, 2–15.
5. C. Kerbrat-Orecchioni, 2004, "Introducing polylogue," *Journal of Pragmatics*, 36(1), 1–24. J. Lambaise, 2010, "Hanging by a thread: topic development and death in an online discussion of breaking news," *Language@Internet*, 7, Article 8.
6. J. Meredith, 2014, "Chatting online: comparing spoken and online written interaction between friends," Doctoral thesis, Loughborough University.
7. E. Goffman, 1979, "Footing," *Semiotica*, 25(1), 1–29. E. Goffman, 1981, *Forms of talk* (Philadelphia: University of Pennsylvania Press).
8. J.J. Gibson, 1979, *The ecological approach to perception* (London: Houghton Mifflin). I. Hutchby, 2001, "Technologies, texts and affordances," *Sociology*, 35(2), 441–456. S. Herring, 2010, "Computer-mediated conversation, Part I: introduction and overview," *Language@internet*, 7, http://www.languageatin-ternet.org/articles/2010/2801. Walther and Jang, "Communication processes in participatory websites," 2–15.. D. Edwards, 2005, "Moaning, whinging and laughing: the subjective side of complaints," *Discourse Studies*, 7(1), 5–29.
9. C. Licoppe, 2012, "Understanding mediated apparitions and their proliferation. The case of the phone ring and the 'crisis of the summons," *New Media & Society*, 14(7), 1073–1091.
10. D.W. Maynard and P.L. Hudak, 2008, "Small talk, high stakes: interactional disattentiveness in the context of prosocial doctor–patient interaction," *Language in Society*, 37, 661–688.
11. https://www.facebook.com/grem.z.vlakom/info?tab=page_info.
12. Edwards, "Moaning, whinging and laughing," 5–29.
13. Kerbrat-Orecchioni, "Introducing polylogue," 3.
14. For example, C. Licoppe and J. Morel, 2012, "Video-in-interaction: 'talking heads' and the multimodal organization of mobile and Skype video calls,"

Research in Language and Social Interaction, 45(4), 399–429; C. Antaki, E. Ardévol, F. Núñez and A. Vayreda, 2005, "For she who knows who she is: managing accountability in online forum messages," *Journal of Computer-Mediated Communication*, 11(1).

15. Licoppe, "Understanding mediated apparitions and their proliferation," 1073–1091.
16. Lee, "Micro-blogging and status updates on Facebook," 110–130.
17. R. Collins, 2004, *Interaction ritual chains* (Princeton and Oxford: Princeton University Press).
18. J. Schönfeldt and A. Golato, 2003, "Repair in chats: a conversation analytic approach," *Research on Language and Social Interaction*, 36(3), 241–284, 272.
19. Edwards, "Moaning, whinging and laughing."
20. E. Rooksby, 2002, *E-mail and ethics: style and ethical relations in computer-mediated communication* (London: Routledge) p. 84
21. SŽ is an abbreviation for the Company "Slovenian Railways."
22. S. Bruxelles and C. Kerbrat-Orecchioni, 2004, "Coalitions in polylogues," *Journal of Pragmatics*, 36(1), 75–113.
23. L. Dersley, 1998, "Complaining and arguing in everyday conversation," Unpublished D.Phil. dissertation, University of York, UK.
24. Meredith, "Chatting online."
25. S. Sigman, 1991, "Handling the discontinuous aspects of continuous social relationships: toward research on the persistence of social forms," *Communication Theory*, 1, 106–127.
26. R. Ide, 1998, "Sorry for your kindness: Japanese interactional ritual in public discourse," *Journal of Pragmatics*, 29, 509–529.
27. S. Orthaber and R. Márquez-Reiter, 2011, "'Talk to the hand': complaints to a public transport company," *Journal of Pragmatics*, 43, 3860–3876.
28. D. Kádár, 2013, *Relational rituals and communication: ritual interaction in groups* (Basingstoke, UK: Palgrave Macmillan).
29. A.H. Jucker and I. Taavitsainen, 2000, "Diachronic speech act analysis: insults from flyting to flaming," *Journal of Historical Pragmatics*, 1(1), 67–95.
30. M. Neurauter-Kessels, 2011, "Im/polite reader responses on British online news sites," *Journal of Politeness Research*, 7(2), 187–214.
31. M. Richins, 1983, "Negative word-of-mouth by dissatisfied customers: a pilot study," *Journal of Marketing*, 47(1), 68–78.
32. Kádár, *Relational rituals and communication*.
33. B. Andrews, 3 June 2014, "Complaining on Twitter may get you better customer service," http://miami.cbslocal.com/.

References

B. Andrews, 3 June 2014, "Complaining on Twitter may get you better customer service," http://miami.cbslocal.com/.

C. Antaki, 1994, *Explaining and arguing: the social organization of accounts* (London: Sage).

C. Antaki, E. Ardévol, F. Núñez and A. Vayreda, 2005, "For she who knows who she is: Managing accountability in online forum messages," *Journal of Computer-Mediated Communication*, 11(1).

Disattending Customer Dissatisfaction on Facebook 125

S. Bruxelles and C. Kerbrat-Orecchioni, 2004, "Coalitions in polylogues," *Journal of Pragmatics*, 36(1), 75–113.

V. Champoux, J. Dugree and L. McGlynn, 2012, "Corporate Facebook pages: when 'fans' attack." *Journal of Business Strategy*, 22(2), 22–30.

R. Collins, 2004, *Interaction ritual chains* (Princeton and Oxford: Princeton University Press).

L. Dersley, 1998, "Complaining and arguing in everyday conversation," Unpublished DPhil dissertation, University of York, UK.

D. Edwards, 2005, "Moaning, whinging and laughing: the subjective side of complaints." *Discourse Studies*, 7(1), 5–29.

J.J. Gibson, 1979, *The ecological approach to perception* (London: Houghton Mifflin).

E. Goffman, 1979, "Footing," *Semiotica*, 25(1): 1–29.

E Goffman, 1981, *Forms of talk* (Philadelphia: University of Pennsylvania Press).

S. Herring, 2010, "Computer-mediated conversation, Part I: Introduction and overview," *Language@internet*, 7, available from http://www.languageatinternet. org/articles/2010/2801.

I. Hutchby, 2001, "Technologies, texts and affordances," *Sociology*, 35(2), 441–456.

R. Ide, 1998, "Sorry for your kindness: Japanese interactional ritual in public discourse," *Journal of Pragmatics*, 29, 509–529.

G. Jefferson, 1973, "A case of precision timing in ordinary conversation: overlapped tag-positioned address terms in closing sequences," *Semiotica*, 9, 47–96.

A.H. Jucker and I. Taavitsainen, 2000, "Diachronic speech act analysis: insults from flyting to flaming." *Journal of Historical Pragmatics*, 1(1), 67–95.

D. Kádár, 2013, *Relational rituals and communication: ritual interaction in groups* (Basingstoke, UK: Palgrave Macmillan).

C. Kerbrat-Orecchioni, 2004, "Introducing polylogue," *Journal of Pragmatics*, 36(1), 1–24.

J. Lambaise, 2010, "Hanging by a thread: topic development and death in an online discussion of breaking news," *Language@Internet*, 7, Article 8.

C.K.M. Lee, 2011, "Micro-blogging and status updates on Facebook: Texts and practices," in C. Thurlow and K. Mroczek (eds), *Digital Discourse: Language in the New Media* (New York: Oxford University Press), 110–130.

C. Licoppe, 2012, "Understanding mediated apparitions and their proliferation. The case of the phone ring and the 'crisis of the summons,'" *New Media & Society*, 14(7), 1073–1091.

C. Licoppe and J. Morel, 2012, "Video-in-interaction: 'talking heads' and the multimodal organization of mobile and Skype video calls," *Research in Language and Social Interaction*, 45(4), 399–429.

W. Glynn Mangold and D.J. Faulds, July–August 2009, "Social media: the new hybrid element of the promotion mix," *Business Horizons*, 52(4), 357–365; Elsevier.

D.W. Maynard and P.L. Hudak, 2008, "Small talk, high stakes: interactional disattentiveness in the context of prosocial doctor–patient interaction," *Language in Society*, 37, 661–688.

J. Meredith, 2014, "Chatting online: comparing spoken and online written interaction between friends," Doctoral thesis, Loughborough University.

M. Neurauter-Kessels, 2011, "Im/polite reader responses on British online news sites," *Journal of Politeness Research*, 7(2), 187–214.

S. Orthaber and R. Márquez-Reiter, 2011, "'Talk to the hand'; complaints to a public transport company," *Journal of Pragmatics*, 43, 3860–3876.

M. Richins, 1983, "Negative word-of-mouth by dissatisfied customers: a pilot study," *Journal of Marketing*, 47(1), 68–78.

E. Rooksby, 2002, *E-mail and ethics: style and ethical relations in computer-mediated communication* (London: Routledge).

H. Sacks, 1992, *Lectures on conversation* Vols 1 and 2, edited by Gail Jefferson (Oxford: Blackwell).

S. Sigman, 1991, "Handling the discontinuous aspects of continuous social relationships: Toward research on the persistence of social forms," *Communication Theory*, 1, 106–127.

J. Schönfeldt and A. Golato, 2003, "Repair in chats: a conversation analytic approach," *Research on Language and Social Interaction*, 36(3), 241–284.

Slovenian Railways, 2012, *Summary of the Annual Report*. Retrieved from: http://www.slo-zeleznice.si/uploads/pictures/gallery/file/LPM_EN11_net.pdf.

J.B. Walther and J. Jang, 2012, "Communication processes in participatory websites," *Journal of Computer Mediated Communication*, 18, 2–15.

8

Cases of Official and Unofficial Business Practices: Examples from Australia, Germany, UK, South Africa, Russia and Pakistan

Andrew Kakabadse, Nada Korac-Kakabadse and Nadeem Khan

Editor's introduction

The authors of this chapter illustrate their case study of international corporate bribery and corruption with examples from the six countries identified in the title. Their central argument is the need for discretionary leadership morality.

Kakabadse and Kakabadse[1] have argued previously that contemporary focus on social and human (as opposed to physical) capital has promoted the emergence of network-based organizations. Network emphasis is on a group view of leadership that includes multiple stakeholders and the negotiation of multiple agendas. A new generation of leaders is now required to exercise *discretion* in addressing the issues they face.

In practice, argue the authors, discretionary leadership means that leaders shape and vary their roles according to the degree of freedom they are allowed. For example, leaders may be assigned limited resources and given specific briefs to pursue prescribed courses of action: they will be able only to leverage existing resources, adequate or not, and may even be directed how to do so. Roles with broader discretion permit the holders to establish their own parameters and directions, to be responsive to changing circumstances, with the potential for profound impact on the strategic future of the relevant enterprise.

Ultimately, discretionary leadership behaviour is not subject to formal role obligations, contracts or rewards. In response to the pace and pressure of organizational change, the nature of discretionary boundaries is increasingly determined by the challenges leaders face and the nature of those with whom they interact. The idiosyncratic nature of the organization, the peculiarities of each leadership role and the characteristics of the relevant individuals are critical considerations in determining role boundaries and parameters.[2]

These factors inevitably are culture-bound; and the examples of bribery and corruption described here may be discussed usefully in terms of culture.

Example #1

The authors describe this Australian example as one of collusion rather than extortion. It is illuminated by Hofstede's[3] definition of "power distance" (PDI): the extent to which a society expects and accepts that power is distributed unequally. He ranked Australian white mainstream culture as low in power distance. This suggests that Australians tend to feel comparatively equal and close to each other in work relationships and to resent autocratic leadership. Hall[4] rated Australian culture as "low context," to suggest that Australians are relatively informal, have equality in interaction and focus on the present and future; Hofstede also ranked Australia high in individualism.

It seems that Jim, in the study that follows, adopts a wide degree of discretion in dealing with his clients, and they with him, on an equal and individualistic basis, which accords with Hofstede's and Hall's findings. Relationships appear to be pragmatic, present-oriented but with an eye to "oiling the wheels" of future business dealings. Kakabadse *et al.* advocate the appointment to senior management positions of "leaders with higher-order social values beyond 'self-interest'" if corruption is to be removed from business practices. The example of Jim cannot be generalized to the whole of Australian business society, but it does suggest that self-interest is effectively a social value, at any rate in the Australian private business sector.

The authors note that perception of corruption in Australia's public sector dropped four points between 2012 and 2013. It is interesting to refer to a 2013 report in The Age[5] by the Independent Broad-based Anti-corruption Commission (IBAC). The Australian National University was commissioned to survey more than 800 employees in the public sector on their perceptions of corruption and found that one in five senior public servants would not know where to report their suspicions or observations of corruption. Moreover, 59% of those surveyed did not know or preferred not to identify corruption risks for their departments.

The researchers suggested that corruption was not part of public servants' "every-day life," but they were concerned that almost half the respondents did not feel confident they would be protected from victimization if they reported corruption. Therefore, it is possible that increased hostility towards "whistle-blowing" accounted at least partly for Australia's drop in the Transparency International (TI) Index.[6] IBAC chief executive Alistair Maclean[7]commented that whistleblower protection laws, enacted earlier in 2013, would help people disclose "improper conduct within the public sector without fear of reprisal."

The research team concluded that the most important instrument against corruption is the spiralling from top down of a culture of integrity, beginning with discretionary leadership.

Example #2

In Germany, an investigative team found that across the companies they examined, the respective directors and CEOs knew that bribery took place as common trading practice in some overseas markets; but chose to turn a blind eye to it and to look instead at the profits.

International business ethics has become an important field of study with the expansion of globalization; and it deals with different issues from those within a single country or legal jurisdiction. In particular, debate is concerned with situations where ethical norms are in conflict owing to different cultural practices and asks which should prevail. One argument is that "when in Rome, do as Rome does" – in practice and in ethics. However, problems arise when, for example, bribery of officials is central to doing business in the host country yet illegal in the home country of the firm – as in the example given in the chapter, of the German firm.

Richard DeGeorge[8] has suggested ten discretionary leadership guidelines for the conduct of multinational firms doing business in less-developed countries. They include avoiding harm, doing good, respecting human rights, respecting the local culture, cooperating with just governments and institutions, accepting ethical responsibility for the firm's actions and making hazardous plants and technologies safe.

The difficulty with all these suggestions is that they make no allowance for the reality of competitive trade under globalization. Writers such as Ronald Green[9] question when and under what conditions "everyone's doing it" might be a moral justification when conducting business transnationally and in competitive markets – as seems to have been the case with this German firm.

Another point of contention is that these moral precepts belong to Western ideologies and may bear little relation to the rest of the world. For example, how cross-culturally to agree on what is a "just" government or institution? The hypothesis of a social contract in itself embodies Western notions of procedural fairness, and the interpretation of the concept of "discretionary leadership morals" is culture-specific. It is likely to be defined differently in China, say, and in Sweden.

Example #3

This is set in the UK and is designed to demonstrate yet another side of leadership discretion: the decisions by those in authority to conceal their true motives behind a smoke screen of "doing the right thing," such as setting up apparently genuine bidding processes (or job interviews, come to that) when the choice has already been made for reasons other than merit.

Example #4

This suggests that a movement to benefit disadvantaged blacks in South Africa has resulted in poorer health care. This is due to corporate cultures more inclined to value low cost over high quality and to corrupt business practices in a competitive industry by which medical professionals demand bribes from suppliers in return for orders.

It is interesting to note that in 2013 in the USA, Porter and Lee[10] argued for a new strategy for national health care that would maximize value for patients by achieving best outcomes at lowest cost. They maintained this would entail moving away from a supply-driven health care system organized around what physicians do and towards a patient-centred system organized around what patients need. The focus would need to be shifted from volume and profitability of services such as physicians' visits, hospitalizations, procedures and tests to achieved patient outcomes. Fragmented systems in which every local provider offers a full range of services should be replaced by a system in which services for particular medical conditions would be concentrated in health-delivery organizations and in the right locations to deliver high-value care.

This would seem to be a good leadership strategy for the South African government to adopt. Theoretically, it should benefit all patients, whether or not socially and economically disadvantaged, and render futile any attempts by medical practitioners to extort money from suppliers in exchange for custom.

Example #5

This concerns widespread and rampant corruption in public and private sectors of Russian society. The Global corruption perceptions index (CPI) 2014[11] measures the perceived levels of public sector corruption in 175 countries and territories. On a scale of 0–100, where 0 is highly corrupt and 100 is very clean, Russia was given a score of 27 and ranked 136/175 countries in the survey. The index, compiled by Transparency International,[12] is a composite – a combination of polls – drawing on corruption-related data collected by a variety of reputable institutions. The CPI reflects the views of observers from around the world, including experts living and working in the countries and territories evaluated.

In 2012, President Vladimir Putin said he wanted to make Russia the fifth-biggest economy in the world (it then stood at number 11).[13] He wanted to boost foreign investment as part of his new economic plan. However, despite Russia's rich resources and its place among the world's fastest-growing economies, there still remains a general feeling that the country is under-performing, falling far short of its potential and failing to attract outside investors.

Reports suggest that the one overriding reason is corruption[14] but alcoholism,[15] widely accepted atheism and a gangster-like view of social morality have hindered Russia ever since Mikhail Gorbachev officially closed the office of the president of the USSR in December 1991. Since then, Russians have been increasingly ravaged by disease and early death. It is the only BRIC country facing a shrinking population. Alcohol-related health problems have led to the life expectancy for men at just 60 years, about the same as in Myanmar and Haiti.

The government acknowledges the damage that corruption does to the economy but seems powerless to combat it, despite a number of anti-corruption decrees and initiatives. In fact, it gets worse year by year. In March 2014, according to Radio Free Europe,[16] Russia's interior minister Vladimir Kolokoltsev told a meeting of ministry officials that the average bribe in Russia had doubled over the past year and now amounted to some 145,000 rubles ($4,000).

Apparently, bureaucrats in charge of state tenders routinely ask for enormous bribes from companies bidding for contracts, which adds to the cost of the bills that the state pays. For example, Roxburgh[17] claimed in 2013 that two or three years previously three senior officials were convicted – a rare occurrence, according to Roxburgh – for demanding $1 m to take the Japanese company Toshiba off a fictitious blacklist, which was preventing it from bidding for a contract.

In 2008, the case of Sergei Magnitsky[18] served as a dire warning to all potential investors. He was an auditor at a Moscow law firm when he discovered what he said was a massive fraud by Russian tax officials and police officers. He uncovered the alleged theft of $230 m (£150 m). After reporting it to the authorities, he was himself detained on suspicion of aiding tax evasion, and died in custody on 16 November 2009 at the age of 37. He acted as a legal adviser for London-based Hermitage Capital Management (HCM), where colleagues still insist the accusations were fabricated to halt his investigations. They point to the fact that dozens of entrepreneurs are in prison on charges trumped up by officials in order to take over their companies.

Despite Magnitsky's death, Russian prosecutors decided to put him on trial – action dismissed as a "circus" by his family and by HCM founder Bill Browder, who was himself tried in absentia. He is now a British citizen, based in London.

Some people have managed to prosper despite the real or perceived corrupt climate. Serguei Beloussov is the founder of Parallels,[19] one of the largest software companies in Russia. He argues that modern Russia's core capitalistic and democratic system can make a huge return; and that people in Russia now live in the best way ever, compared to the last 1,000 years, in terms of both freedom and in their material wealth.

The country is trying to position itself economically as a well-respected and modern emerging market leader. Political leaders are well aware that bureaucratic corruption not only deters big international fund managers like Foxhall Capital Management from investing in Russia, it also discourages foreign companies and hurts the local economy. Elected officials, civil servants and police are viewed as the most corrupt,[20] and one of the ways the government has tried to change this image is by removing all government officials from chairman of the board positions at state-owned enterprises like natural gas giant Gazprom.

Example #5 confirms that many Russian businessmen also hate the climate of corruption but face the problem of how to root out corrupt officials when, to quote a Russian saying, "the fish rots from the head down." According to some figures,[21] Russian citizens are the least likely of their global peers to believe they can make a difference in the fight against corruption. Only 45% believe it, compared to 62% in Asia Pacific, 73% in Latin America and 81% in North Africa and the Middle East. This example illustrates poignantly the helplessness many Russians feel because of lack of leadership morality.

Example #6

This example from Pakistan again refers to the 2014 Corruption Perceptions Index[22] that measures the perceived levels of public sector corruption in 175 countries and territories. Pakistan was ranked 29 in 2014 compared to 27 in 2012 on a scale where 0 is a perception that the country's public sector is "highly corrupt" and 100 is "very clean." The example describes a retired academic's struggle to get a state pension in a system where the payment of a bribe is a prerequisite for a successful application.

Reference is made to a public protest movement against nepotism within the civil service that has created a major divide between the elite ruling class and the main population – another indication of the need for discretionary leadership morality.

Abstract:

Six examples illustrate business interactions within different cultural contexts and sectors. Corruption and bribery are the common themes. Cross-comparison reveals that weak discretionary leadership morals result in a cultural gap between official and unofficial business practices. This becomes entrenched within the relevant organizational culture and maintained in behaviour learned by members for self-interest and corporate survival.

The studies reveal how communication channels (news and social media, lobbying outlets, political power games, etc.) may include hidden agendas in which bribery and corruption are critical items. These agendas distort official business practices and damage the longer term "common good"; hence, the need for leaders with higher-order social values beyond self-interest. Such values are pre-requisites for broader early-stage stakeholder engagement, accountability and transparency in inter-connected business practices.

Keywords: bribery, business practice, corruption, discretionary leadership, hidden agendas, transparency

Introduction

Corruption and bribery are major concerns of international business and both popular press and academic research – such as that of Jones[23] – testify that this behaviour is on the increase. This is in spite of continuing reforms, stricter enforcement of industry and national regulations, stronger legal constraints on directors and employees and ever-increasing fines following high-profile company fraud exposures.

Global interconnectedness benefits trade but reveals a widening difference between official and unofficial business norms in international dealings. Weak discretionary leadership morals pose systemic risks to institutions and companies with partial shared knowledge of the realities. The following examples illustrate that reforms are often a matter or pursuing self-interested companies or individuals too late, after damage

has been done to the common good. Consequently, local civil societies – in developed or developing countries – learn to distrust government efforts to impose business transparency and accountability.

Further, some international business leaders stake illegitimate advantage of differences in national governance systems. For example, in
2009, according to the US Department of Justice,[24] US, French, British
and German corporations and companies paid over US$1 billion in
fines or as settlements for violations of the US Foreign Corrupt Practices
Act (FCPAS) of 1977. The FCPA[25] is part of a broader international
networked agenda to combat bribery, not so much for ethical reasons
as because bribery is deemed to be bad for business. The most recent EU
anti-corruption report attributed a cost of 120 bn Euros per year to the
EU economy. Bribery increases the cost of doing business, poses a threat
to democratic institutions, induces social problems, reduces public
trust, threatens market integrity, undermines the rule of law and forces
economic disparity.

Karpoff[26] is only one of many writers to affirm that the costs associated with detection and prosecution, reputational and financial losses all
destroy firm value. The gap is widening between those countries that can
and those that cannot control such unofficial practices. Brinded[27] has
calculated that corruption is to blame for loss of more than $1 tn in each
of the poorest economies and – for associated reasons – 3.6 m deaths.

Transparency International[28] collates indices to rank countries
according to how corrupt their public, private and third sectors are
perceived to be. The following examples concern six countries whose
Corruption Perceptions Indices (CPI 2013) range from low (Australia,
Germany and the UK) to relatively high (South Africa, Russia and
Pakistan) (Table 8.1).

Table 8.1   Transparency International Corruption Indices

	Australia	Germany	UK	South Africa	Russia	Pakistan
Corruption Perceptions Index (CPI 2013)						
CPI Score (0–100)	81	78	76	42	28	28
Country Rank (1–177)	9	12	14	72	127	127
Global Corruption Barometer (GCB) 2013: Perceived Corruption (in %)						
Business Corruption	47	61	49	54	57	43
NGOs	23	31	18	43	45	39

Continued

Table 8.1   Continued

	Australia	Germany	UK	South Africa	Russia	Pakistan
Parliament/ Legislation	36	48	55	70	83	63
Public Officials Civil Servants	35	49	45	74	92	82
Judiciary	28	20	24	50	84	45
Media	58	54	69	40	59	36
Willingness to say stop corruption	74	49	68	68	44	69
Global Corruption Barometer (GCB) 2013: Reported Bribing (in %)						
Judiciary	5	No data available	21	30	No data available	36
Medical/Health Service	1		3	9		23
Police	2		8	36		65
Registry/Permit Services	2		11	39		45
Utilities	1		3	13		57
Tax Revenue	1		4	16		55
Land Services	3		11	20		75
Educational Services	1		7	11		16
Bribe Payers Index (BPI) 2011						
BP Score (0–10)	8.5	8.6	8.3	Not included	6.1	Not included
Country Rank (1–28)	6	4	8		28	

Source: Adapted by authors from various indices.

Case presentation

Example #1. Quid pro quo: the Australian case

Jim (name changed for confidentiality) is a successful Australian entrepreneur who runs his own IT network company.[29] Often when he signs a contract to supply products and/or services, he is asked to "throw in" a couple of iPads or to include a couple of days of free consultancy in the price of the goods (the official fee to be skimmed off by the contracting party). Reportedly, this is common practice in the Australian IT industry regardless of sector, size of firms, state government or third sector; they all expect some kind of "kick back."

When quizzed on whether he complies with this practice, Jim smiled and replied:

> I have to run my business and play the game. In my industry a few "extras" are the quid pro quo for being awarded a contract. I throw in whatever is requested as "commission" by my client. It is part of the negotiated agreement. I calculate this in to my quotation one way or another. Either I increase the price or I use second-hand material and equipment. They are fine and in working order – but not new, as stipulated in the contract.

Negotiations such as these are decided ahead of contract, maybe over an informal dinner. Although they constitute a form of bribery, there is what Wrage[30] describes as collusion between the two parties rather than one party extorting a bribe from the other; and in practice, according to Kranacher *et al.*,[31] it is seen as a mechanism to "grease the wheel of the contracting machine" or – in Jim's words – as a *quid pro quo*.

Example #2. Sacrificing the general manager: tribulation of a German company secretary

During a high-level executive development programme for an international German engineering firm, the company secretary Angelika (name changed for confidentiality) approached Dieter (name changed), the organizer, privately to share a dilemma. The newly appointed CEO had stipulated that any manager found to be giving or taking bribes would not receive any financial or legal support from the company. However, the firm operated principally in countries holding considerably different governance principles from those of Germany.

Angelika was the confidante of many general managers who held roles of country presidents of the firm, and did not know how to respond to their angry and astounded reaction to the CEO's stipulation that bribery would no longer receive any company support. More than 90% of company profits were through bribery. Most contracts were with the governments of the countries in which the firm operated – which involved dealing with a mountain of corrupt officials and ministers. All foreign companies in the company's sector behaved in the same way, and in fact the German managers believed they were far less corrupt than their British and US competitors.

Angelika was deeply concerned that loyal servants of the company would be betrayed; and finally felt she could not support the CEO's and the Board's public sacrifice of the General Management population. Shortly after talking to the training programme organizer, she resigned her position. Troubled by the whole matter, Dieter formed a team to make an extensive qualitative investigation of the practices of companies that operate internationally.

They discovered that bribery is dramatically on the increase across most countries and numerous sectors. There exists an unspoken practice of using governance protocols to protect Boards of Directors from being held accountable for corrupt practice. This leaves the general manager population unduly exposed to censure, without support from their employers, when they operate in countries with blatantly corrupt practices.

In all the companies examined, their directors and CEOs knew that bribery took place as common trading practice in particular markets. Many general managers reported that their sales targets had increased year by year, but still they were told not to give or take bribes. When they explained to their masters that the only way to continue increasing sales targets was to bribe even more, the standard response was: "Well, you're paid enough. Sort this out for yourself." Only occasionally, especially in high media profile cases, were senior executives or company directors forced into resignation.

Example #3. It is how you pre-package the offer: the glass walls of the UK

John (name changed), an entrepreneur, successfully negotiated a government-backed SME ("small and medium business enterprise") bank loan and bought a packaging business run by two partners who had built up the business from scratch and were retiring. As part of the handover process, John was introduced to suppliers and customers accompanied by an outgoing partner.

On the way to meeting his largest new customer, the retiring partner explained to John:

> I always take this buyer out to lunch once a month and I give him a discrete Christmas bonus on the side. That way we keep the business and he lets me know if competitors are quoting cheaper prices.

This was an unexpected ethical dilemma for John. In principle, he was opposed to any form of bribery but this customer accounted for 20% of turnover. Over the next few months, he did take the buyer out for a meal but did not offer any bonus. Fortunately, the individual in question left his firm and John was able to retain its custom on a merit basis.

However, a year or so later, he tendered to supply packaging to a local factory. The tendering process had reached a point of decision when the factory buyer asked John to meet him privately. She told him she ran her own business as a sideline and needed some additional packaging. She asked him to quote for supplying it by using one of codes in the factory's IT system. This meant she would get the goods for her private company but the factory would be invoiced. The woman made it plain that this arrangement was an unwritten condition of John's firm being awarded the (very large and lucrative) factory contract. John refused and lost the contract.

Nevertheless, in time his business became well established and was growing strongly. Then he was invited "out of the blue" by a closed bidding agency to submit a quotation for a huge packaging contract with a corporate client. This would entail increased inventory costs, floor space and delivery pressures; moreover, the contract was loaded with terms and conditions – such as late delivery fines. After much anxious deliberation, he sought a private meeting with the agency representative, with whom he had developed a good rapport. She told him in confidence that his bid was most unlikely to succeed in any case; the decision had been already made, based on internal factors. John did not submit a bid.

These incidents demonstrate how intricate, subtle and sophisticated influences affect business dealings in competitive markets that have nothing to do with outward appearances. Thus, requests are made in secret under threat of reprisals if refused; or honest traders are made to "go through the motions" of competing for business, merely to justify predetermined decisions that exclude them. This UK example supports the argument in the introduction that the public at large – worldwide – has learned almost to take for granted a lack of transparency and accountability in day-to-day business practices.

Example #4. Securing market share: the case of South African medical device companies

South Africa is the most recent member of the BRICS, the acronym for an association of five major emerging national economies: Brazil, Russia, India, China and, in 2010, South Africa.

They represent an emerging market in which there is an increasing cluster of middle-income earners. The South African government encourages the black majority population to join the economic mainstream, including government transactions with black-owned companies as primary suppliers.

The impact of worldwide recession has driven a movement towards "broad-based black economic empowerment" (BBBEE or B-BBEE as written by the South African government). Its aim is to distribute wealth across as broad a spectrum of previously disadvantaged South African society as possible.

However, volume increase has become the focus of B-BBEE companies; they compete by offering low prices to undercut the foreign multinationals, and one way of doing so is to provide generic products from manufacturing countries such as China and India, adept at product copying and "low price" strategies. Government trade alliances with these countries further promote these imports and force companies to sell products at a cost determined by class of goods, irrespective of the quality and benefits to patients. The result has been that the health care system in South Africa has developed a corporate culture inclined to accept low-cost products despite poorer medicinal outcomes for patients – a custom that inevitably increases the overall cost health care because of treatment failure.

The policy of low cost over quality has been encouraged by single exit pricing[32] as a feature of the South African Health Care system. It is part of a recently (2004) introduced fee structure by the Board of Healthcare Funders of Southern Africa (BHF)[33] to discourage inappropriate use of high-cost products with the laudable objectives of making medical scheme contributions more affordable and assisting government and funders to make private health care accessible to more South Africans. The new regulations put a stop to discounts and additional levies on medicines, providing only for the addition of a dispensing fee to the single exit price. The downside of single exit pricing is that it escalates competition between medical suppliers.

Competition and rivalry are fierce not only in the South African medical industry device but also in other sectors. There is a high number of similar products competing for the same business. This has fuelled a price war initiated by the smaller companies and negatively impacts the large multi-nationals. The price war works in favour of the medical funders whose sole intent is to drive down operational costs regardless of quality.

Suppliers are focused on generating sales to increase market share; therefore, there are many cheap substitutes for medical equipment, an example being artificial implants used for joint reconstructive surgery. Cost differentiation is a limiting factor, negatively affecting long-term share value and profitability. The South African medical device environment is highly regulated and competitive, with decision-making power in the hands of funders, hospital groups, government and health care professionals. The market is open to global manufacturers with lower cost producers more likely to receive high levels of reimbursement.

One study[34] reveals that the pressure on medical device employees to achieve sales and profit targets is immense, due to the desire of companies to meet their targets and satisfy their shareholders and investors. In the words of one (anonymous) participant in the study:

> Increase in sales drives poor behaviour. There are too many companies and to meet sales targets, most of time you have to be creative.

This view was shared by the majority of respondents, for example, one (anonymous) regional company representative complained:

> Business pressure to achieve sales figures, as the competition increases, makes it more difficult to deliver the targets. So these guys offer incentives, be it financial, travel, free products – it's about securing market share.

Another (anonymous) company representative said:

> In the highly competitive medical device environment, where pressure to deliver financial goals is high, business practices are sharp.

Another explained:

> Enforcement of codes of conducts and regulatory requirements is lax. I am not aware of anyone who enforces regulation or manages compliance of what we may or may not do.

Thus, the lack of prosecution from unethical business dealings facilitates the current behaviour patterns in South Africa. There are also health care professionals who seem to encourage unethical behaviour.

One (anonymous) sales representative reported:

> It is (health care professionals') brazen and total disrespect for the law and regulations which make them believe that they are entitled to receive kickbacks. The basis of this sense of entitlement is the fact that it is their usage which is the main source for product utilization and sales.

Other respondents specifically blamed surgeons. A typical comment was:

> Surgeons ask for (bribes) so what I am to do? It is the greed of surgeons who want to capitalize on their power as customers.

In contrast, surgeons complain of onerous performance management requirements and targets set by the health care system: but their demands for financial inducements influence the industry to adopt corrupt business practices in order to beat the competition.

Thus, lack of strategic leadership planning and coordination between different government bodies, and corrupt corporate leadership, has resulted in a paradox: that measures designed to help poor sick people have in effect disadvantaged them even further.

Example #5: Desire for a new world: local reaction to corruption in Russia

A talented Russian MBA student Oleg (name changed to avoid identification) returned home after graduation from an overseas university. As an experienced financial entrepreneur, he quickly become finance director of a major manufacturing enterprise. Astute negotiations with various financial and public bodies gained him the reputation of being an exceptionally talented deal maker.

Oleg came to the attention of a major Russian bank, and his career rise was meteoric. He quickly gained the trust of the CEO and the Chairman through working closely with both on numerous global projects. Oleg even liaised with the Russian central government and pulled together finance for major federal projects including investment in infrastructure and the re-equipment of the military.

At the height of his ascendency, Oleg lunched with a friend in Moscow and surprised her by telling he just resigned from the Bank and now held a lower paid position in a financial institution of much lower status. Why? She asked him. He replied:

> The corruption I had to deal with become more than I could tolerate. Corruption in Russia is simply appalling. On certain deals, various members of government can even take up to 20% as a bribery payment. Even in the Bank it's taken for granted that a certain percentage of every deal goes into the pockets of various senior managers. I have developed an international reputation as a person who can put together the most complex financial deals. This means that I can very easily loose this reputation if I am seen to be part of the corrupt network that surrounds me.

Oleg said he had never taken a bribe, but because of his growing global exposure, he was now being identified as a part of the Russian mafia.

I wondered for a long time whether I should leave the Bank. Finally, I decided that I must. Yes, this was strongly motivated by my concern for the loss of my reputation, but I have also become more and more aware of the damage being done to my country. An increasing number of my generation is totally sick of the corruption that surrounds us all. They are making their concerns heard. I do not wish them to see me as corrupt as those around me. My thinking started with me worrying about my reputation abroad. I am now worried about my reputation at home.

Also, I am deeply troubled by the legacy I am leaving my children who are already in their early teens. What probably will trouble me most is the prospect of my children, in a few years' time, accusing me not only of having done nothing to make the world better for them, but of being part of the corrupt hierarchy that made our country so bad for them. I am not unusual, there is a growing intelligence that things are not as they should be.

Example #6: Desire for a new world: local reaction to corruption in Pakistan

A Pakistani professor of surgery named Tariq Bajar (name changed to avoid identification), combined his passion for surgery with high personal moral integrity. His international experience included over a decade in the UK National Health Service and over a decade in Riyadh, the capital of Saudi Arabia. He taught medicine at a prestigious medical university in Pakistan.

Two years after his retirement, he was asked in an interview how he found it. His answer clearly revealed frustration:

I spend my days making trips to the Punjab Secretariat in an attempt to get my pension. The reality is I spend more in monthly petrol costs than the pension is worth and they still have not cleared it, so I am waiting to receive a pension in my home country, yet I got my entitlement for service in UK the day I retired.

He said the local civil servant in charge of pensions was delaying the paperwork until he was paid a cash bribe. The only way Tariq could get his pension without bribery would be if he were a member of a power network within the system. He said:

It is unfortunate but an honest man like me cannot survive or have merit-based career opportunities here – this is why I have worked most of my career abroad.

He was in the fortunate position of being non-dependent on the need for a government pension. It gave him financial freedom to take an ethical stand. Those who need the pension are forced to pay a cash bribe to get it. According to the professor, this has become the norm in a culture of power incentivized by self-interest, in which honest people are hopelessly disadvantaged.

In 2013, Pakistan scores 30 on the Gini-index[35] (see Table 8.1, page 134). This measures the degree of inequality in the distribution of family income in a country. The more nearly equal a country's income distribution, the lower its Gini index, for example, Denmark, with an index of 25 in 2011.[36] The more unequal a country's income distribution, the higher its Gini index, for example, South Africa with an index of 63. However, despite rising per capita income, a most recent report published by Oxfam highlights multiple inequalities[37] in Pakistan. An advisor to Chief Minister of Baluchistan has claimed there is a Pakistan for the elites and a Pakistan for the public. In 2014, this has resulted in rising disparity.[38]

Pakistan is the fifth most populous nation on the planet. In 2013, the population was close to 200 m. However, over half is living below the poverty line and despite claiming the youngest Nobel peace prize winner (Malala Yousafzai, 2014), about 25 m children do not attend school even though the constitution establishes free and compulsory education.

Currently, there is a political stand-off between the status-quo parties (PML-N; PPP) with the more recently formed PTI party[39] claiming that the last elections were rigged. In recent months, this has evolved into a people's movement of peaceful protests seeking an end to bribery and corruption practices. Protesters maintain these are supported by a high level of nepotism within institutions, and this has created a major divide between the elite ruling class and the main population.

Outcomes

Bribery and corruption exist in both developed and developing countries. In developed markets, it assumes a subtle, refined form which remains hidden; whilst in developing markets corrupt practices are more open, as official salaries are low and cost of living is high. Table 8.2 summarizes the dominant cultural impact of covert strategies illustrated by the aforementioned examples.

Table 8.2   Outcomes of unofficial covert strategies

Markets	Case	Unofficial covert strategy	Cultural outcome
Developed	Australia	Inbuilt kickbacks	Collusive trust
	Germany	Protocol to protect boards	Distancing accountability
	United Kingdom	Pre-determined processes	Groomed networking
Developing	South Africa	Incentivizing the powerful	Control of the office holder
	Russia	Developing a reputation	Building internal groups
	Pakistan	Using the job for self-interest	Isolation and frustration

Source: Author's own.

Ultimately, covert communication through media, politics, lobbying and powerful groups drives hidden agendas within each culture that gradually erode cultural cohesion and damage the common good. However, there is increasing transparency in private, public and NGO organizations; for example, recently whistle blowing has begun to encourage more open communication within organizations: but ultimately building trust and integrity needs to be firmly on boards' agendas.

The authors of this case study argue that reform involves recognition that the pursuit of financial gain for self-interest can only lead to the weakest possible outcomes because it fosters isolation. Humans are social beings who need to be part of a "common good" and a common will to achieve higher order outcomes. Financial gain should be the outcome from delivering value in fair and progressive markets that operate well with each other in an open, civic minded, cosmopolitan approach to doing business. This requires a culture of truth, in which people say what they mean and do what they say.

Discretionary leadership[40] depends on a level of freedom within role. With greater freedom, responsibility shifts from "doing what you are told to do" to more "making judgements and value adding contributions." This demands self-questioning, self-regulation of behaviour and action in context of the greater good or leadership team. It emerges as a "leadership morality" where leaders form reputations.

More often, leaders are competitively selected as suitable fit based upon crafted experiences and economic achievements. However, it is their morality which, when open to testing in a free-market, can either preserve or damage an organization, society and ultimately self. Leadership morality calls upon individuals to know themselves and keep learning.

The risk is that discretionary leadership is inclined towards self-belief, self-confidence and hierarchical power-based decision-making. The outcomes driven by self-interest range from "collusive" to "extortionate" practices. Leaders are entrusted to make decisions about how to (re)position sets of resources (financial, social, intellectual) in order to archive organizational goals that are (re)defined by themselves. These decisions have moral consequences, depending on how goals are achieved, but only outcomes are measured as performance – that is, financial targets. Contrastingly, a culture of transparency, accountability, co-operation and shared decision making supports "common good" outcomes in which leadership's success is when the whole is greater than the sum of individual's output combined.

It is the unofficial and informal boundaries of leadership that are irreplaceable and the legacy good leaders leave behind – ethics govern economics and morality impacts greater than short-term profit.

Notes

1. Nada Kakabadse and Andrew Kakabadse, 2005, "Leadership and the art of discretion: London Business School," *Business Strategy Review Autumn* 59–64, http://bsr.london.edu/lbs-article/330/index.html.
2. Ibid., 59.
3. G. Hofstede, 1980, *Culture's consequences: international differences in work-related values* (Sage).
4. E. Hall, 1976, *Beyond culture* (New York: Anchor Books).
5. J. Lee, 18 September 2013, "Public servants in the dark on corruption," http://www.theage.com.au/.
6. http://www.transparency.org/, accessed 8 December 2014.
7. Lee, "Public servants in the dark on corruption."
8. R. DeGeorge, 1993, *Competing with integrity in international business* (Oxford University Press).
9. R. Green, 1991, "When is 'everyone's doing it' a moral justification?" *Business Ethics Quarterly*, 1(1), 75–93.
10. M.E. Porter and T.H. Lee, "The strategy that will fix health care," October 2013 issue, *Harvard Business Review*, www.hbr.org/.
11. A. Willis, 4 December 2014, "Global corruption index 2014: the world's most corrupt countries in one amazing interactive map," https://metro.co.uk/.
12. http://www.transparency.org/, accessed 8 December 2014.

13. J. Melik, 28 June 2012, "Russia's growth stifled by corruption," *Business Daily*, BBC World Service, http://www.bbc.com/.
14. K. Raposa, 17 June 2011, "Russia Plagued by Corruption Perception," http://www.forbes.com/.
15. J. Golloher, 28 March 2011, "Trying to stay sober in Russia," PRI's The World, http://www.pri.org/.
16. Radio Free Europe, 6 December 2014, "Average Russian bribe doubles to $4,000 over past year," http://www.rferl.org/.
17. A. Roxburgh, 2013, *The strongman: Vladimir Putin and the struggle for Russia* (I.B.Tauris).
18. "Q&A: The Magnitsky affair, 11 July 2013," http://www.bbc.com/.
19. http://sp.parallels.com/, accessed 8 December 2014.
20. http://www.transparency.org/, accessed 8 December 2014.
21. Raposa, "Russia Plagued by Corruption Perception."
22. http://www.transparency.org/cpi2014.
23. J. Day, 27 December 2013, "Anti-corruption regulation survey of select countries 2013," http://www.mycorporateresource.com/.
24. http://www.justice.gov/criminal/fraud/fcpa/, accessed 9 December 2014.
25. http://www.fcpablog.com/#, accessed 9 December 2014.
26. J.M. Karpoff, D.S. Lee and G.S. Martin, 27 February 2012, "The impact of anti-bribery enforcement actions on targeted firms," http://www.baylor.edu/.
27. L. Brinded, 2014, "Corruption costs poorest countries $1Tn each a year," *International Business Times*, 3 September 2014, http://www.ibtimes.co.uk.
28. http://www.transparency.org/, accessed 8 December 2014.
29. In 2013, Davidson reported that Australia was labelled as one of "the biggest decliners" in the TI table, alongside nations including Syria, Libya, Mali, Spain, Iceland and Guatemala. The perception of corruption in Australia's public sector declined four points from 85 in 2012 to 81 in 2013, though the country is still ranked ninth cleanest globally, and third in the Asia-Pacific region. H. Davidson, 3 December 2013, "Australia rated alongside Syria as 'big decliner' in corruption perception," http://www.theguardian.com/.
30. A.A. Wrage, 2007, *Bribery and extortion: undermining business, governments, and security* (, Westport: Praeger Publishers), 7.
31. M. Kranacher, R. Riley and J.T. Wells, 2010, *Forensic accounting and fraud examination* (Hoboken, NJ: Wiley).
32. S. Swanepoel, 11 November 2006, "Single exit price: new dispensing fees are good for you," http://www.bhfglobal.com/.
33. http://www.bhfglobal.com/, accessed 8 December 2014.
34. Kakabadse and Kakabadse, "Leadership and the art of discretion."
35. http://data.worldbank.org/, accessed 8 December 2014.
36. https://www.cia.gov, accessed 8 December 2014.
37. http://www.oxfam.org/en/research/time-end-extreme-inequality, accessed 8 December 2014.
38. http://tribune.com.pk/story/783732/rising-disparity-over-30m-malnourished-in-pakistan/, accessed 8 December 2014.
39. B. Sattar, 20 October 2014, "Changing political landscape," http://www.dawn.com/.
40. A. Kakabadse, J. Bank and S. Vinnicombe, 2004, *Working in organisations* (Gower Publishing, Ltd.).

References

Bribe Payers Index Report, 2011, http://bpi.transparency.org/bpi2011/results/.

"Broad-based black economic empowerment," 2014 (no author), http://www.southafrica.doingbusinessguide.co.uk/.

L. Brinded, 3 September 2014, "Corruption costs poorest countries $1Tn each a year," *International Business Times*, http://www.ibtimes.co.uk.

CMS Guide to Anti-Bribery and Corruption Laws, 2 September 2014, http://www.cmslegal.com/.

H. Davidson, 3 December 2013, "Australia rated alongside Syria as 'big decliner' in corruption perception," http://www.theguardian.com/.

J. Day, 27 December 2013, "Anti-corruption regulation survey of select countries 2013," http://www.mycorporateresource.com/.

R. DeGeorge, 1993, *Competing with integrity in international business* (Oxford University Press).

A.I.J. Dyck, A. Morse and L. Zingales, January 2007, "Who blows the whistle on corporate fraud?" University of Chicago, CRSP Working Paper No. 618, European Corporate Governance Institute ECGI – Finance Working Paper No. 156/2007, http://faculty.chicagobooth.edu/.

FCPADigest, Cases and Review Releases Relating to Bribes to Foreign Officials under the Foreign Corrupt Practices Act of 1977, January 2014, http://www.shearman.com/.

J. Golloher, 28 March 2011, "Trying to stay sober in Russia," PRI's The World, http://www.pri.org/.

R. Green, 1991, "When is 'everyone's doing it' a moral justification?" *Business Ethics Quarterly*, 1(1): 75–93.

E. Hall, 1976, *Beyond culture* (New York: Anchor Books).

G. Hofstede, 1980, *Culture's consequences: international differences in work-related values* (Sage).

C.L. Jones and S.E. Weingram, "The effects of insider trading, seasoned equity offerings, corporate announcements, accounting restatements, and SEC enforcement actions on 10b-5 litigation risk," Social Science Research Network, http://papers.ssrn.com/.

N. Kakabadse and A. Kakabadse, 2005, "Leadership and the art of discretion; London Business School," *Business Strategy Review Autumn*, 59–64, http://bsr.london.edu/lbs-article/330/index.html.

J.M. Karpoff, D. Scott Lee and G.S. Martin, 27 February 2012, "The impact of anti-bribery enforcement actions on targeted firms," http://www.baylor.edu/.

M. Kranacher, R. Riley and J.T. Wells, 2010, *Forensic accounting and fraud examination* (Hoboken, NJ: Wiley).

J. Lee, 18 September 2013, "Public servants in the dark on corruption," http://www.theage.com.au/.

J. Melik, 28 June 2012, "Russia's growth stifled by corruption," *Business Daily*, BBC World Service, http://www.bbc.com/.

M.E. Porter and T.H. Lee, October 2013, "The strategy that will fix health care," *Harvard Business Review*, www.hbr.org/.

C. Provost, 3 December 2013, "Is Transparency International's measure of corruption still valid?," http://www.theguardian.com/.

C. Provost and M. Chalabi, 9 July 2013, "Global corruption barometer – Get the data," http://www.theguardian.com/.

K. Raposa, 17 June 2011, "Russia plagued by corruption perception," http://www.forbes.com/.

S. Rogers, 5 December 2012, "Corruption index 2012 from Transparency International: find out how countries compare," http://www.theguardian.com/.

R. Rose, 19 February 2013, "Bribery and public services: a global comparison," http://www.cspp.strath.ac.uk/lse%20bribery.pdf.

A. Roxburgh, 2013, *The strongman: Vladimir Putin and the struggle for Russia* (I.B.Tauris).

B. Sattar, 20 October 2014, "Changing political landscape," http://www.dawn.com/, Shearman & Sterling's recent trends and patterns in the enforcement of the Foreign Corrupt Practices Act (FCPA)/FCPA Digest, 21 July 2014; http://www.shearman.com/.

S. Swanepoel, 11 November 2006, "Single exit price: new dispensing fees are good for you," http://www.bhfglobal.com/.

Transparency International, 2011, "Bribe Payers Index report," http://bpi.transparency.org/.

Transparency International, 2013, "The global corruption barometer 2013 is the biggest ever survey tracking world-wide public opinion on corruption," http://www.transparency.org/.

Transparency International, 2014, "The 2014 corruption perceptions index measures the perceived levels of public sector corruption in 175 countries and territories," http://www.transparency.org.

US Securities and Exchange Commission, 9 April 2014, "Spotlight on Foreign Corrupt Practices Act," https://www.sec.gov.

A. Willis, 4 December 2014, "Global corruption index 2014: The world's most corrupt countries in one amazing interactive map," https://metro.co.uk/.

A.A. Wrage, 2007, *Bribery and extortion: undermining business, governments, and security* (Westport: Praeger Publishers).

9

Business Ethics and Self-Initiated Expatriates

Catherine Pereira and Anne Marie Zwerg-Villegas

Editor's introduction

This detailed case study is of the results of cultural differences between a member of a highly individualistic culture – that of the US – and representatives of a particularly collectivist section of Colombian society – the Department of Antioquia. According to Hofstede's[1] "6-D" model, US mainstream culture ranks 91 for *individualism* in contrast to that of Columbia's ranking of 13.[2]

Moreover, the authors draw on a number of writers in the field of cross-studies, and of business ethics, to explain how a US academic member of a Colombian university came to be so much at odds with her colleagues that she felt the need to resign her post.

As the authors point out, the potential for problems such as this increases as companies more and more operate across borders, and their managers have to contend with different values, norms and cultural behaviour in different countries.

The following case illustrates clearly the need for individuals who have to make important decisions in cross-cultural settings to take local as well as personal values into account. The main protagonist in this story is Susan, whose refusal to compromise her moral standards proved disastrous not only for herself but also for the harmony of her organizational environment. Her antagonist was the Colombian university Chancellor, who does seem to have understood Susan's position, at least to some extent. However, his attempt to negotiate with her was based on such culture-specific assumptions that no compromise was possible: a case of an irresistible force meeting an immovable object.

Abstract:

This study explores the participation of an expatriate in a decision-making body of a large private university in which she felt pressured to act against her ethical values. The case is discussed within the literature of business and cross-cultural ethics, and analyses the expatriate's experience as an example of how culture affects individual ethical reasoning. It provides useful insights to the field of cross-cultural management.

Keywords: cross-culture, decision-making, ethical reasoning, expatriate

Introduction

Background to the case

As Susan (fictitious name) was clearing her personal belongings from her office and saying good-bye to her colleagues (those who would still speak to her), she wondered, "How could things have gone from so good to so bad so quickly?"

US-born Susan thought she had adapted and integrated well after many years living in Antioquia, Colombia. No longer the adventure-seeking self-initiated expatriate, she was a contented immigrant permanently residing with her Colombian husband and her dual-nationality children. She was employed with a Colombian institution under Colombian labour law and standards. She really felt she had become a culturally intelligent, culturally agile, contributing member of an active community.

Suddenly, all that changed. She had never felt so foreign and out-of-place; she questioned how she ever got herself into this predicament and how she could possibly get herself out of it. She felt she had done the right thing, and her family and friends in the US agreed and encouraged her; however, she doubted herself. Maybe she had been culturally insensitive; maybe she had even been culturally arrogant.

In the beginning, her Colombian colleagues seemed to support her. They called her "brave," which seemed to be a strange way of describing her actions; it was only later, once things had gone too far, that she understood their choice of word. Now some of her closest colleagues, including those she considered friends, limited their contact with her, especially on work premises, and resorted to sending something akin to sympathy messages to and from private email accounts. Even her husband accused her of acting irrationally, of essentially committing professional suicide and sacrificing the family's well-being to benefit colleagues who would never appreciate what she had done and who certainly would never have done the same.

Susan reconsidered all her decisions over the past two decades. Would she ever fit in to Colombian culture? Should she return to the United States? Or was there even such thing as Colombian culture? Maybe this was just an issue of one organization's culture?

Case presentation

Setting

The setting for Susan's case is a medium-sized private university in the northwestern part of Colombia, South America. The university is located in the Department of Antioquia – a region initially founded in 1569 but recognized in 1886 as a territory – which today contributes more than 13% of the country's GDP,[3] is home to one of Colombia's most developed industrial belts, has a highly motivated and industrious population and is nationally renowned for its idiosyncratic nature.

Statistically, the Colombian population is one of the most homogeneous in the world with 58% of the population self-identifying as mestizo, 20% as white, 14% as mulato, 4% as black, 3% as black-indigenous and 1% as indigenous.[4] The predominant religion is Roman Catholicism with over 90% of the population professing some degree of affiliation,[5] and Colombia has one official language, Spanish, spoken by the overwhelming majority of the population.[6] Less than 0.3% of total population has originated elsewhere.

In Antioquia, topographical conditions have led to geographic isolation and distinct patterns of socio-cultural-economic development. It is nestled in the steep valley created by the intersection of two corridors of the Andean mountains. This remote location provided safety for early settlers from pirate and other outsider attacks. Today, it serves to buffer inhabitants from outside cultural influences.

The university has a strong regional presence and aims to gain an international presence in the medium term. It employs approximately 1,250 faculty members and serves 12,500 full-time undergraduate and postgraduate students, of whom over 15% benefit from scholarships. The university offers both undergraduate and postgraduate programmes in business and economics, engineering, natural sciences, law and music, among others, and its mission is ideological pluralism and the maintenance of a democratic and open institutional culture. Its motto "Open to the World" reflects this aim for ideological tolerance as well as its internationalization goals.

Susan

Susan is a 35-year-old economist who was born and raised in the US and graduated from a well-known east-coast university. She visited Colombia on a gap year adventure, having just graduated with a master's degree and wanting to travel anywhere in Spanish-speaking Latin America before either joining the corporate world or continuing with doctoral studies. She had no money saved and did not count on her family's approval – and therefore financial support; so rather than the typical gap year backpacking activities, she decided to find salaried work in a job that would advance her professional career.

Before departing the US, she was able to land a full-time contract as an economic analyst with the Antioquia branch of an international bank. Thus began her self-initiated expatriate experience. During the first year, she suffered moments of "culture shock" – sometimes reducing her to tears; but for the most part, she enjoyed her foreign adventure. She met and fell in love with a native Colombian. The two moved back and forth between the US, Colombia and several other countries, enjoying something of a globetrotting lifestyle. It was when they decided to start a family that they made the decision to establish roots in Colombia. At this point, Susan shed her identification as a self-initiated expat and identified herself as being an immigrant with permanent residency.

Now that adventure had taken second place to motherhood, Susan tried even harder to fit in to the local culture. She preferred to socialize with other Colombian families rather than with the foreign community; she enrolled her two children in traditional, Spanish-language, Catholic school despite being of another religion herself and having several English-language options; and she decided to pursue her academic and professional goals as a PhD student and lecturer at a Colombian university.

Over the next six years, Susan loved every minute of her work with the university and developed excellent relationships with her colleagues and superiors. Then, despite her initial reluctance, her colleagues convinced her to run for Faculty Representative to the Superior Council; and she was extremely proud when elected to represent her fellow professors at the main decision-making body of the organization. Members of the Superior Council who represent faculty carry out their duties without any monetary compensation. They are elected to serve a one-year term but may be reelected as long as they continue to work at the university.

The Superior Council is constituted by the Chancellor, the Vice-Chancellors, General Counsel, President of the Board of Directors, and representatives of different sectors including alumni, the business community, students and professors. Some Council members are nominated by the university and others – faculty and student representatives – are elected by their peers. Regardless of their selection or election, all members have the right to vote and voice their opinions on equal terms.

At the time of Susan's election, the Superior Council faced two important decisions. The first was the appointment of a new Dean to the Faculty of Economics. The second was the design of a system to rate, hire and compensate faculty when they joined the university; to establish commitments in terms of teaching hours and research production; and to characterize the tenure track system which would be implemented within the organization.

Dean's appointment

Most organizations, and particularly universities, represent a wide variety of interests, backgrounds and professions. This plurality usually implies that decisions on appointment of heads of schools and faculties should be made between a number of candidates from different backgrounds. Each should be able to represent different perspectives and visions of academia; be competent in use of financial resources; possess leadership skills in achieving specific group goals and coordinating the efforts of individual members. Based on these requirements, it is often the case that a university requires a Dean to epitomise the qualities of a good educator, an experienced researcher, and a competent administrator.

The University's Chancellor presented three candidates to be considered by the Council for the post of Dean of the Economics Faculty. The first was one of the Vice-Chancellors, who had been the Dean a decade ago. The second was an MBA with industry and teaching experience but no track record in scientific research; and the third – who was nephew to the Chancellor – was a recently graduated PhD who had published a book based on his dissertation but with no experience in the management of an academic unit.

System design for hiring and compensating academic staff and establishing the terms of their employment.

The university's faculty had been traditionally hired and compensated following a system that took into account undergraduate and post-graduate degrees, doctoral and post-doctoral studies, as well as years of professional experience. Academic staff was expected to average 12 hours of lectures a week, to publish at least one annual research paper and to participate in such activities as national and international academic events, academic missions and media relations.

As part of its policy-making responsibilities, the Superior Council was considering a new system that would require professors to lecture on average 18 hours a week instead of the previous 12, publish at least three articles a year, instead of one, in top-quality peer-reviewed journals and to engage in a specified number of activities associated with social projection.

Susan's dilemmas

Although Susan had worked at the university for over five years, had assimilated the local culture and learned to understand the traditional responses of the local population with regards to different situations and initiatives, she was confronted by her personal background and beliefs regarding the appointment of the Dean and the new grading system for the faculty. In fact, her vote on both decisions would be different from the votes cast by the rest of the Council members.

In the matter of the Dean's appointment, Susan expressed concern that none of the candidates was suitable for the post and requested recruitment of additional candidates. The Chancellor argued convincingly that this was an urgent matter; that selecting more candidates would be needlessly time-consuming; and that the most suitable candidate – his recently graduated nephew – had already been identified. According to the Chancellor, his nephew was a person "of confidence," someone he could count on and work with easily.

Susan's reaction was to ask the council to review in detail the experience contained in each candidate's curriculum in order to highlight their strengths and weaknesses in relation to the post. Based on her observations, she thought it reasonable to ask the Council to continue the search for suitable candidates. However, a vote was taken and all members voted in favour of the Chancellor's recommendation, with only Susan abstaining.

For several members of the council, including the Chancellor, Susan's opposition was nothing short of scandalous. In fact, it seemed so outrageous that an elected member of the Council should question the wisdom of the Chancellor with regards to the appointment that she was quickly summoned after the meeting to sign retroactively the minutes of the Council's proceedings and was pressured to alter the record of her abstention vote to one in favour of the preferred candidate.

At this point, Susan had first-hand knowledge of how the Superior Council reacted to what it understood as opposition. Albeit, she was faced with another decision: whether to approve or reject the proposed new system to hire, compensate and establish teaching and publishing commitments for professors. Susan felt morally obliged to present the view of the majority of academic faculty members, since she was their elected representative, and they were clearly against the proposal. However, the Superior Council was in favour of the proposed, more demanding, terms on the grounds they would guarantee quality improvements in both teaching and research in the future. The Vice-Chancellor and the General Counsel provided a thorough review of the long-term benefits of the new system and expected Susan to vote in favour of the plan.

Personally, Susan agreed with many parts of it. Certainly, it would be comparable to systems in the most respected institutions around the world and it would better position her university in international rankings. In fact, she herself would benefit from the new system since she was advancing along a research-focused track. However, as she saw it, her vote as an elected official should represent the views of her constituents, not her own. In particular, there was no way she could vote in favour of a system that increased effective classroom hours by 50% without corresponding compensation.

Faced with this situation, Susan decided to gather opinions formally from faculty members with regards to the new criteria. Accompanied by several elected officials to other decision-making bodies, Susan called town-hall-style meetings in each faculty to hear and register her constituents' concerns and proposals.

Once the proposal for the new system was presented before the Council, Susan shared with her fellow Council members the views and opinions that she had collected among the faculty; and voted accordingly against the proposal while the rest of the votes were in favour. The Chancellor made no effort to hide his disapproval of Susan's actions, but this time he did not bother to summon Susan to change her vote. Instead, he summoned Susan's Department Head, who coincidentally was the Chancellor's god-daughter, and instructed her to "control" Susan.

These two collisions between Susan and the others of the Superior Council paved the way to a generalized view that Susan was an anti-establishment figure who had taken advantage of the support she had in the teaching community to go against the long-term interests of the university. This perception hindered Susan's work at the university, and just one day after her landslide reelection to the Superior Council, she resigned.

Outcomes

Theoretical framework

In an increasingly globalized world, it is often hard for organizations to reconcile policies with the diverse cultural norms of their members. While the term "culture" can refer to a particular group's ideas and customs, it can also refer to socially accepted attitudes and behaviour.[7] Thus, the variety of elements that constitute an organizational culture is often broad and may differ in many respects from the national culture within which it operates.[8] This may present a management challenge when integrating individual employees with achievement of organizational goals.[9]

In addition to the seminal work by Hofstede[10] and others who have contributed to the field of cross-cultural management, some researchers[11] have found that culture-based ethical values of individual staff members of any organization may affect their perceptions of management decisions,[12] and members of some cultures are more sensitive than others to the ethics of decision-making.[13]

While some studies have concentrated on analysing the broad relationship between ethical behaviour and culture, others have focused on what is known as descriptive ethics,[14] which studies decision-making and aims to explain the behaviour of individuals in a management context. Among others, authors such as Bass and Cohen[15] have contributed to the field of business ethics by using the concept of cognitive moral development. This concept originates in the field of psychology and maintains that an individual's conception of what is moral, that is, what is "right" or "wrong," progresses as the person matures.

Other contributions to descriptive ethics include Jones,[16] who set criteria to determine how factors such as social consensus and the intensity of moral consequences are involved in business ethics. Trevino *et al.*[17] also contributed to these studies with the concept of ethical climate and ethical culture. In addition, within the field of ethical decision-making, perhaps one of the main contributions is the four-step framework proposed by Rest.[18] Regarding the association between ethical behaviour and culture, authors such as Thorne and Saunders[19] explore ways in which ethical values might be instilled within an organization. All these studies of ethical decision-making in cross-cultural management literature are helpful in analysing the case of Susan, the expatriate-turned immigrant who felt pressured to make unethical decisions within an organization whose cultural values were different from her own.

While the movement of workers across geographic boundaries is not a recent phenomenon,[20] since the turn of the century, other forms of international mobility have increased significantly and self-initiated expatriates now out-number traditional expatriates.[21] Such individuals embark on the expatriate experience on their own, without a corporate sponsor. Their motives for relocating and their participation in the foreign community are quite distinct from those of traditional expats. Their cultural interaction and the potential for cultural conflict are much more extensive than those of their corporate-sponsored contemporaries. Both the individuals and the organizations receiving them face distinct cultural challenges.

The first of four steps in a conceptual framework proposed by Rest[22] to study moral decisions is that of *moral perception*, the ability to interpret a situation as moral. In Susan's case, despite her understanding of the local "way things work," her perception was that she had a moral responsibility to represent accurately her peers who had elected her into office and that it was morally wrong for the Council to influence her vote on the Dean's appointment, much less retroactively to change it. She felt the need to argue objectively on each candidate's merits and to suggest that the council should search for more suitable candidates.

Rest's second step in the process of ethical decision-making is *moral judgment*. Susan's understanding was that she had been elected to represent a large and diverse number of professors, the majority of whom had negative views on aspects of the proposal and had expressed opinions about how the system could be modified. Much as she wanted to integrate with the other members of the Council and to demonstrate her loyalty to the institution, its Chancellor and its governing bodies, Susan's moral judgement was that she could not agree to vote in favour of a candidate who in her view was not sufficiently qualified for the job of Dean, regardless of the fact that he might be a good member of the Chancellor's team. Also, she decided to report to the Council the opposition expressed by the faculty about the proposed modification to the current employment system and to raise the possibility for a change in the proposal.

The Council members did not understand that her position was underpinned by what Rest describes in his framework as *moral intent* – a third step in ethical decisions. Susan set her moral values above considerations of expediency and good team work, and to implement her moral intention she engaged in what Rest calls *moral behaviour* as a fourth step. She refrained from voting for any of the three candidates and voted against the proposed system to hire, evaluate and compensate faculty. Both decisions were contrary to what the Council wanted and expected.

However, Rest's ethical reasoning framework is not altogether sufficient to explain both Susan's reasoning and the Council's reaction; the cultural backgrounds of all parties need to be taken into account. Six cultural dimensions seem to be relevant and are identified in the work of Hofstede and Trompenaars.[23]

The first dimension is *individualism/collectivism*, identified by Hofstede and Trompenaars (*individualism/communitarianism*): the extent to which individuals feel integrated with groups. Susan was born, raised and educated in the US, a nation characterized by a highly individualistic culture. She began her life in Colombia as a self-initiated expatriate; thus, in general, individualism appears to shape her ethical reasoning and personal judgements.

On the other hand, Colombia is one of the most collectivist countries in the world (topped only by Ecuador, Panama and Guatemala).[24] Loyalty to group membership and deference to group opinion are extremely important, as is the value of supporting extended family members. Not surprisingly, the members of the Council – predominantly Colombian – expected Susan to side with the decision of the group under the leadership of the Chancellor.

Hofstede's second cultural dimension is *power distance*.[25] If individuals within a given culture perceive a relatively small difference in terms of respect between those with influence and power and those without, they are more likely to support democratic social and political behaviour. In cultures of high power, distance members are more likely to accept a social and political hierarchy in which some members have the right to more privileges than others and are entitled to more obedience and respect.

In this case, it is valid to say that individuals in Colombia tend not to question the exercise of power within a hierarchy. As a result, most members of the Superior Council were willing – much more easily than Susan – to follow the Chancellor's lead on how they should vote; but Susan belongs to a culture of comparatively low power distance and is therefore more democratic minded, which makes it natural for her to question other individuals' decisions, no matter who they are.

Susan herself, in the midst of these conflicts, reflected upon how she came upon her life in Colombia. Thinking back on those decisions she made as a young adventurer, she thinks that part of her decision to leave the US (supposedly temporarily) was an exercise of questioning authority. She wanted to break away from her family's influence, she wanted to stall her involvement in hierarchical institutions (whether corporate or academic) and she wanted to experience life outside of the US hegemony.

A third dimension identified by Hofstede that is useful to analyze how culture influenced Susan's individual behaviour is *femininity versus masculinity*.[26] Colombia and the US, on average, rank as *masculine* societies, driven by competition, achievement and the will to succeed. However, as members of a culture both *masculine* and *collectivist*, Colombians tend to compete against out-groups rather than against members of their own in-groups.

Susan displays more *feminine* characteristics, that is, she is more prone to value relationships and a better quality of life over competition and achievement. Part of the reason she chose to travel to Colombia in the first place was to delay participation in the competitive corporate or academic world. In the earlier case, she clearly valued her relationship with faculty peers more highly than personal gain from bowing to the council's influence. Her attitude created misunderstanding in the Council, whose predominantly Colombian makeup valued more *masculine* characteristics consistent with support for a more demanding system to evaluate faculty.

Moreover, Trompenaars[27] has found cultural distinctions between the values of *achievement* and *ascription*. In *achievement*-oriented societies, such as the US, people's worth is assessed in terms of performance, of what they have achieved, no matter what their background or social status, and they reward and recognize good performance appropriately. On the other hand, *ascriptive* societies value their members according to their place in society. Power, title and position matter in these cultures, and power roles define behaviour. Therefore, it is not surprising that Council members were scandalized by Susan's refusal to accept the Chancellor's leadership.

Susan's view was that appointing the less-than-appropriately qualified nephew of the Chancellor as Dean of the Economics Faculty was closer to nepotism than recognition of merit. The Chancellor's view, supported by the majority of Council members, was that the preferred candidate had the status – culturally synonymous with merit – to be named Dean.

Trompenaars also found that individuals within a given culture may be more or less comfortable in accepting *universalistic* or *particularistic*[28] rules of morals and ethics. In a *universalist* society, such as that of the US, rules and contracts are presumed to apply in any situation. Therefore, Susan relied on what she understood to be the rules governing academic appointments and argued for the Dean's appointment from a wide range of candidates selected solely for their academic qualifications. However, Colombia, as argued by Trompenaars, owns a *particularistic* culture in which people look at relationships and circumstances in any specific situation to decide what is right. Thus, in appointing a new Dean, the Council members took the general rules for academic appointments only as a starting point for a final agreement based on the relationships in the given circumstances.

As the situation unfolded, it seems that the Chancellor might have understood that Susan's accusation of lack of impartiality had some substance, which may be why he summoned her to his office to persuade her to sign retroactively a set of Council minutes that recorded her as voting in favour of the appointment. Had she not done so, the new Dean might have been received with less legitimacy in the wider, and more culturally heterogeneous, university community.

A final dimension that might shed light on Susan's decisions is what Trompenaars[29] refers to as *analysis/integration*. At one end of this dimension, individuals in any given society are more inclined to value detailed analysis of facts, situations and events; at the other end, they look first at "the big picture" to find integrating elements in order to reach true understanding of the whole. In this case, Susan behaved in an analytical manner, focusing on the details of the Dean's appointment and the proposed system to hire and evaluate faculty, whereas Council members took an integrated view that included relationships as well as rules and favoured quality improvements as a whole over individual faculty objections.

Conclusion

The experience of Susan reinforces the view that culture affects individuals' ethical reasoning and highlights to what extent different cultural dimensions may affect reasoning and behaviour. It seems that six such dimensions, identified in the literature, predominately characterized her reasoning: *individualism/collectivism, power distance, femininity/masculinity, achievement/ascription, universalism/particularism* and *analysis/integration*.

Susan believed that individual interests best serve the community at large, but this clashed with other council members' perceptions of collective interests and loyalties. The fact that power distance is low in Susan's culture allowed her to reason and discuss with the Chancellor on equal terms, but this simply promoted the view within the council that

Susan was an anti-establishment member. As a woman, Susan tends to own more *feminine* values than those of her national *masculine* culture and, therefore, was inclined to put her relationship with the faculty over the Council's objectives. However, she conformed to the characteristics of US culture in general by perceiving that merit (*achievement*) should be regarded much more highly than status or social position; and she was inclined to take a more *analytical* view of the two problems confronting the Council than the other, Colombian, members who sought *integration* of the various components.

More research is required to corroborate a relationship between individual culture and ethical reasoning,[30] but cases such as this tend to suggest that globalization and labour market mobility challenge how organizations promote values and standards. The discussion in this chapter suggests organizations that ignore culture's influence on individual decision-making may do so by risking the cohesion of corporate goals and hampering both internal communication and employee perception of the consistency with which it performs.

Notes

1. http://geert-hofstede.com/united-states.html, 2 January 2015.
2. http://geert-hofstede.com/colombia.html, 2 January 2015.
3. DANE-Departamento Nacional de Estadísticas, 2014.
4. http://www.indexmundi.com/colombia/population.html, 23 August 2014.
5. http://www.studylands.com/guide/CO-religion.htm, 19 June 2014.
6. http://www.ethnologue.com/country/CO, 2014.
7. G. Hofstede, 1991, *Cultures and organizations: software of the mind* (London: McGraw Hill).
8. N. Adler, 1997, *International dimensions of organisational behavior*, 3rd edition (Cincinnati, OH: South Western College Publishing).
9. Hofstede, *Cultures and organizations*. G. Hofstede, 1980, *Cultures consequences: international differences in work related values* (Beverly Hills CA: Sage Publications). C. Hampden-Turner and F. Trompenaars, 1994, *The seven cultures of capitalism: value systems for creating wealth in the United States, Britain, Japan, Germany, France, Sweden, and the Netherlands* (Piatkus). F. Trompenaars, 1993, *Riding the waves of culture: understanding cultural diversity in business* (Economist Books).
10. Hofstede, *Cultures and organizations*.
11. T. Jackson and M. Artola, 1997, "Ethical beliefs and management behavior: a cross-cultural comparison," *Journal of Business Ethics*, 16, 1163–1173. S.J. Vitell, S.L. Nwachukwu and J.H. Barnes, 1993, "The effects of culture on ethical decision-making: an application of Hofstede's typology," *Journal of Business Ethics*, 12, 753–760.
12. G. Macdonald, 2000, "Cross-cultural methodological issues in ethical research," *Journal of Business Ethics*, 27(1/2), 89–104.

13. Jackson and Artola, "Ethical beliefs and management behaviour." D. Izraeli, 1988, "Ethical beliefs and behavior among managers: a cross-cultural perspective," *Journal of Business Ethics*, 7, 263–271; J.R. Cohen, L.W. Pant and D.J. Sharp, 2001, "An examination of differences in ethical-decision making between Canadian business students and accounting professionals," *Journal of Business Ethics*, 30(4), 319–336; J. Cohen, L. Pant and D. Sharp, 1992, "Cultural and socio-economic constraints on international codes of ethics: lessons from accounting," *Journal of Business Ethics*, 11, 687–700.

14. P.H. Werhane, 1994, "The normative/descriptive distinction in methodologies of business ethics," *Business Ethics Quarterly*, 4(2) April, 175–180.

15. K. Bass, T. Barnett and G. Brown, 1999, "Individual difference variables, ethical judgments, and ethical behavioral intentions," *Business Ethics Quarterly*, 9(2), 183–205. Cohen *et al.*, "An examination of differences in ethical-decision making."

16. T. Jones, 1991, "Ethical decision-making by individuals in organization: an issue-contingent model," *Academy of Management Review*, 16(2), 366–395.

17. L.K. Trevino, K.D. Butterfield and D.L. McCabe, 1998, "The ethical context in organizations: influences on employee attitudes and behaviors," *Business Ethics Quarterly*, 8(3), 447–476.

18. J.R. Rest, 1986, *Moral development: advances in research and theory* (New York: Praeger).

19. L. Thorne and S.B. Saunders, 2002, "The socio-cultural embeddedness of individuals' ethical reasoning in organizations," *California Management Review*, 44(3), 37–54.

20. B.W. Husted, J.B. Dozier, J.T. McMahon and M.W. Kattan, 1996, "The impact of cross-national carriers of business ethics on attitudes about questionable practices and form of moral reasoning," *Journal of International Business Studies*, 27(2) (2nd Qtr.), 391–411, Palgrave Macmillan Journals.

21. T. Jokinen, C. Brewster and V. Suutari, 2008, "Career capital during international work experience: contrasting self-initiated expatriate experience and assigned expatriation," *International Journal of Human Resource Management*, 19(6), 979–999.

22. Rest, *Moral development*.

23. Hofstede, *Cultures consequences*. Hampden-Turner and Trompenaars, *The seven cultures of capitalism*.

24. Hofstede Center, 2014, Cultural Tools, http://geert-hofstede.com/colombia.html.

25. Ibid.

26. Ibid.

27. Trompenaars, *Riding the waves of culture*.

28. Ibid.

29. Ibid.

30. See, for example, Lin Ge, 2004, "Culture and gender effects on ethical reasoning in an auditing context: a comparison of Canada and mainland China," http://hdl.handle.net/10133/602; https://www.uleth.ca/. N.A. Granitz, 2003, "Individual, social and organizational sources of sharing and variation in the ethical reasoning of managers," *Journal of Business Ethics*, Springer. N.A. Granitz and J.C. Ward, "Actual and perceived sharing of ethical reasoning and moral intent among in-group and out-group members," *Journal*

of Business Ethics, Springer. Husted *et al.*, "The impact of cross-national carriers of business ethics," 391–411, Palgrave Macmillan Journals. C. Robertson and P.A. Fadil, 1999, "Ethical decision making in multinational organizations: a culture-based model," *Journal of Business Ethics*, Springer. L. Thorne and S.B. Saunders, 2002, "The socio-cultural embeddedness of individuals' ethical reasoning in organizations," *Journal of Business Ethics*, Springer. J. Tsui and C. Windsor, 2001, "Some cross-cultural evidence on ethical reasoning," *Journal of Business Ethics*, Springer. S.J. Vitell, S.L. Nwachukwu and J.H. Barnes, 1993, "The effects of culture on ethical decision-making: an application of Hofstede's typology," *Journal of Business Ethics*, Springer.

References

N. Adler, 1997, *International dimensions of organizational behavior*, 3rd edition (Cincinnati, OH: South Western College Publishing).

K. Bass, T. Barnett and G. Brown, 1999, "Individual difference variables, ethical judgments, and ethical behavioral intentions," *Business Ethics Quarterly*, 9(2), 183–205.

J. R. Cohen, L. W. Pant and D. J. Sharp, 1992, "Cultural and socio-economic constraints on international codes of ethics: Lessons from accounting," *Journal of Business Ethics*, 11, 687–700.

J. R. Cohen, L. W. Pant and D. J. Sharp, 2001, "An examination of differences in ethical decision making between Canadian business students and accounting professionals," *Journal of Business Ethics*, 30(4), 319–336.

DANE-Departamento Nacional de Estadísticas, 2014, http://www.dane.gov.co/.

Lin Ge, 2004, "Culture and gender effects on ethical reasoning in an auditing context: a comparison of Canada and mainland China," https://www.uleth.ca/dspace/handle/10133/602.

N.A. Granitz, December 2002, "Individual, social and organizational sources of sharing and variation in the ethical reasoning of managers," *Journal of Business Ethics*, 42(2), 101–124.

N.A. Granitz and J.C. Ward, 2001, "Actual and perceived sharing of ethical reasoning and moral intent among in-group and out-group members," *Journal of Business Ethics*, 33, 299–322; Springer.

C. Hampden-Turner and F. Trompenaars, 1993, *The seven cultures of capitalism* (New York: Currency Press: Doubleday).

Hofstede Center, 2014, "Cultural tools," http://geert-hofstede.com/colombia.html.

G. Hofstede, 1980, *Cultures consequences: international differences in work related values* (Beverly Hills CA: Sage Publications).

G. Hofstede, 1991, *Cultures and organizations: software of the mind* (London: McGraw Hill).

B.W. Husted, J.B. Dozier, J.T. McMahon and M.W. Kattan, 1996, "The impact of cross-national carriers of business ethics on attitudes about questionable practices and form of moral reasoning," *Journal of International Business Studies*, 27(2) (2nd Qtr.), 391–411; Palgrave Macmillan Journals.

D. Izraeli, 1988, "Ethical beliefs and behavior among managers: a cross-cultural perspective," *Journal of Business Ethics*, 7, 263–271.

T. Jackson and M. Artola, 1997, "Ethical beliefs and management behavior: a cross-cultural comparison," *Journal of Business Ethics*, 16, 1163–1173.

T. Jokinen, C. Brewster and V. Suutari, 2008, "Career capital during international work experience: Contrasting self-initiated expatriate experience and assigned expatriation," *International Journal of Human Resource Management*, 19(6), 979–999.

T. Jones, 1991, "Ethical decision-making by individuals in organization: an issue-contingent model," *Academy of Management Review*, 16(2), 366–395.

G. Macdonald, 2000, "Cross-cultural methodological issues in ethical research," *Journal of Business Ethics*, 27(1/2), 89–104.

J.R. Rest, 1986, *Moral development: advances in research and theory* (New York: Praeger).

C. Robertson and P.A. Fadil, 1999, "Ethical decision making in multinational organizations: a culture-based model," *Journal of Business Ethics*, 19(4), 385–92; Springer.

L. Thorne and S.B. Saunders, 2002, "The socio-cultural embeddedness of individuals' ethical reasoning in organizations," *California Management Review*, 44(3), 37–54.

L.K. Trevino, K.D. Butterfield and D.L. McCabe, 1998, "The ethical context in organizations: influences on employee attitudes and behaviors," *Business Ethics Quarterly*, 8(3), 447–476.

J. Tsui and C. Windsor, 2001, "Some cross-cultural evidence on ethical reasoning," *Journal of Business Ethics*, 31(2), 143–150; Springer.

S.J. Vitell, S.L. Nwachukwu and J.H. Barnes, 1993, "The effects of culture on ethical decision-making: An application of Hofstede's typology," *Journal of Business Ethics*, 12, 753–760.

P.H. Werhane, April 1994, "The normative/descriptive distinction in methodologies of business ethics," *Business Ethics Quarterly*, 4(2), 175–180.

10

Electronic Sub-titles for Opera Librettos: The Case of Figaro

Geoffrey Webb

Editor's introduction

All the case studies in this collection offer unique insights into aspects of international management and intercultural communication. This case study in this chapter is a unique contribution in four ways.

First, its setting is musical performance, a form of international and cross-cultural communication not always recognized as such, though it transcends all boundaries and unites listeners from all nations. The 2015 Eurovision Song Contest, for example,[1] featured artists from Armenia to Australia, Italy to Iceland and Sweden to Serbia.

Second, it deals with a unique form of technology-mediated communication. Third, the case is one of project management, the only one in the book, and another example of inter- and intra-team communication. Finally, it offers a new perspective on the effects of space on communication (Andrew Harrison also writes on this subject in Volume 2, Chapter 11).

Music

Opera music belongs to a unique and magnificent musical genre; but this case is based on the fact that in opera it is often difficult to understand the plot, and librettos are not always crystal clear.

One solution over the years has been for aficionados to bring a book and a torch to the auditorium; and many did so. Then, in 1983, Lotfollah Mansouri, General Director of the Canadian Opera Company and latter director of the San Francisco Opera, pioneered a way to project opera sub-titles on the proscenium above the stage so the audience could follow the libretto during the performance.[2]

Since then, many opera houses all over the world have mounted similar huge screens; but they all suffer from the same disadvantages. One is that people risk stiff necks watching sub-titles located so high above the stage. Another is that they focus attention on the titles instead of on the stage; they cannot be switched off and loom distractingly large when displayed in several languages. This case study is of a new way to read sub-titles while enjoying an opera performance on stage.

Technology-mediated communication

The case describes a system, Simultext®, located within hands' reach of opera-goers, on the back of the seat immediately ahead of each of them: an electronic libretto system by which patrons can read the libretto in a chosen language or switch it off during a performance, as easily as they can watch a movie on an airline flight.

Project management

The Project Management Institute[3] defines projects as temporary group activities designed to specific ends. They are temporary, with defined beginnings and ends in time, scope and resources. Every project consists of a specific set of operations to accomplish a particular goal. Project teams often include people who do not usually work together – sometimes from different organizations, internationally and cross-culturally. They work together under expert management to deliver on-time, on-budget results and to provide learning and integration that organizations need.

Project management is the application of knowledge, skills and techniques to execute these programmes effectively and efficiently. It represents a strategic competency that enables organizations to tie results to business goals, the better to compete in their markets.

The following account of Figaro's[4] project to install an electronic sub-titles system in an Italian opera house is effectively a perfect example of project management with all its ups and downs.

The effects of space on communication

In Volume 2, Chapter 11, Andrew Harrison writes of the need to redesign traditional learning spaces such as lecture rooms and even whole buildings to take account of innovative teaching and learning methods, including the use of technology. Webb, in the following study, offers a vivid account of the redesign of the interior an opera theatre to enhance the learning and enjoyment of audiences.

Abstract:

This is an account of an installation for an opera sub-titling system by a US-based firm Figaro Systems, Inc, in a theatre in Italy in 2001. It describes how the project began, its process through various negotiations and setbacks and its final success.

Keywords: electronic sub-titles, opera theatres, project management

Introduction

In 2001, Paulo, the director of la Canzone, an Italian opera house, approached Figaro with a proposal to install a sub-titling system on seatbacks in the theatre. Paulo was aware that the firm had completed similar international projects but also that the Italian public is very protective about opera performances and would resist any threat to tradition. However, he knew that sub-titles for performances were becoming a necessity. Those that Figaro had installed at the Metropolitan Opera in New York, for example, had boosted sales by some 12%, and electronic sub-titles were part of an irresistible wave of new technology. Paulo's plan was to close la Canzone for refurbishment and refitting and in meantime to find another theatre in which to install the system as an experiment. If opera patrons could experience the system first in this theatre, they would be more likely to accept, and indeed support, a later installation in la Canzone.

As it turned out, Paulo's predictions were vindicated because after the première of the system in a suburban theatre, the notoriously savage Italian opera critics voiced unanimous praise for this new addition to opera and Simultext® became a prerequisite for la Canzone renovations.

Case presentation

While Paulo was seeking a temporary theatre, an old factory outside the city centre was being rezoned and reconstructed for public housing. Approval for rezoning the area from industrial to residential was conditional on the inclusion of public works for the community at large. The owner was eager to comply and entered into an agreement with Paulo for the construction of a theatre on the site, to be called the Teatro degli Fabbrica.

The project was not without problems, the first being open resistance – and active hostility – by the commissioned architect to alter his original design to include Figaro's need for modifications to the seats and major changes to the infrastructure that would be essential for installation of the sub-title system. His objections were eventually overcome by Paulo, who was paying his bill, but because of existing building contracts, which could not be changed, everything that Figaro needed had to be added in as inconspicuous a manner as possible to what was already there.

Divertimento, a theatre buildings restoration and maintenance firm, already had a contract with la Canzone's management for maintenance of the house. This firm became Figaro's partner, as a huge handicap for these sensitive negotiations was that Figaro is a US-based company. None of its representatives or technicians spoke Italian, so working with architects, subcontractors and engineers who spoke little or no English presented major problems. An interpreter was needed for every meeting, logistical discussion, design issue or planning detail, and it was a boon to have Divertimento as a partnering company who could deal with matters such as explaining technical requirements and giving instructions to local subcontractors. However, even this intervention was not without its problems because Divertimento had no previous experience with installations of this technology or on this scale, and so they needed supervision and direction.

Figaro visited the site, identified problems or potential difficulties and then decided with the Divertimento team how best to obtain approvals for the work and get the necessary equipment and manpower. All parties involved in the project had something to learn and something to give to the collaboration.

Another challenge was that the building was not even close to being finished before the theatre was scheduled to open. About a month before the set date, the whole construction process was changed and the team began closing off large portions of the building with sheet rock walls. Then, a great deal of effort was spent on finishing and furnishing the foyer and the auditorium so the public could attend the theatre for the one advertised opening performance. It was a "smoke and mirrors" illusion involving politics, the city and construction companies and was out of Figaro's hands. All its people could do was wait, and after the "opening," the theatre was closed again for two months to complete the installation of the sub-title system.

La Canzone was even more complicated because it is a historic building and many of the fittings date back to the 18th century. Installation of the system involved refurbishing the building itself, the buildings behind, demolishing the stage house and constructing new buildings in their stead.

The stage is very old, and its hydraulic lifts were still powered by water. They leaked and so had to be replaced, as did all rope line sets, which were updated to electric winches, and a computer-controlled operating system. Most of the decorative elements in the auditorium were showing signs of two hundred years of wear so the installation team members re-plastered walls, fixed mouldings, restored original frescos and re-gilded with real gold leaf. They put a new floor in the orchestra section of the house and replaced the old seats with new ones of minimal upholstery to return the sound closer to its original state – livelier and clearer – when the theatre was new.

However, despite bringing the opera house into the modern era, the original design, look and feel of the house had to be preserved; therefore, approval for Figaro's design for la Canzone underwent much more scrutiny than it had for the Teatro degli Fabbrica. In addition to the management, the architect overseeing the refurbishment, the construction company and technical staff, there was also a Historical Committee whose members added aesthetic and political dimensions to the approval process. It even including individuals such as technical supervisors, whose decisions were not essential on every issue but who could derail the process if they felt they had not been adequately consulted. This could lengthen the time it took to make decisions, but was essential politically for the installation to move forward.

Figaro's approach was not to try and disguise the technology but to make it clearly an addition that is visible yet not obvious, being visually quiet and subservient to the architecture and décor. The system, if removed, would return the building to its original condition. After submitting designs for consideration, lengthy discussions and many meetings, including a deal of reassurance, Figaro eventually managed to get approval from all those involved, though there were still many decisions to be made throughout the installation.

The system has three primary installation steps: first to install the central hub and computers that operate the entire system; second, the infrastructure for the data and the power, with cabinets scattered throughout the auditorium containing power supplies, switches and so forth; and third, the actual electronic displays attached to the seats or walls or other structures. Each step needed labour and attention, and there was a lot of work in figuring out how to run cables and wires in a discreet way without changing the structure of the building; and then to attach the screens to the seats, built into a recess at the back. Fortunately, Figaro could design the seat integration before the seats were built, so they could be included in the contract.

However, most of these decisions were not easy with a great many Italians all talking rather passionately at once, and Figaro relying on its partner, Divertimento, for translation and understanding of concerns and answering questions. It often took several restatements of an issue in different ways, first for the interpreter to understand the problem and then to communicate it to the other party. It took a lot of persistence and repetition, drawings or other visual aids, to convey highly technical concepts. Only when information was clearly understood could decisions be made.

As for logistics, it was quite difficult to find a space that could be used as a "control room" for the system. The theatre auditorium is usually where it is sited; but there was a lot of argument by architects and theatre management that there just wasn't enough room. Figaro had to find a remote location, and there was an enormous amount of political in-fighting by various departments as to where this would be – it was a turf war. There were several locations offered. Only one was workable, but it was in demand by two other factions within la Canzone: an electrical maintenance crew, and the stage management people who wanted it for their offices because it was convenient to the stage.

After considerable wrangling and in-fighting, it was eventually decided that Figaro could have the space, so from there they could lead the cables to different areas. Drawings needed to be made, reviewed by engineers and coordinated with the electrical engineers to ensure the system's power had a place in the main switch with enough capacity to operate. A lot of co-ordination was necessary.

The location of the cabinets throughout the theatre was again more complicated because of the Historic Committee. Figaro needed the cabinets to be located within a certain position or zone within the theatre so the cables could be run with feeds to them and on to other places, connecting them as necessary. Much work was involved in deciding each and every one of these places and where they could go, including crawling all over the building and physically investigating every possible space. All cables had to be "invisible." It took a tremendous amount of time to organize.

After satisfying the Committee, and bearing in mind that each choice needed to be practical and within budget, they were all reviewed by the architect and construction team. The architect was concerned about the tremendous number of other services within the theatre; Figaro had to ensure the system components were not in the way of any other systems, cables or pipelines. All this was done through an interpreter.

Some decisions were easy, others took a couple of months of negotiation, with about 20 cabinets being installed in all. One of the locations was on the site of some ancient Roman ruins, possibly a graveyard – and there was the additional and unexpected dilemma that one of the deeply superstitious crew members refused to enter it for fear of spirits.

Eventually, all the cabinets were recessed into the available wall in each location with a very plain cover, but typically in store rooms off anterooms – not public spaces – so they were in place but not visible.

The last part of the project was fitting the actual displays to the back of each seat. There were some constraints already on the size, and what could be done with the casings, but the architect was responsible for this decision. The Committee reiterated that as long as the displays could be removed if necessary, and would not affect the structure or historic nature of the theatre, they would approve. Different designs and proto-types were discussed with the architect to find an aesthetically pleasing device. Meanwhile, Figaro consulted with the manufacturer for the design of the electronics and possibilities for cabling and mounting.

Figaro also had to work with the seat manufacturer because in the parkett or the orchestra section of the theatre, the displays were to be mounted directly into the seatbacks. A sample seat with built-in parts was made for the architect and Historical Committee to approve, including a screen, case and the cabling loom.

There was a lot of back-and-forth in discussions about the mounting. The seemingly simple task of making a hole in the back of the seats had some unexpected problems due to the structure of the laminated plywood chairs and the need to ensure they retained strength after sustaining cuts that would allow cables to run through them. This was all part of the normal process of design and construction, but in this case, Figaro was dealing with other contractors who didn't speak English. It was a challenge to communicate each other's technical constraints and trying to arrive at a solution that would satisfy everyone. All concerned had to learn the art of communicating effectively and precisely through an interpreter.

Outcomes

As with many projects under time constraints, and with the addition of communication issues, there are always unexpected delays; and tensions were high towards the end of this one. However, la Canzone – being better organized in its refitting than the Teatro degli Fabbrica – opened with a completed theatre and public spaces. Although some ancillary office spaces were not finished, Figaro's installation was successfully completed in time for the reopening, an event graced with prominent politicians and European royalty.

Notes

All names are fictitious with the exception of Figaro Systems Inc, of which the author is director.

1. http://www.eurovision.tv/.
2. Ramzi Saidani, 6 February 2014, "Access to culture: opera subtitles help!" http://opera-digital.com/.
3. http://www.pmi.org/.
4. Figaro Systems, Inc, "Titling and captioning solutions for the performing arts," http://www.figaro-systems.com/, 15 February 2015.

Reference

Ramzi Saidani, 6 February 2014, "Access to culture: opera subtitles help!" http://opera-digital.com/.

11

The Case for Games and Iconography in Multicultural Technology Training

Vincent Ferravanti

Editor's introduction

The topic of games for learning is fairly well covered in the literature and accepted generally as an effective teaching medium (see, e.g., Christopher and Smith[1]; *Simulation & Gaming* (S&G),[2] an international journal of theory, practice and research; Steinkuehler *et al.*[3]).

Jessica Trybus,[4] in a 2014 article titled "Game-based learning: what it is, why it works, and where it's going," included a tabular comparison of traditional training and hands-on and game-based learning (see Table 11.1)

Table 11.1 Comparisons of learning methods

	Traditional training (lectures, online tutorials)	Hands-on training	Game-based learning
Cost-effective	X		X
Low physical risk/liability	X		X
Standardized assessments allowing student-to-student comparisons	X		X
Highly engaging		X	X
Learning pace tailored to individual students		X	X
Immediate feedback in response to student mistakes		X	X
Students can easily transfer learning to real-world environment		X	X
Learners are actively engaged		X	X

Source: Editor.

However, there is little literature on games for technology training, or for what Ferravanti describes as "iconography" as a training medium. The Transportation Research Board[5] has published a "decision game and facilitation" for training in new technologies; and Sivasailam Thiagarajan[6] has written on enhancing training with interactive games; but most relevant literature deals with video or computer game–based learning. Ferravanti's application of a popular children's game as a teaching tool for a technological process is original if not unique.

Haig Kouyoumdjian[7] has written on learning through visuals, and there are a number of publications about learning language and vocabulary through use of images, for example, by the LEO network[8]; but Ferravanti again has broken new ground with his account of IT teaching through pictures.

Ferravanti's innovative methods call to mind two more examples of graphics in place of written instructions as international communication tools. One is road signs (Figure 11.1) and the other is assembly diagrams (Figure 11.2).[9] However, these are not really training tools; and it is for this reason that Ferravanti's use of such 'icons' is remarkable.

Figure 11.1   Road signs
Source: Compiled by editor from various sources.

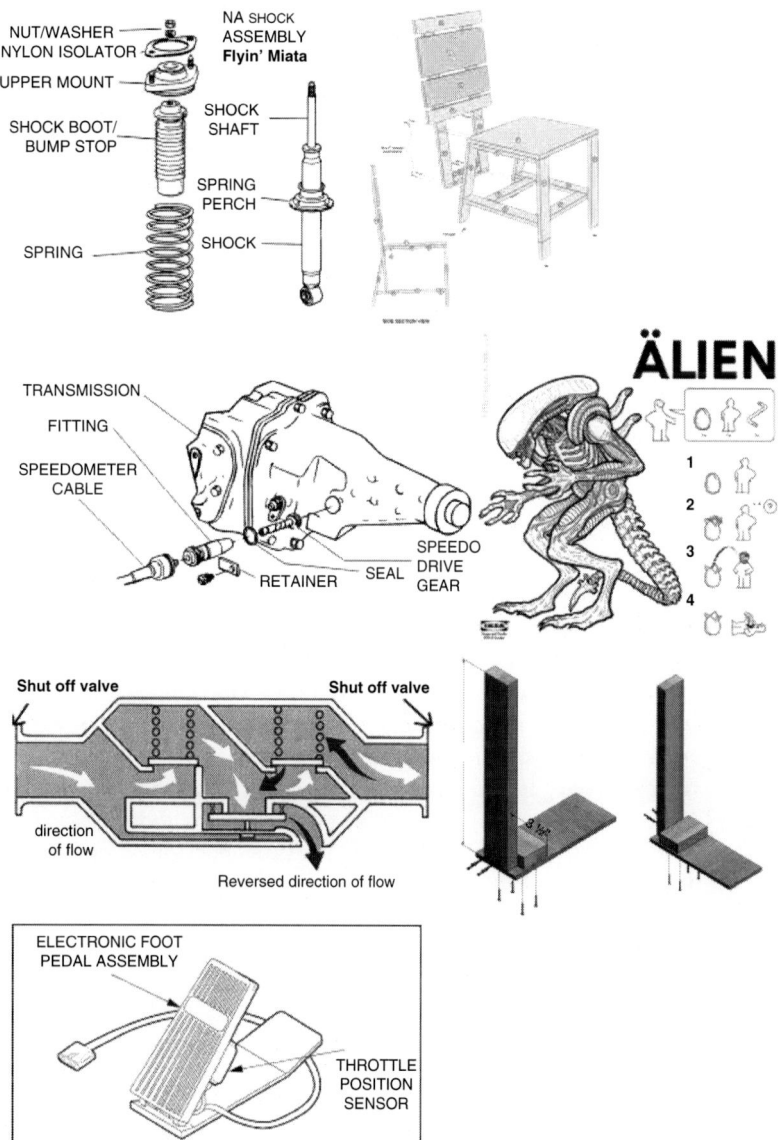

Figure 11.2 Assembly diagrams

Source: Compiled by editor from various sources.

Abstract:

Multi-national companies are reducing costs and improving information flow by implementing technological solutions globally. This poses a problem in the production of standardized training materials and training practices. This case concerns the production and use of icon-based training materials. It describes the use of gaming to introduce the techniques of barcode data entry, first to a production group with English as a second language and then to an Italian-speaking audience using the same training materials and procedures.

Keywords: gaming, iconography, technology, training, multicultural

Introduction

Barcode data collection was a relatively new technology when this began. The hardware used was quite different from the supermarket checkout systems now in use. Rather than swiping the barcode past a sensor, users needed to "wand" it. "Wanding" is the act of gliding a metal pen with a glass tip over the barcode. The trick was to cross the whole barcode while maintaining a constant speed, and this took some practice. Moreover, the whole process of transacting shop floor activity required the "wanding" of multiple barcodes in a specific order, some attached to the objects being worked on and some attached to a barcode data entry station.

The reason for using barcoding is accuracy and speed. Long part numbers are easy to key in incorrectly when typed. The particular set up in the case study that follows also allowed for the ability to weight count the parts, again using barcode prompts, and to produce barcoded labels. The project ran from 1990 to 1992 but the technology used is still relevant and used in many organizations.

Case presentation

A gaming approach

This case shows how a combination of icon-based training materials and simple gaming techniques can be used to introduce complex technology to culturally diverse groups with no modification, reducing implementation costs and insuring standardization.

The implementation of sophisticated technologies demands innovative and creative approaches to user training. As companies become more international, they require training methods that insure consistent results across multiple cultures. A company's success depends on user acceptance and understanding of new technologies. If the technology is unused or, worse, misused, all of its benefits are lost.

System implementers need to identify what information users must be given. The difficulty is in finding a single method to present it that will span the global work force. Companies are faced with a diverse pool of employees with varying degrees of education, language skills, technical competency and cultural background. Training techniques need to be developed to span these groups and insure a consistent understanding of new technologies. This case describes the introduction of gaming and iconography to training methods that span the diverse backgrounds of the user community.

Over the past two years, the manufacturing information systems group at ABACUS (fictitious name) has implemented barcode data collection systems in three facilities in two countries. These system implementations have enabled the firm to develop and test new approaches to systems training.

One successful training method that spans diverse groups is gaming. The introduction of barcode data collection meant that users needed to be comfortable using barcode wands. While supermarket barcode readers are ubiquitous, barcode wands work differently and can be intimidating to employees unused to highly technical equipment.

To introduce barcode equipment to the user community, ABACUS developed a simple, "low-tech" game based on a popular paper-and-pencil game called Tic-tac-toe, or Noughts and Crosses, or Xs and Os. It is for two players, X and O, who take turns marking the spaces in a 3×3 grid. The player who succeeds in placing three respective marks in a horizontal, vertical, or diagonal row wins the game.

The goal of this training game is to get users confident and competent with barcode wands. Using a game framework has several advantages. First, it varies the traditional form of training sessions, in which a large amount of time is spent lecturing. This is a passive form of learning, while game playing is active. ABACUS found it advantageous to schedule a Tic-tac-toe game in the middle of training sessions to break up the monotony of lecturing. Because game playing is an active form of learning, it also acts as an ice breaker, forcing communication between trainers and trainees who might otherwise have remained silent during lectures.

Second, Tic-tac-toe has no relevance to the tasks the trainees will be performing with the new barcode system. This separates the game from any anxiety the participants may have about changes to their work routine and focuses them on learning how to use a barcode wand.

Third, the game is mildly competitive, providing an incentive for learning and helping trainers to learn how class members interact with each other.

The mechanics of the game are very simple. Game boards were printed. The board is a simple Tic-tac-toe grid of 3×3. Each square contains a barcoded sequence. The sequence should be long enough to make the "wanding" challenging but not so long as to be too difficult. A length of seven characters seems to work well. The characters used in the barcode sequence are unimportant. The game centres on the fact that the barcode reader beeps when the player successfully completes a scan and thus wins the square.

To play the game, members of training groups are divided into pairs of opponents, each pair having a game board. All players get one try to claim the square they want. If the barcode device beeps, the relevant player claims the square by placing either an X or an O in the square, opponents alternately trying to claim squares. If any player fails to make the device beep on their turn, their opponent can try to take the square. The rules for winning are the same as in Tic-tac-toe – three across, down or diagonal wins.

More complex variations of the game are possible but the simplicity of the game allows trainers to play it with diverse groups with minimum instruction on the games rules; and in fact all training groups across multiple countries have been found to understand Tic-tac-toe, so all the time spent on the game is focused on using the barcode device rather than explaining the game.

The question ABACUS needed to answer was: "Does gaming actually teach users anything?" At the end of these Tic-tac-toe games, everyone in each training session knew how to handle a wand and no one was the least bit timid about picking one up when it came time to hands-on training on the shop floor system.

Iconographic instructions

User instructions are the "leave behind" items of a training session. They reinforce training by acting as a reminder of correct procedures. However, in a global implementation, word-heavy instructions would require a lot of time and cost to translate; and in any case, it is questionable whether users would bother to read them while carrying out the relevant task.

ABACUS decided to limit the use of words as much as possible in user instructions and to rely instead on iconography. This means simplified but recognizable representations of real-life objects. The first step was to design a page format that would lend itself to icon-based instructions.

This was accomplished by dividing the page in half, vertically. Barcode systems require users first to read the device's prompt and then to wand the correct barcoded field. Dividing the page in two, vertically, created one space in which to track what the barcode system is prompting and another in which to display where to get the information to scan. On the right-hand side of the page, ABACUS placed pictures of the barcode device display with its messages. On the left-hand side of the page is a picture of the appropriate source document/barcode.

The second step was to tie the two sides together. For this, ABACUS developed the wand icon, simply a stylized drawing of a barcode wand. Whenever the system requires users to wand in information, the right side of the page will display this icon followed by the words "Wand the -." On the left side of the page is the image of the source document from which the information will come. Superimposed over this document is the same wand icon pointing to the appropriate barcoded field (Figure 11.3).

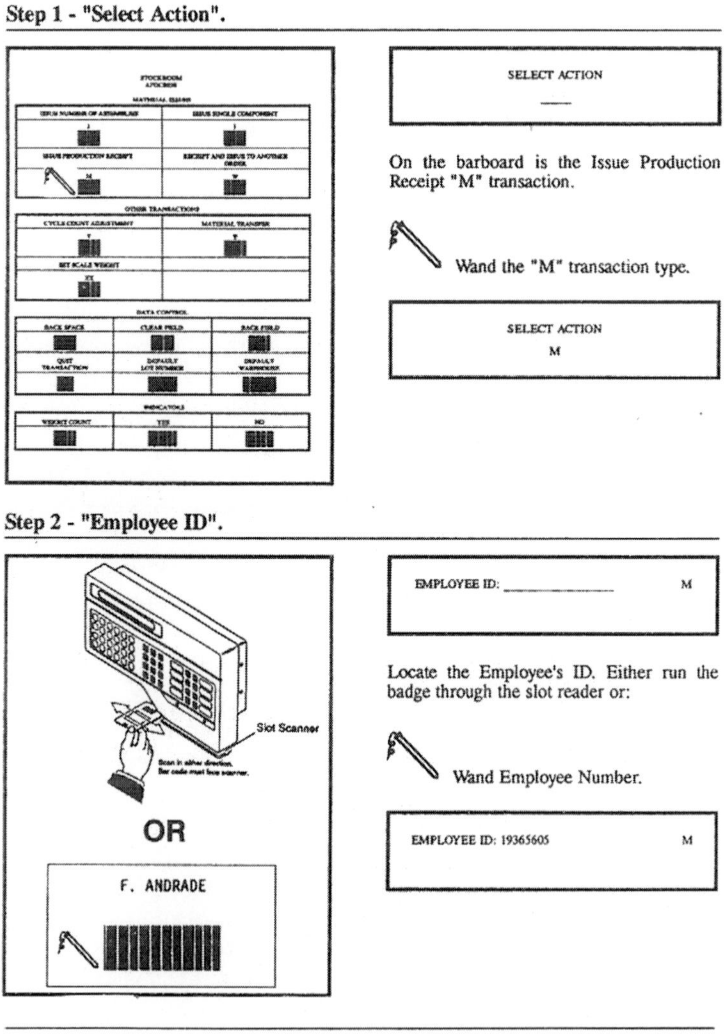

Step 1 - "Select Action".

On the barboard is the Issue Production Receipt "M" transaction.

Wand the "M" transaction type.

SELECT ACTION

M

Step 2 - "Employee ID".

EMPLOYEE ID: _____   M

Locate the Employee's ID. Either run the badge through the slot reader or:

Wand Employee Number.

EMPLOYEE ID: 19365605   M

Figure 11.3   Barcode instructions

In this way, users can match the barcode system's prompts with the barcoded field they need to wand. All they have to do is look to the left-hand side of the page to see what they need to wand.

The rest of the organization of the instructions is straightforward. Each chapter corresponds to a major task, such as entering labour hours or down time. Each chapter is broken up into steps, each consisting of one barcode system prompt and its appropriate response.

At each step, the barcode device screen is pictured before and after the required field has been "wanded." Between the two displays, the wand icon is shown. There are about two steps per page. Some steps take up more space because there is more than one possible source for the information. In this case, one icon is shown on the right side of the page while multiple icons are depicted on the left side, indicating the multiple sources. Situations of multiple sources are kept to a minimum so as not to confuse users. The instructions are not completely free of words and users must still be able to recognize frequently used words such as "work centre" or "item number."

The use of icons reduces the amount of reading to simple words or phrases. As a result, the barcode system has been implemented in English in several non-English-speaking countries. These user populations – while not fluent in English – became familiar with the key English words used by the system. This has allowed ABACUS to use the same hardware and user instructions throughout its global implementation.

Outcomes

As a result of these two techniques, gaming and iconography, one set of user instructions and training techniques has been used globally to successfully implement the barcode data collection system. This has reduced implementation costs and insured consistency in implementation across the company.

Training materials, such as user instructions, can benefit from a fresh look and an understanding of the increasing scope of users' abilities. Globalization is requiring companies to train user populations with varying familiarity with technology and multi-cultural backgrounds. Being able to develop single training solutions that can be utilized across a global organization can both reduce costs and ensure consistency. The use of gaming techniques and iconographic user instructions are two techniques that can help produce global training programmes.

The success of the Tick-tack-toe game is due to the its universality. This limits the time needed to explain the game and maximizes its effectiveness as a training tool. The iconographic user instructions work because core English phrases are recognizable to all of the company's employees worldwide – though the limited use of English in the instructions would have made the translation of them relatively easy and inexpensive if required.

Conclusion

Good form cannot compensate for poor content. All the basics that go into defining material that needs to be taught still apply. However, the best-prepared material may fail to reach its audience if the form in which it is presented is not one with which the audience is comfortable.

Notes

1. E.M. Christopher and L.E. Smith, 1991, *Negotiation training through gaming: strategies, tactics, and manoeuvres* (Kogan Page).
2. http://sag.sagepub.com/, accessed 28 July 2014.
3. C. Steinkuehler, K. Squire and S. Barab, 2012, *Games, learning, and society: learning and meaning in the digital age* (Google eBook: Cambridge University Press).
4. http://www.newmedia.org/game-based-learning – what-it-is-why-it-works-and-where-its-going.html, 2014.
5. "Determining training for new technologies: a decision game and facilitation" (Transportation Research Board, 2003), http://www.trb.org/.
6. S. Thiagarajan, 2005, *Thiagi's interactive lectures: power up your training with interactive games and exercises* (Google eBook, American Society for Training and Development).
7. H. Kouyoumdjian, 20 July 2012, "Learning through visuals: visual imagery in the classroom," http://www.psychologytoday.com/blog/get-psyched/201207/learning-through-visuals.
8. http://www.learnenglish.de/pictures.html, accessed 28 July 2014.
9. http://visualdictionaryonline.com.

References

E.M. Christopher and L.E. Smith, 1991, *Negotiation training through gaming: strategies, tactics, and manoeuvres* (Kogan Page).
H. Kouyoumdjian, 20 July 2012, "Learning through visuals: visual imagery in the classroom," http://www.psychologytoday.com/blog/get-psyched/201207/learning-through-visuals.

C. Steinkuehler, K. Squire and S. Barab, 2012, *Games, learning, and society: learning and meaning in the digital age* (Google eBook: Cambridge University Press).

S. Thiagarajan, 2005, *Thiagi's interactive lectures: power up your training with interactive games and exercises* (Google eBook: American Society for Training and Development).

Index

Printed and bound by CPI Group (UK) Ltd, Croydon, CR0 4YY